Universities cannot decide your fate,
but you can!

MANAGEMENT BEYOND ACADEMICS

MAGADA

BlueRose ONE
Stories Matter
NewDelhi • London

BLUEROSE PUBLISHERS
India | U.K.

For permissions requests or inquiries regarding this publication, please contact:

BLUEROSE PUBLISHERS
www.BlueRoseONE.com
info@bluerosepublishers.com
+91 8882 898 898
+4407342408967

ISBN: 978-93-7542-565-6

Typesetting: Manisha Rawat

First Edition: March 2026

"

Dedicated to my wife Rekha, son Reshi Magada, my source of inspiration 'Gangamma' —my mother

"

Foreword...

I have spent years making one-minute videos to educate and inspire people about the finance and investment. I always say: *I can show you the dots, but connecting them is your job.* The real power of learning lies not just in information, but in your ability to make sense of it, act on it, and change your life.

That is precisely why this book, *Management Beyond Academics,* authored by my father, Dr. Shivakumar Magada, matters so much. I feel deeply fortunate to write the foreword to my own father's work. It does something rare—it **connects the dots for you**. It takes years of wisdom, real-life experiences, and deep reflections, and turns them into practical lessons that help you make wiser decisions. Whether you are building a business, managing people, or simply navigating life, this book will guide you to think beyond the classroom and beyond conventional theories.

The best lessons are often lived, not taught. And this book is full of those lived lessons—honest, thoughtful, and powerful. My hope is that as you go through these pages, you won't just learn... you will also *act*. Because winning in life is not about knowing more; it's about **doing better**.

I'm excited for you to read this. May it inspire you to take charge of your journey and connect your own dots—one decision at a time.

Reshi Magada
Founder ROB Media &
Producer, NAS Company, Singapore

Preface

I can only think like me...

The title of this book was conceived long ago, back in 2005, while attending a conference at Central College in Bangalore. Yet, the subtitle took shape two decades later, a testament to the evolving nature of thought. When I shared this with my friend Ashoka, he said, 'Why don't you write it in Kannada?' His tone felt quite judgmental. Although he said it in a complimentary way, appreciating my command over Kannada, I sensed that he perhaps assumed I couldn't grasp English well — which, in essence, conveyed the same meaning. It's unfortunate, but my instinct often rebels against instruction — I tend to walk the path opposite to what others suggest. Throughout my life, I have always been an independent thinker, an opinion maker. From a young age, I embraced my own ideologies and beliefs, expressing them through plays and poems by the time I was 19. However, this kind of writing felt distant from my usual creative form.

There were times when I mentioned the idea of writing a book with my friends, only to be dismissed, made to believe I lacked the competence for such a task. But deep inside, I knew it was only a matter of time before I would disprove them, and that time has now arrived. Of course, already, I have written 24 books/handbooks related to my science profession.

This one third one in a series. When I crafted the subtitle, "Universities cannot decide your fate, but you can!", I initially felt a pang of doubt, wondering if I had been too bold, even arrogant. But, as is my way, I consoled myself with the understanding that the message wasn't arrogant at all—it was deeply philosophical. The statement embodies a universal truth: while education holds value, it does not dictate the entirety of one's life. Long before universities existed, humanity thrived. Our ancestors shaped their fates with wisdom, experience, and resilience. Institutions can guide, but they cannot define.

The essence of this sentiment lies in personal empowerment, in the belief that one's fate is a reflection of one's choices and actions. Self-reliance, growth, and a deeper understanding of life's purpose arise from within—not from external forces. By embracing this message, I sought to send a strong and uplifting reminder that our destinies are in our hands, and this truth is timeless.

Thus, I held firm to the subtitle, knowing that its strength lies in its call for individual responsibility and its recognition of the inherent power we each possess.

Read this book with an open mind, free from prejudice or preconceptions. Its purpose is to help you orient yourself in the right direction—towards clarity, purpose, and positive impact. Just like a diamond that reflects more light when cut and polished correctly, your thoughts and actions, once aligned, can illuminate not only your own path but also help dispel the darkness and ignorance that shadow our society.

You hold the power to create wonders—Yes,

let that truth echo in your soul.
For if you've known my spirit well,
Despair could never take its toll. Yes. You can do wonders. Yes.
You read it right!

"If you know me, you can't be a PESSIMIST"

Dr Shivakumar **Magada**
Mangalore, India

Contents

"Practice makes man/women perfect;
make sure that you chose the best practice-**Magada**"

Introduction: Redefining Your Destiny

Imagine standing at the crossroads of your life, equipped with endless paths and possibilities. Education, society tells us, determines the road we must take—shaping our fate, defining our success. Yet, is our destiny truly carved out by universities and grades? Can institutions genuinely decide the trajectory of our lives, or is it, in reality, a choice that lies firmly within our own hands? In fact, universities are designed to equip you with the critical thinking skills, knowledge, and analytical tools necessary to deepen your understanding of the world around you. Through diverse academic disciplines, exposure to different perspectives, and engagement in research and discussion, they help you develop a more informed, thoughtful, and nuanced view of complex global issues. In reality, the actual learning starts after the university program.

Globally, education is a powerful tool for building a comfortable and successful life. However, education alone does not guarantee success. It is passion and creativity that set individuals apart from the average, enabling them to shape their own destiny irrespective of the educational qualifications.

In "MBA: Management Beyond Academics," we explore a profound truth often obscured by conventional wisdom: true success and fulfilment cannot be fully dictated by formal education alone. Instead, it is deeply rooted in our capacity for independent thought, the courage to question the status quo, and the determination to create meaningful change.

This book was born not merely out of theoretical contemplation but out of real-world experiences, personal reflections, and candid observations accumulated over decades. It emerged from conversations, debates, challenges, and victories witnessed first-hand—from classrooms to boardrooms, from inspiring personal journeys to thought-provoking historical accounts.

Through the chapters ahead, you will embark on a transformative journey. We'll begin by revisiting history, learning from past and their invaluable contributions to global education. We'll critically examine the evolution of educational systems, identifying their strengths and their flaws. This book doesn't shy away from bold discussions on societal pressures, consumerism, and the hidden traps of conformity.

Yet, beyond mere critique, "MBA" offers a hopeful, empowering message: You have the innate power to shape your own destiny. Education should never be about blind acceptance of facts but should foster curiosity, creativity, and critical thinking. The journey you're about to undertake aims to help you find clarity in chaos, uncover purpose amidst uncertainty, and inspire action where there might otherwise be hesitation.

As you read, keep your mind open and your spirit curious. Let these words challenge and guide you to look beyond the superficial metrics of success and into the true essence of personal achievement and societal contribution. Remember, the greatest accomplishments are those born from original thought, fearless questioning, and a sincere commitment to growth—not just academically, but holistically.

Welcome to a new paradigm of learning and living—welcome to your own MBA program.

"Do not be satisfied with the stories that comes before you. Unfold your own myth -**Rumi**"

The Last Chapter

Among the many humorous statements and witty one-liners I've come across on T-shirts, one in particular left a lasting impression on me. It read: "*I was born intelligent; education ruined me.*" On the surface, it was just another cheeky slogan meant to evoke a chuckle. But for some reason, this line refused to stay just a joke. It followed me, echoed in my thoughts, and slowly began to feel more profound than it initially appeared. Behind its playful irony was a compelling reflection on the disconnect between our natural curiosity and the traditional structures of formal education.

The beauty of the line lies in its contradiction—it suggests that intelligence is something innate, an original gift that we are born with, while education, which is supposedly designed to nurture and sharpen that intelligence, somehow dampens or even distorts it. In many ways, that irony holds a kernel of truth. As children, we are naturally curious. We ask questions endlessly, poke at mysteries, and embrace wonder without inhibition. But once we step into structured classrooms and standardized curriculums, that innate curiosity is often forced to conform. We're told what to think, how to write, when to speak, and in which format to answer. The spontaneity of thought gives way to rote learning, memorization, and the constant pursuit of grades over genuine understanding.

That witty slogan also made me reflect on how intelligence is measured and perceived. Schools and colleges often have narrow parameters for evaluating brilliance—grades, percentages, and rankings. Those who think differently or struggle to fit into these moulds are often labelled as underachievers or troublemakers, even if their natural intellect is sharp and creative. The pressure to perform within these frameworks can sometimes suppress originality and erode confidence. I've known brilliant minds who could explain complex concepts effortlessly in conversation but stumbled when asked to write them down within strict exam formats.

This isn't to say that education, in itself, is detrimental. On the contrary, true education is liberating—it broadens perspectives, fosters critical thinking, and opens doors to the world. But when education becomes synonymous with conformity, when it becomes more about compliance than curiosity, then it risks doing exactly what the T-shirt warned: dulling the sharpness we were born with. The quote, humorous as it is, invites us to reimagine education not as a system that tries to "fix" intelligence, but one that cultivates and celebrates it in all its diverse forms. Intelligence doesn't always show up in exams—it sings in music, it plays on sports fields, it whispers through poetry, and it questions through rebellion.

So yes, I laughed when I first saw that T-shirt. But then I thought deeply about it. And in that mix of humour and truth, I found a quiet challenge—a call to preserve the intelligence we are born with, and to fight for an education that fuels it rather than ruins it.

Gajendra Moksha – The Liberation of the Elephant

It was in the year 1983, my language teacher Mrs M J John narrated a story of Gajendra Moksha which goes as "Once upon a time, there was a noble elephant king named Gajendra, who ruled over a beautiful forest and lived peacefully with his herd. One day, while bathing in a lake with his companions, a crocodile (Makara) suddenly caught hold of his leg and began dragging him into the water.

Despite his great strength, Gajendra couldn't free himself. The struggle went on for several hours, symbolizing the relentless grip of worldly suffering. Eventually, realizing he was powerless, Gajendra raised his trunk to the sky and surrendered to Lord Vishnu, chanting his name with full devotion. Touched by the elephant's complete surrender and unwavering faith, Lord Vishnu appeared instantly, riding on Garuda, his divine eagle. He hurled his 'Sudarshan Chakra' — A circular deadly weapon and killed the crocodile, freeing Gajendra."

As the Supreme God and Creator, it struck me that even the crocodile was part of His own creation. If He is the source of all life, isn't it a contradiction for Him to destroy any of it? With that thought lingering in my mind, I casually remarked, "He shouldn't have killed the crocodile." Our teacher, Madam, paused for a moment, clearly amused, and then, with a sharp smile and a touch of sarcasm, replied in Kannada, "*Adenu nimmappanda*?" — "Is that crocodile your father's or what?" The entire class burst into laughter.

I, too, smiled along—half embarrassed, half thoughtful. I knew my question might've sounded naive or irreverent, but to me, it was a genuine curiosity. Of course, all my classmates were clever enough to stay in the teacher's good books. They laughed, not just at the joke, but also at my innocence. But somewhere deep down, I still held on to that question.

"It is often said that *"It's safer to go with the wrong majority than to be right alone"*. But I have never subscribed to that philosophy." I chose to stay true to my convictions, even when they went against the tide. I continued to question what didn't make sense to me—not out of defiance, but out of genuine curiosity and a desire to understand. After all, isn't that what education is meant for?

True education is not about blind acceptance of information; it's about developing the ability to think independently, to question, to innovate, and to make sense of the world through logic and reasoning. It should empower students to analyze issues critically, solve real-world problems, and create new knowledge, rather than simply memorize existing facts.

Unfortunately, the system often gets it wrong—teachers are frequently selected based on their academic scores or paper qualifications, not on their ability to teach, their communication skills, or their natural aptitude for inspiring and engaging students. This misjudgement in recruitment is not a minor oversight; it is a systemic flaw with far-reaching consequences.

Who are our teachers

We turned out well because we had good teachers. If students today are struggling, teachers can't place the blame solely on society—some part of the responsibility lies with them too. After all, teachers are usually selected based on their merit and academic qualifications. But a single poor hiring decision can ripple through generations—misguided minds shaping young ones, passing on confusion instead of clarity, suppression instead of stimulation. And today, we are witnessing the effects of such mistakes in the form of the Gen-Z generation—smart, questioning, and vibrant, but often at odds with a system that hasn't evolved to nurture their potential. It is also an undeniable reality that many from the Gen-Z generation have gradually stopped asking questions, assuming that everything they need to know is just a click away on Google. This easy access to information, while revolutionary, has ironically dulled the very spark of curiosity that drives true learning.

These so-called "Google kids" often rely heavily on quick answers and instant solutions, without dwelling deeper into understanding the 'why' and 'how' behind things. In doing so, they risk losing touch with their own innate creativity, critical thinking, and human ingenuity—the very qualities that distinguish us from machines.

The convenience of search engines has created an illusion that knowledge is merely information, ignoring the fact that true wisdom comes from reflection, analysis, experience, and questioning. The art of struggling with a problem, brainstorming ideas, failing and trying again—these are essential aspects of learning that are slowly fading.

In essence, the tragedy isn't that Gen-Z or Gen-alpha lacks intelligence—far from it. It is that their potential is often left untapped, as they substitute genuine curiosity with copy-paste answers, and original thought with algorithm-fed conclusions. It's akin to learning how to walk using a white cane — the mobility aid designed for those without sight — while we ourselves have perfect vision. It feels unnatural, even paradoxical. In the same way, as technology advances, it begins to guide us through life's decisions and directions, even when we are fully capable of seeing and thinking for ourselves. What was once meant to assist us has started to imitate — and in some cases, replace — our very thought processes. That's where the danger lies. When we allow machines to think *like* us, we run the risk of forgetting *how* to think for ourselves. We are in a position to prove our computers that we are not 'Robots.' Great, we've advanced so far that we're doing CAPTCHA tests to prove to our computers we're not their cousins. It's not the presence of Google or ChatGPT that's the issue, but the absence of a questioning mindset, the very trait that education is meant to nurture.

Recently, I had the opportunity to address a large gathering of students in a beautiful auditorium. The setting was just right for a session on personality development—comfortable seating, a great sound system, and an atmosphere that encouraged focus and reflection.

However, as I began speaking, I noticed something disappointing: most of the students were looking down, not out of shyness or deep thought, but because they had their mobile phones tucked discreetly between their legs. Their attention was divided—physically present, but mentally elsewhere. Sensing the disconnect, I paused and asked them, "Do you want your country to progress and achieve greatness?"

A unanimous "Yes" echoed through the hall. I smiled and continued, "Then how can you expect your country to rise when you're constantly looking down? If you truly want progress, you must lift your gaze—look ahead, look up. Progress doesn't happen with heads bowed down to screens. It starts with awareness, with vision." There was a moment of silence. A few glanced up, some nodded, and gradually, the room filled with a quiet sense of realization. That collective sigh wasn't just a breath—it was a moment of awakening.

In a college that houses the dreams and aspirations of over a thousand young minds, the absence of genuine engagement during their own college function was disheartening. A celebration meant to recognize talent, dedication, and collective spirit became a reflection of a changing generational pulse. Of the many enrolled, barely 150 students sat inside the auditorium, while over 200 loitered outside—immersed not in the event itself, but in curating their own visual narratives through photos and reels.

Their eyes weren't on the stage where fellow students were being recognized for academic or extracurricular achievements, but on their phones, on their outfits, and on the promise of a DJ night and fashion show that awaited after the formalities. As the winners walked up to the dais—moments that should have been marked with thunderous applause and warm cheers—they were instead met with silence, a vacuum of appreciation. Even the sports teacher, once a commanding voice in the field, had to resort to urging the students to "make some noise."

This quiet isn't just about sound—it's about disconnect. A cultural shift seems underway, where instant gratification and social validation often outweigh the value of shared institutional pride. Gen-Z, raised in a hyper-digital age, is arguably more expressive online than present in reality. Their sense of celebration is more personal than communal, more aesthetic than participatory.

But this is not a condemnation—rather, a call for reflection. Are we, as educators and institutions, failing to evolve our formats, failing to bridge their world with ours? Or are we witnessing the growing pains of a generation grappling with identity, relevance, and meaning in ways we've yet to fully understand?

True engagement cannot be demanded; it must be inspired. And perhaps it is time to reimagine college affairs not as routines to be followed, but as experiences to be felt, owned, and shaped by the students themselves.

Because of my straightforward and bold approach in such interactions, I've noticed that many people have quietly distanced themselves from me. They've stopped calling or inviting me, and to be honest—I'm perfectly fine with that. In fact, I'm grateful. I have no desire to address people who are not serious about learning, growing, or engaging with sincerity. Their absence saves me time and energy, which I can now invest in those who are truly open to thought, dialogue, and change.

We live in a society where being passive is often mistaken for being virtuous. Many people want to be labelled as "good" by simply avoiding controversy or conflict. They don't ask questions, they don't participate meaningfully, and they carefully keep themselves at a distance from anything that demands accountability or courage. Ironically, this passive detachment earns them the tag of being "good people"—not because of what they do, but because of what they avoid.

But this mindset brings to mind two powerful quote:

"You can also commit injustice by doing nothing— *Marcus Aurelius* "

"The world is not destroyed by the violence of bad people, but by the silence of good people." **Mostly** said by *Albert Einstein* and many others

The real danger doesn't always come from those who act with malice—but from those who choose to stay silent, look away, or disengage when their voice and action could have made a difference.

I would rather be seen as inconvenient than irrelevant. Because growth doesn't come from silence, and progress doesn't come from avoidance. It comes from the courage to speak, to question, and to confront what needs change.

Ironically, while universities are meant to cultivate independent thinking, their structure often does the opposite—especially in the Indian context. Students are expected to follow a rigid schedule, attend lectures during fixed hours, and passively absorb information from teachers. The learning process is largely unidirectional, with limited opportunities for real-time engagement, critical dialogue, or independent exploration.

Although the teaching methodologies in Indian universities—such as lectures, practical sessions, seminars, field visits, project-based learning, and research at the postgraduate and doctoral levels—mirror those of Western education systems, the real gap lies in execution and exposure. In many Western institutions, there is a far greater emphasis on hands-on learning, access to advanced tools, and a culture that promotes inquisitiveness and innovation. What often holds Indian institutions back is not the curriculum, but factors like:

- Limited access to well-functioning instruments and lab infrastructure.
- Inconsistent or inadequate exposure of students to modern equipment and technology.
- Financial limitations that restrict investments in internal quality assurance systems, laboratory enhancements, and the pursuit of uncompromised, full-scale research initiatives.

As a result, while the educational framework may appear similar on paper, the depth of experience and quality of learning can differ significantly. To truly foster independent, analytical thinkers, we need not only structural reforms but also serious investments in infrastructure, teaching capability, and academic culture.

I'm going by the general average across the institutes. This observation may not fully apply to institutions like the Indian Institute of Technologies (IITs) and other premier technical institutes, where the standards of education and infrastructure have indeed reached global benchmarks. The nation has invested heavily—financially, intellectually, and emotionally—in nurturing these centres of excellence, with the sincere aim of empowering young minds with world-class knowledge and skills.

Yet, there lies a paradox.

Many of these exceptionally gifted individuals, shaped by the very soil that raised them, eventually set sail for foreign lands. There, they apply their brilliance to solve the challenges of other nations, often criticizing the very country that enabled their rise. In doing so, it seems as if the country's investment becomes an offering to the progress of the West, rather than a solution to its own pressing needs.

While the remittances they send may add to our economic numbers, and their global achievements may fill us with pride, that was never the true purpose of education. Education, at its core, is not merely about success or earning potential—it is about service, responsibility, and transformation. The nation doesn't just seek applause for the minds it produces; it yearns for their contribution to its own evolution, for answers to the problems that still plague its people.

"A brain that escapes may win the world,
But a brain that stays back may help heal its own."

Today, many of the brightest minds—graduates from top-tier institutions like the IITs and premier MBA programs—are serving the economies of affluent nations. Their skills are harnessed to build better systems, create wealth, and solve complex challenges elsewhere. Meanwhile, those who have chosen to remain in India carry the responsibility—and the opportunity—of nation-building.

But let's be clear: progress doesn't come from blaming the system, pointing fingers at the country, its universities, or those who chose to leave. Growth begins with acceptance, purpose, and proactive effort. It is not about lamenting what we lack, but about maximizing what we have.

Not every graduate or postgraduate will walk into their dream job. That's a reality we must embrace. But that doesn't mean the road ends there. For those who have the courage to think differently, to look at problems not as roadblocks but as potential pathways, there exists an ocean of opportunities.

Every challenge, every gap in the system, every inefficiency—these are hidden invitations to innovate, to create solutions, and to make a real impact. India is not just one nation; it is a mosaic of more than thirty culturally and economically diverse regions, each with its own unique challenges and possibilities.

"Incredible India" is not just a slogan—it reflects the extraordinary complexity and potential of this land. And yes, along with incredible beauty and diversity come 'Incredible Problems'—but these are not curses; they are calls to action.

Nature, or perhaps God, has gifted you with the chance to make a difference. The question is not whether opportunities exist, but whether you are willing to open your eyes, roll up your sleeves, and take responsibility—not just for your career, but for your country.

In fact, I am not suggesting that you engage in charity. However, it is entirely possible to align profit-making with nation-building. As you strive for financial success, remember that your enterprise can also serve a greater purpose. I encourage you to take an unconventional approach: begin by reading the final chapter of this book first. Then, retire to bed—but resist the urge to sleep immediately. Instead, allow your mind to wander freely. Think deeply. Think ambitiously. Envision possibilities without restraint. Let every idea, no matter how random or unconventional, surface. Do not suppress your thoughts—embrace them all.

Once you've gathered this pool of potential ideas, apply rigorous scrutiny. Discard the weak and impractical. Evaluate the remaining options with strategic clarity. Identify the most compelling and viable idea. If this mental exercise keeps you awake until 4:30 a.m., consider it a valuable night. Paradoxically, if you sleep peacefully, it likely means the ideas were not powerful enough to stir your spirit. But if you find yourself restless and consumed by a singular, compelling vision—that is your breakthrough moment. That's the idea worth pursuing. Note it, nurture it, and only then, return to complete the rest of this book.

This book is not merely about imparting knowledge; it is about transforming the very way you learn. It guides you beyond the surface of conventional understanding, encouraging you to read between the lines and extract insights that are often overlooked. Rather than providing ready-made answers, it empowers you to frame your own problem statements—an essential skill in the modern management landscape. Through this process of intellectual engagement and critical thinking, your perspective on employment undergoes a fundamental shift.

You no longer see yourself as a job seeker constrained by predefined roles. Instead, you begin to identify gaps, opportunities, and innovations—traits that shape you into a job creator, an entrepreneur, and a leader. This book becomes a catalyst for a mindset change—from dependency to enterprise, from compliance to innovations.

This book is designed to equip you with the mindset and tools to:

- Think independently and form your own opinions
- Analyze situations with logic and clarity
- Cultivate healthy skepticism grounded in reason
- Nurture a sense of organized curiosity

- Ask meaningful and challenging questions
- Build the courage to stand by your convictions
- Achieve success in life on your own terms
- Ultimately, lead a life of fulfilment and happiness.

"You have to win; otherwise, weaker genes prevail
-Magada"

The Life on the Earth

Before jumping into business, try to get a feel for what life on Earth is really all about. Established science suggests that life on Earth began approximately 4.24 billion years ago. The earliest life forms to appear were Blue Green Algae (BGA), also known as cyanobacteria, which are primitive primary producers. These simple organisms were pivotal in shaping the Earth's atmosphere, contributing to the oxygen we now rely on, and forming the foundation of the food chain.

Today, it's estimated that there are about 8.7 million species of living organisms on Earth, with approximately 2.6 million inhabiting aquatic environments and around 6.1 million residing on land. However, these figures are based on scientific approximations and logical estimations. The true number of species could be much higher, as there are likely millions of organisms that have yet to be discovered or identified by human researchers. Given the limits of our current technology and understanding, much of Earth's biodiversity remains hidden or unknown, leading scientists to use broad terms like "numerous" and "Infinite" to describe the sheer variety of life forms that inhabit our planet.

This estimation of biodiversity is a reminder of the vast complexity of life on Earth. It highlights the ever-evolving relationship between humans and the natural world, where discoveries continue to expand our understanding of the ecosystems that sustain us. New species are constantly being discovered, especially in remote or less-explored regions such as deep oceans and dense rainforests, suggesting that life on Earth is far more intricate and diverse than we can fully comprehend at present.

When I first began studying fisheries science back in 1988, the textbooks of that time listed the total number of fish species in India as approximately 2,200. Fast forward to today, and that number has surged to 3,250. In the span of just 35 years, over 1,000 new species have been identified and catalogued. This remarkable growth in our knowledge of fish biodiversity reflects the rapid advancements in science and technology, particularly in fields such as taxonomy, genetics, and environmental research.

Thanks to modern tools and techniques—ranging from DNA analysis to improved underwater exploration—our ability to discover and classify new species has accelerated tremendously. The rate at which we are uncovering new fish species, as well as other forms of life, is increasing at a pace unimaginable decades ago. It's not uncommon now to see new species being documented every month, highlighting the dynamic and ever-evolving nature of biological research.

This ongoing discovery process isn't limited to fishes alone. As science advances, our understanding of all types of organisms—both terrestrial and aquatic—is expanding, leading to the identification of previously unknown species across the board. This growth in knowledge underscores how vast and rich Earth's biodiversity truly is, with much of it still waiting to be explored and understood.

Moreover, this richness of life—from microscopic algae to massive land and marine animals—represents an intricate web of interdependence. It underscores the importance of protecting ecosystems, as the extinction of even a single species can have profound ripple effects across the entire biological network. In this way, life on Earth is not only numerous but also interconnected, revealing a delicate balance that has been shaped over billions of years of evolution.

From Simple Cells to Complex Life

For billions of years, life remained simple, with single-celled organisms dominating the planet. The next major leap in the genesis of life occurred with the evolution of eukaryotic cells, which are more complex than prokaryotic cells (like bacteria). Eukaryotic cells contain a nucleus and other specialized structures called organelles, which allowed for greater complexity and diversity in life forms. This evolutionary development eventually led to the emergence of multicellular organisms.

The "Cambrian Explosion," which occurred about 541 million years ago, marked a critical turning point in the evolution of life. During this relatively short period in geological time, an unprecedented diversity of life forms appeared, including many of the major animal groups that still exist today. It was a time when complex organisms, with specialized tissues and organs, rapidly diversified and spread across the planet.

No life forms on Earth are without purpose. Every species, from the tiniest microorganism to the largest mammal, plays a vital role in the delicate balance of nature. The existence of each life form is tied to a larger, interconnected web of biodiversity that sustains life on our planet. It is a mistake to assume that the '*Value of a species is determined solely by its direct utility to human beings*'. The Earth is not designed for *Homo sapiens* alone, but for all forms of life, each contributing to the ecosystem in ways that may not be immediately apparent.

Human beings are just one species among millions, and evolved like many other species. Though, we have developed technologies, built societies, and claimed dominance over the planet, we remain part of the vast network of biodiversity. This network includes not only the animals and plants that we benefit from directly but also the microorganisms, insects, fungi, and viruses that contribute to the health and functioning of ecosystems. Without these seemingly insignificant life forms, the entire natural balance could collapse.

Even life forms that are perceived as harmful to humans, such as the AIDS virus or Ebola virus, have a right to exist. These viruses, although deadly, are part of the natural world and follow the same biological principles that govern all life. While human beings work tirelessly to combat diseases and prevent the spread of such viruses, it is essential to acknowledge that their existence is not inherently malevolent—it is simply another expression of life's adaptability and survival. These viruses, like all organisms, are driven by the fundamental instinct to propagate and survive.

We must remember that Earth's ecosystems are deeply interdependent. The survival of one species often relies on the presence of others, even if those others seem irrelevant or harmful '***only***' from a human perspective. For example, predators regulate prey populations, insects pollinate plants, and bacteria decompose organic matter, enriching the soil. Each species, no matter how small or seemingly inconsequential, has a role to play in maintaining ecological balance. To lose one species can set off a chain reaction, affecting countless others in ways that might be impossible to predict.

This is a humbling reminder that the Earth's biodiversity was not crafted with humans at the centre. We are part of this intricate system, but we are not its masters. Our survival is deeply intertwined with the survival of countless other species, from the microorganisms in the soil to the great whales in the oceans. The air we breathe, the food we eat, and the climate we live in are all dependent on a thriving, healthy ecosystem.

In recognizing the intrinsic value of all life forms, we must also rethink our role as stewards of the planet. Conservation efforts should not be limited to species that are directly beneficial to humans but should extend to all organisms that contribute to the web of life. Preserving biodiversity is not just about saving animals or plants—it's about maintaining the stability and resilience of the natural systems that make life possible for all beings, including humans.

Our perspective needs to shift from viewing nature as a resource for human consumption to seeing it as a complex and interdependent system where every life form, no matter how small or seemingly dangerous, has a place. By acknowledging the purpose of every species, we cultivate a deeper respect for the natural world and recognize that life on Earth is a shared existence. Every creature has a right to be here, contributing to the richness and diversity of this planet, which, in turn, sustains us all.

The Purpose of Life

The biological aim of life is grounded in two fundamental imperatives: "To live" and "To reproduce." These twin objectives drive the behaviour of all living organisms, as life itself hinges on survival and the perpetuation of the species. Every animal, regardless of its size or complexity, has evolved its own strategies to meet these objectives. From microscopic organisms to complex mammals, each species has developed mechanisms to extract energy from their surroundings—whether through food, sunlight, or chemical processes—and to ensure the transmission of its genes to future generations.

Survival is the foremost priority of every animal. It is the basic instinct that underlies behaviours such as seeking food, avoiding predators, and maintaining homeostasis. Each animal is equipped with adaptations—physical, behavioural, or biochemical—that enhance its chances of survival in the specific environment it inhabits. However, survival alone is not enough; reproduction ensures that the species continues to exist beyond the lifespan of individual members. Animals invest considerable energy into finding mates, reproducing, and often caring for their offspring, ensuring that their genetic material persists into future generations. Natural selection always favours the best to exist and pass on to the next generation.

You may have noticed that the female part of a flower, known as the pistil, is composed of the stigma, style, and ovary, while the male part, the anther, produces thousands of pollen grains. Similarly, in the animal kingdom, females typically produce fewer eggs, while males generate millions of sperm. One might wonder why nature doesn't produce these in a one-to-one ratio. However, this imbalance is part of nature's strategy: by producing an abundance of pollen or sperm, only the strongest and most viable will successfully reach the egg, ensuring the creation of new life with the best possible chance of survival and growth. This selection process promotes the resilience and adaptability of future generations. It in this context, I say "Everyone is a born winner."

In an ideal world, these processes would unfold in balanced, undisturbed ecosystems, where every species coexists within a web of life. In such environments, predator-prey dynamics, competition for resources, and reproductive success are in a delicate equilibrium, allowing life to flourish without significant external disruption. However, in reality, such untouched ecosystems are exceedingly rare. Human activity—through industrialization, deforestation, pollution, and habitat destruction—has altered the natural balance of nearly every ecosystem on Earth. As a result, many species struggle to adapt to rapidly changing environments, and biodiversity faces threats from extinction.

Humans, as a species, have outpaced other animals in terms of survival strategies. Through the process of evolution and the development of advanced cognitive abilities, humans have devised ingenious ways to extract energy from their environment. From mastering fire and agriculture to harnessing fossil fuels and renewable energy, humans have continuously improved their ability to secure food, shelter, and resources. Moreover, technological advancements and social structures have vastly enhanced human reproductive success, allowing for significant population growth.

Unlike other animals, whose survival is intricately tied to their natural environment, humans have the unique ability to modify and reshape ecosystems to suit their needs. This adaptability has contributed to human dominance over the planet, but it has also come at a cost. The exploitation of natural resources, environmental degradation, and climate change are direct consequences of human ingenuity and survival strategies. As humans continue to push the boundaries of energy consumption and resource extraction, they increasingly disrupt the natural balance that other species rely on for survival.

In summary, while the biological aim of life is universal—to survive and to reproduce—the methods by which different species achieve this vary greatly. Humans, in particular, have developed extraordinary strategies for survival, far surpassing other animals. Yet, this progress has disrupted natural ecosystems, posing challenges for the long-term survival of not only humans but also countless other species. As evolution continues, humans must find ways to balance their ingenuity with the preservation of the planet's delicate ecosystems.

Moreover, purpose and resilience are deeply embedded in the natural world. Every organism follows the biological imperative to survive and reproduce, evolving over generations to refine these instincts. Likewise, in the world of management, every action—whether in strategy, communication, or innovation—is driven by the desire to survive in competitive markets and to replicate success. Strong organizations, like resilient species, constantly adapt to changing environments and learn from failures.

Nature also teaches us about selection, excellence, and sustainability. For instance, a flower doesn't produce a single pollen grain per ovule—it produces thousands, ensuring that only the fittest contribute to the next generation. This mirrors how the best business decisions emerge from a wide array of possibilities, rigorous testing, and iteration. Natural selection parallels performance management—where merit, adaptability, and value creation determine who leads, who follows, and who thrives.

However, human activities have disrupted this natural balance. Industrialization, deforestation, and climate change now threaten many species. Similarly, when management loses sight of ethics, sustainability, and long-term vision, organizations risk collapse. The modern manager's role, then, is not just to lead efficiently but to lead responsibly—understanding the broader impact of decisions on people, society, and the planet.

The lesson here is powerful: just as life on Earth thrives through diversity, adaptability, and interconnection, successful management thrives when it embraces real-world learning, nurtures diverse talent, fosters innovation, and respects ecological and human boundaries.

In the end, "Management Beyond Academics" is about learning from nature, cultivating an ecosystem of purpose, responsibility, and growth—mirroring the complex, beautiful, and interconnected web of life on our planet. It reminds us that leadership, like evolution, is not about domination, but about co-existence, stewardship, and shaping a future where all can thrive.

"Do not compete with your enemies;
instead, make them irrelevant-**Magada**"

Last But One Chapter

Genesis of Education System

The origins of the education system are a captivating tale that stretches across millennia, mirroring humanity's growth, ambitions, and the progression of how knowledge is shared. The structure we know today traces its beginnings to ancient civilizations, where the need to pass on knowledge, skills, culture, and values from one generation to the next became crucial for the advancement of society. Much like instinct in animals, every society believed in its own superiority and sought to preserve itself at all costs. As a result, survival skills were passed down through generations, either through direct inheritance or through more formalized, organized systems of learning. Over time, these systems evolved into structured educational institutions, ensuring that each new generation was equipped with the tools needed to thrive.

Prehistoric and Early Education

In prehistoric times, education was informal and deeply integrated into daily life. Elders passed down survival skills, such as hunting, gathering, and farming, through oral traditions and hands-on learning. Knowledge of tools, fire, shelter construction, and the rhythms of nature was shared within tight-knit communities. Early humans learned through observation, imitation, and direct experience, which were critical for survival.

Early Formal Education: Mesopotamia, Egypt, and China

The birth of formal education systems can be traced back to the rise of early civilizations around 3000 BCE. As societies became more complex, with the development of agriculture, trade, and governance, a more structured system of knowledge transmission emerged.

1. **Mesopotamia**: One of the earliest examples of formal education was found in ancient Mesopotamia (modern-day Iraq). The Sumerians established schools known as "edubbas" around 2500 BCE, where students—primarily boys—were taught to read, write, and perform arithmetic using cuneiform script. The primary purpose was to train scribes who could manage administrative tasks in the early bureaucracies of cities.
2. **Ancient Egypt**: Similarly, ancient Egypt had a system of education designed for scribes, priests, and government officials. Temples were centres of learning where students were taught hieroglyphic writing, mathematics, and astronomy. Education was vital for the management of Egypt's large bureaucracy, agricultural production, and monumental construction projects like the pyramids.
3. **Ancient China**: In ancient China, formal education systems were closely tied to Confucian philosophy, beginning around 1000 BCE. Education focused on moral development, civic responsibility, and governance. The "Six Arts" (ritual, music, archery, chariot-riding, calligraphy, and mathematics) were essential subjects, and Confucian scholars held prestigious roles in the government. This education system influenced the Chinese imperial examination system, which selected government officials based on merit rather than lineage.

Greek and Roman Education

The ancient Greeks and Romans contributed significantly to the structure and content of modern education systems.

1. **Ancient Greece**: In Greece, particularly in Athens, education focused on developing well-rounded citizens. The Greeks introduced the concept of liberal arts education, which included philosophy, mathematics, literature, rhetoric, and physical education. The famous Academy, founded by Plato, and the Lyceum, established by Aristotle, became centres of philosophical thought and scientific inquiry. In contrast, Sparta focused on a militaristic education system, training boys for warfare and discipline.
2. **Ancient Rome**: The Romans borrowed much from the Greeks but placed greater emphasis on practical skills, such as law, rhetoric, and engineering. Roman education was highly stratified; the elite received private tutoring in grammar, literature, and public speaking, while the masses often had access to only rudimentary education. The Roman education system was instrumental in shaping Western legal and administrative traditions.

The Middle Ages and the Rise of Religious Education

With the fall of the Roman Empire in the 5th century CE, Europe entered the Middle Ages. During this time, education was largely preserved and promoted by religious institutions.

1. **Monastic Schools**: Monasteries became centres of learning during the early Middle Ages (500-1000 CE). Monks copied and preserved ancient texts, taught religious doctrine, and educated the clergy. These monastic schools were often the only places of formal education in Europe at the time.
2. **Cathedral and Scholastic Schools**: By the 11th century, cathedral schools began to emerge, providing education to

both clergy and laypeople. These schools were precursors to medieval universities. The curriculum was based on the trivium (grammar, rhetoric, and logic) and the quadrivium (arithmetic, geometry, music, and astronomy), reflecting the influence of ancient Greek philosophy and the Christian worldview.

3. **Islamic Golden Age**: During the Islamic Golden Age (8th–14th centuries), scholars in the Middle East and North Africa made significant advances in education, science, and philosophy. Institutions like the House of Wisdom in Baghdad became centres of learning, where scholars translated and built upon Greek, Persian, and Indian knowledge. The Islamic world's contributions to mathematics, astronomy, medicine, and philosophy had a profound impact on both Eastern and Western education systems.

The Birth of Universities

The modern university system has its roots in the Middle Ages. The first universities emerged in Europe in the 11th and 12th centuries. These institutions were initially established to train clergy and bureaucrats but gradually expanded to include a broader range of subjects.

1. **University of Bologna (1088)**: Often regarded as the first university, Bologna in Italy was founded to study law. It established the model of a community of scholars, where students and professors worked together in the pursuit of knowledge.
2. **University of Paris (1150)**: The University of Paris, particularly its theology faculty, became one of the most influential centres of learning in Europe. The scholastic method, which sought to reconcile faith and reason, was

developed by scholars like Thomas Aquinas during this time.

3. **University of Oxford and University of Cambridge**: These institutions, founded in the 12th and 13th centuries, became centres of learning in England and have continued to be prestigious educational institutions to this day.

Nalanda University:

Nalanda University in India is one of the most iconic and ancient centres of learning in world history. Established around the 5th century CE in present-day Bihar, India, it was a flourishing centre of higher education long before modern universities came into existence. Nalanda's profound contributions to knowledge, education, and global culture make it a symbol of India's rich academic and intellectual heritage.

Historical Background

Founding and Establishment: Nalanda University was founded in the 5th century CE during the reign of Gupta Emperor Kumara Gupta I (circa 415-455 CE). It is believed that Nalanda began as a monastery, with an emphasis on teaching and learning, and gradually expanded into a full-fledged residential university that attracted scholars from across India and abroad. The university was heavily supported by royal patronage, and successive rulers contributed to its growth.

Location: Located near the ancient city of Rajagriha (modern-day Rajgir), Nalanda was strategically positioned in the Magadha region, a major cultural and intellectual hub. Its proximity to the ancient capital cities and trade routes helped the university flourish as a centre for knowledge exchange

Academic Prowess and Curriculum

Subjects Taught: Nalanda was a pioneer in multidisciplinary education, offering a wide range of subjects. The curriculum included Buddhist studies, philosophy, logic, mathematics, astronomy, medicine, grammar, metaphysics, and the Vedas. Buddhist teachings and philosophies were central to its intellectual discourse, but it was not limited to religious education. Scholars also studied secular subjects like law and natural sciences, making Nalanda an early example of a university with a broad, well-rounded curriculum.

Prominent Scholars: Nalanda attracted renowned scholars from all over Asia, including China, Korea, Japan, Tibet, and Central Asia. Some of the most celebrated figures associated with Nalanda include:

- **Xuan Zang (Hiuen Tsang)**: The famous Chinese monk and traveller who studied and taught at Nalanda during the 7th century CE. His detailed accounts of Nalanda have provided valuable insights into the university's structure and function.
- **Shilabhadra**: A great scholar and the abbot of Nalanda who was a teacher of Xuan Zang. He is known for his contributions to Buddhist philosophy.
- **Dharmapala** and **Vasubandhu**: Great Buddhist philosophers associated with Nalanda, particularly in the development of Mahayana Buddhism.

International Influence: Nalanda was a global institution that attracted students and scholars from across Asia. Xuan Zang, who studied at Nalanda, described it as a vibrant community where knowledge was exchanged between people of diverse cultures and countries. This cross-cultural exchange contributed to the spread of Indian philosophy and science to other parts of Asia, especially China, Korea, Japan, and Southeast Asia.

Structure and Facilities

Nalanda University was a large residential institution, housing over 10,000 students and around 2,000 teachers at its peak. It had extensive facilities, including:

- **Libraries**: Nalanda had an impressive library system, often described as one of the largest and finest in the ancient world. It was said to have three large buildings, one of which was nine stories high, housing thousands of manuscripts. The library collections included scriptures, philosophical texts, and scientific treatises.
- **Monasteries (Viharas)**: The campus had several viharas (monastic dormitories) where students lived and studied. These were well-equipped with amenities for long-term residence.
- **Temples and Stupas**: The university complex was also home to numerous temples and stupas, reflecting its Buddhist roots. These religious structures were often centres of teaching and worship.

The Decline and Destruction of Nalanda

The decline of Nalanda began in the 12th century, primarily due to the changing political landscape in northern India. The arrival of the Turkic Muslim invaders and the weakening of Buddhist patronage played a significant role in the university's decline.

- **Destruction by Bakhtiyar Khilji (1193 CE)**: In 1193 CE, the university suffered a devastating blow when it was attacked and destroyed by the Turkic general Bakhtiyar Khilji, a military commander in the army of Qutb-ud-din Aibak, the first ruler of the Delhi Sultanate. Khilji's army set fire to the libraries and other structures. According to historical accounts, the vast collection of manuscripts burned for months. Many monks were killed, and the remnants of the university community scattered, marking the end of Nalanda as a centre of learning.

- **End of Buddhist Influence**: The destruction of Nalanda was also part of the larger decline of Buddhism in India, as the religion began to lose royal patronage and faced increasing competition from resurgent Hinduism and the spread of Islam.

Revival in the Modern Era

After centuries of lying in ruins, interest in Nalanda's legacy began to resurface in the 19th and 20th centuries, when archaeological excavations revealed the grandeur of its ancient structures. Scholars, historians, and governments recognized its significance as a symbol of India's ancient academic prowess.

- **Archaeological Excavations**: British archaeologists in the 19th century began excavations that revealed parts of the university's ruins, including temples, stupas, and monasteries. Later, in the 20th century, the Archaeological Survey of India (ASI) carried out extensive excavations, leading to the discovery of inscriptions, sculptures, and other relics that shed light on the university's history.
- **Revival of Nalanda University (21st century)**: In 2010, the Indian government, with support from various Asian countries, initiated a project to revive Nalanda University. The new Nalanda University, established in 2014 near the original site, aims to emulate the ancient institution's spirit of international collaboration and multidisciplinary learning. It is positioned as a global university focusing on subjects like ecology, historical studies, and Buddhist studies.

Nalanda University stands as a monumental symbol of ancient India's intellectual and cultural achievements. It was not just a centre for Buddhist studies but a beacon of global learning that influenced scholars across Asia. The destruction of Nalanda represents a tragic loss to world heritage, but its revival in the modern era is a testament to the enduring legacy of knowledge and education that transcends time and borders.

Renaissance and Enlightenment: Broadening Education

The Renaissance (14th–17th centuries) revived interest in classical learning and led to significant changes in education. Humanism, which emphasized the study of humanities (history, literature, and moral philosophy), became central to education. Education was no longer seen as just for the clergy or elite; it was viewed as a means of developing the individual's full potential.

During the Enlightenment (17th–18th centuries), education became more secular and democratized. Thinkers like John Locke and Jean-Jacques Rousseau emphasized education as a right for all people, not just the privileged few. Rousseau's "Emile" proposed that education should be child-cantered and focus on developing practical skills and moral character rather than rote memorization.

Industrial Revolution and Modern Education

The Industrial Revolution of the 18th and 19th centuries dramatically transformed societies and education. As industrialization spread, there was an increasing demand for literate and skilled workers. This led to the establishment of public education systems in many countries.

1. **Compulsory Education**: By the late 19th century, many countries in Europe and North America introduced compulsory education laws, ensuring that children from all social backgrounds had access to basic education. This marked a significant shift from education being a privilege to it being a universal right.

2. **Standardized Curriculum**: The development of standardized curricula, examinations, and teacher training became essential to meet the demands of modern, industrialized societies. Subjects like mathematics, science, history, and literacy became central to the curriculum, with the goal of creating informed citizens and a competent workforce.

Education in the 20th and 21st Century

The 20th century saw the rise of global education systems, driven by technological advancements, social movements, and international cooperation.

1. **Universal Access**: Education became recognized as a human right, with international organizations like UNESCO advocating for universal access to primary and secondary education. Education systems in many countries have continued to expand, including access to higher education.
2. **Technological Integration**: The 21st century has seen the rapid integration of technology into education, transforming how knowledge is delivered and consumed. The rise of the internet, online learning platforms, and digital resources has democratized education, making it more accessible to people worldwide.
3. **Lifelong Learning**: The modern education system increasingly emphasizes lifelong learning, as the rapid pace of change in the modern world requires individuals to continuously acquire new skills and knowledge throughout their lives.

The genesis of the education system reflects the evolution of human societies, values, and the quest for knowledge. From its earliest roots in oral traditions and religious teachings to the establishment of universities and modern technological integration, education has continually adapted to meet the needs of individuals and societies.

As we move forward, the education system will continue to evolve, shaped by the challenges and opportunities of the future.

Indian Education System

Looking back at history, it's important to note that languages like Tamil and Kannada in India were already well-established when the now globally dominant language, English, was still in its infancy. In fact, English, despite its worldwide influence today, still does not have its own original script and has borrowed heavily from other languages. When Nalanda University was flourishing in India, a centre of knowledge attracting scholars from all over the world, there was no country called 'Canada'—or many other nations that exist today. Some countries that are now powerful did not have a long-standing history or culture of their own, while others, especially colonized nations, were deeply rooted in rich histories.

The cultural imprints left by colonial powers became integrated into the identities of many countries. Colonialism not only altered political boundaries but also influenced the customs, traditions, and languages of colonized nations. The culture of the colonial rulers often became intertwined with the native practices, leading to a hybrid identity in many regions. This colonial legacy still lingers in the education, governance, and social systems of many post-colonial nations. The Indian education system has a rich and diverse history, evolving over millennia and reflecting the country's cultural, philosophical, and spiritual heritage. It has passed through various phases—from the ancient Gurukula system to modern institutions—each contributing to the development of knowledge and learning in the subcontinent.

1. Ancient Indian Education (Vedic Period)

- **Gurukula System:** In ancient India, education primarily took place in Gurukulas, where students lived with their teacher, or guru, and learned through close, personal instruction. The education focused on holistic development—physical, mental, and spiritual. Subjects like philosophy, mathematics, medicine, astronomy, and martial arts were taught, along with religious texts such as the Vedas and Upanishads.

- **Oral Tradition:** Knowledge was passed on orally from the teacher to the student, and memorization was a key aspect of the learning process. The emphasis was on understanding and wisdom, rather than rote learning.
- **Inclusivity and Exclusivity:** While the system provided deep knowledge, it was largely limited to certain castes and privileged groups, particularly the Brahmins, and excluded large sections of society like women and lower castes.

2. Classical Indian Education (Buddhist and Jain Influence)

- **Buddhist Monastic Universities:** During the 5th century BCE, with the rise of Buddhism and Jainism, education became more accessible, and large monastic universities like Nalanda, Takshashila, and Vikramashila flourished. These institutions attracted students from across the world and taught a wide range of subjects, from logic and grammar to medicine and metaphysics.
- **Emphasis on Critical Thinking:** Unlike the rigid caste-based system of the Vedic period, Buddhist institutions promoted critical thinking, open debate, and inquiry. This era is often considered a golden age of Indian education.

3. Medieval Period (Islamic Influence)

- **Madrasas and Islamic Centres:** With the arrival of Islamic rulers in the medieval period, the education system in India diversified. Madrasas were established as centres of learning, primarily focused on Islamic theology, philosophy, and the sciences. Subjects like mathematics, astronomy, medicine, and literature also flourished during this period.

- Integration of Knowledge: The blending of Hindu, Buddhist, and Islamic knowledge created a rich intellectual landscape, with scholars from various disciplines engaging in dialogue and exchanging ideas.

4. Colonial Period (British Influence)

- **Introduction of Western Education:** During British rule, the Indian education system underwent significant changes. The British introduced the Western model of education through schools and universities, with an emphasis on English language instruction. This led to the establishment of institutions like the University of Calcutta, Bombay, and Madras in the mid-19th century.
- **Macaulay's Minute:** The infamous Macaulay's Minute of 1835 advocated for an education system that focused on producing a class of English-educated Indians who would serve as intermediaries between the British rulers and the Indian population. This led to a decline in traditional Indian systems of education.
- **Impact on Social Structure:** While the British system helped modernize certain aspects of education, it also reinforced social hierarchies, side-lining indigenous knowledge systems, and further marginalizing the lower classes.

5. Post-Independence Era

- **Democratization of Education:** After India gained independence in 1947, there was a strong push to democratize education and make it accessible to all sections of society. The Indian Constitution guaranteed the right to education, and various initiatives were undertaken to expand the reach of primary, secondary, and higher education.

- **Expansion of Universities and Technical Institutes:** The post-independence period saw the establishment of prestigious institutions like the Indian Institutes of Technology (IITs), Indian Institutes of Management (IIMs), and Indian Institutes of Science Education and Research (IISERs), which contributed to India's growing reputation in science, technology, and management.
- **Focus on Literacy and Inclusion:** Numerous policies aimed at improving literacy rates and promoting inclusivity, especially for women and marginalized communities, were introduced. Programs like the Mid-Day Meal Scheme and Sarva Shiksha Abhiyan were launched to encourage school attendance and reduce dropout rates.

6. Contemporary Indian Education

- **Diverse and Complex:** Today, the Indian education system is one of the largest in the world, with millions of schools and thousands of higher education institutions. It is characterized by a mix of public and private schools, along with a variety of curricula, including state boards, Central Board of Secondary Education (CBSE), Indian Certificate of Secondary Education (ICSE), and international programs.
- **Challenges:** Despite significant progress, the system still faces challenges such as inequality in access, poor infrastructure, quality of teaching, and a gap between urban and rural education. There is also a strong focus on rote learning, which often stifles creativity and critical thinking.
- **Recent Reforms:** The National Education Policy (NEP) 2020 introduced major reforms aimed at overhauling the education system. It emphasizes holistic, flexible learning, the integration of vocational education, and a focus on

critical thinking and creativity. The NEP also aims to make higher education more inclusive and accessible while promoting the use of technology in education.

7. Global Impact and Indian Diaspora

- **Contribution to Global Education:** Indian-origin professionals and academics have made significant contributions to the global education system, particularly in fields like science, technology, and engineering. The Indian diaspora plays a key role in shaping research and development worldwide.
- **Increasing Globalization:** Indian education is also increasingly globalized, with many Indian students studying abroad and foreign universities collaborating with Indian institutions.

The Indian education system has evolved through a blend of indigenous traditions and external influences, from ancient Gurukulas to modern universities. While it has made great strides, the system continues to evolve to meet the needs of a rapidly changing world. The focus now is on creating an education system that not only imparts knowledge but also fosters innovation, inclusivity, and holistic development, ensuring that it keeps pace with global standards while preserving its cultural roots.

"Knowledge is not a power,
until it is applied-**Dr Myles Munroe**"

Education in Modern India

As of January 29, 2024, India boasts a total of 1,113 universities, comprising various types such as central, state, deemed, and private universities. Among these, there are 56 central universities and 67 agricultural universities actively functioning across the country.

One of the oldest universities in India is the Serampore College, established in 1818, which attained university status in 1829, making it 201 years old. Historically, India's education system was designed primarily to impart knowledge, rather than prepare individuals for specific jobs. The focus was on learning for the sake of wisdom and enlightenment. However, as society evolved and became more organized, those who were highly educated naturally began to hold influential positions, including in the king's court and other areas of governance and administration. Over time, education became a crucial pathway not only for intellectual growth but also for gaining employment and securing important roles in society.

Today, universities continue to play a vital role in shaping the careers and future of individuals in a more structured and professionalized manner. During 1960 to 1990, they maintained their sanctity and professionalism. Later universities, become miniature of the governments because of too much involvement of the government machinery. Government and Governor used to nominate intellectuals, social workers and other visionaries as 'Members of Board of Management or Syndicate Members.' However, all the members will not be nominated by the government. Few members will be nominate the Chancellor. Some governments have expressed a desire to assume complete control by curtailing the powers of the governor. However, this has not been implemented.

The Universities

Estimating the exact number of universities worldwide is challenging due to varying definitions of what constitutes a university and differences in national education systems. However, as of 2023, several sources provide approximate figures.

- Erudera, an education search platform, reports approximately 23,624 schools and universities offering study programs globally.
- The Centre for World University Rankings (CWUR) evaluated 20,531 institutions in its 2023 assessment, with the top institutions making it to their Global 2000 list.
- Statista indicates that, as of July 2023, India alone had an estimated 5,350 universities.

These variations highlight the complexities in defining and counting universities across different countries and educational frameworks. Various sources give different numbers of educational institutes. Even in the era of digital revolution, some institutes do not get listed in the list of official data.

"People who bite the hand feeds them usually lick the boot that kicks them-**Eric Hoffer**"

Laws of Nature

Energy Flow in Nature: From Higher to Lower Gradients. In natural systems, energy does not stay still—it constantly seeks equilibrium. A fundamental principle across physical sciences is that energy flows from regions of high potential (or concentration) to regions of low potential. This is observed in various forms of energy transfer, most notably heat and water movement.

1. Heat: Guided by the Laws of Thermodynamics

Heat energy naturally flows from a hotter object (higher thermal gradient) to a colder object (lower thermal gradient). This behaviour is described by the Second Law of Thermodynamics, which states:

"In an isolated system, heat will always flow from a region of higher temperature to a region of lower temperature until thermal equilibrium is reached."

- This is why your coffee cools down in a cold room, or why heat radiates from the Sun to Earth.
- The driving force is the difference in temperature, which is a gradient of thermal energy.

Water: Governed by Gravitational Laws

Water movement in natural environments—like rivers, rain runoff, or groundwater flow—is primarily driven by gravitational potential energy.

"Water flows from higher elevation (higher gravitational potential) to lower elevation (lower gravitational potential) due to gravity."

- When water is stored in a tank or reservoir at a height, it has more gravitational potential energy.
- As it flows downward, this energy is converted to kinetic energy, powering its movement.

This is governed by Bernoulli's Principle and Hydraulic Head in fluid dynamics, which combine elevation, pressure, and velocity components to describe how and why fluids move.

General Principle: Gradient-Driven Flow

Whether it's thermal energy, water, electric current, or even concentration of chemicals, the natural world operates through the principle of gradient dissipation:

- Heat → Thermal gradient
- Water → Gravitational (elevation) gradient
- Electricity → Voltage (electric potential) gradient
- Diffusion of gases or solutes → Concentration gradient

In each case, energy or matter flows to balance or equalize the system, often releasing usable energy or performing work in the process.

So, when we say "energy flows from higher to lower gradient," we are referring to a universal behaviour in physics and nature—driven by laws like gravity, thermodynamics, and fluid mechanics. Understanding these gradients allows engineers, environmental scientists, and energy experts to design systems like hydropower, thermal engines, and irrigation channels that mimic or harness these natural flows efficiently.

Flow of Knowledge

In earlier times, a scholar or teacher was regarded as the ultimate authority on knowledge, and learning flowed in one direction—from the knowledgeable to the unlearned, much like water flowing from a higher to a lower gradient. Debate and discussion were rare, as the relationship between master and student was often one of passive instruction. The teacher's authority was seldom, if ever, questioned, and education took the form of preaching rather than interactive learning.

Moreover, education was a privilege reserved for a select few, often restricted to certain communities, castes, or the ruling class. The vast majority of the working class was either denied access to education or could not afford it. This exclusion was a widespread practice, rooted in social hierarchies and economic inequalities. Across different regions and religions, for most of human history, education was systematically withheld from large sections of society. We can assert, without hesitation, that this denial of education was a global phenomenon, affecting many cultures throughout history. Many of the challenges the world faces today are the by-products of discrimination based on caste, creed, and religion.

Supremacy and discrimination in human society come at a tremendous cost in various forms. Sadly, the instinct for competition—rooted in animal behaviour—has been adopted by humans. Yet, unlike animals, humanity has the capacity to thrive through cooperation, not rivalry. Unfortunately, the imperial instincts of the Mughals and Europeans disrupted the prosperity of a nation as rich as India, dismantling its well-established education system.

Education systems were well established in ancient times in regions like Greece, Egypt, India, and Iran, each with its own distinct methodology and curriculum. These early civilizations had a rich intellectual tradition, creating institutions of learning that shaped the foundation of knowledge in their respective societies. For example, while Greece was known for its philosophical teachings and Egypt for its wisdom in mathematics and astronomy, India was home to some of the world's earliest universities like Nalanda, where scholars from all over the world came to study.

The wealth looted by European colonial powers played a significant role in helping them build robust economic structures and become prosperous nations. During the colonial era, countries like Britain, Spain, Portugal, France, and the Netherlands amassed immense wealth by exploiting the natural resources, labour, and raw materials of the colonies they controlled in Asia, Africa, and the Americas. Here are some ways looted wealth contributed to the economic development of European countries:

1. **Resource Extraction**: Colonies were rich in valuable resources like gold, silver, spices, cotton, tea, sugar, and later, industrial raw materials like rubber and minerals. These resources were extracted and sent to Europe, providing the capital needed to fuel industrialization.
2. **Cheap Labour and Slave Trade**: European colonial powers exploited cheap labour in their colonies and participated in the transatlantic slave trade. Millions of Africans were forcibly transported to work on plantations in the Americas, which significantly contributed to the economic prosperity of European powers, particularly through agricultural products like sugar, tobacco, and cotton.
3. **Trade Monopolies**: European countries established monopolies on trade with their colonies. By controlling trade routes and markets, they ensured that colonial wealth flowed back to Europe, enhancing their economies and allowing them to invest in infrastructure, industry, and military power.
4. **Industrialization**: The resources extracted from colonies fuelled the Industrial Revolution in Europe. Raw materials like cotton from India and sugar from the Caribbean helped create new industries, while the wealth generated allowed European powers to build factories, railways, and modern infrastructure, accelerating their economic growth.

5. **Financial and Banking Institutions**: The profits made from colonial exploitation also led to the development of robust financial institutions in Europe. Banking, insurance, and stock markets thrived on the back of colonial wealth, allowing these economies to stabilize and expand.
6. **Social Stability**: The wealth generated from colonies helped stabilize European societies by creating a more affluent middle class, funding public services, and reducing the tax burden on the local population, thus contributing to social and political stability.

The wealth and resources extracted from colonies were instrumental in the development of Europe's economic might. This exploitation allowed European countries to industrialize faster, accumulate capital, and build stronger, more robust economies that continue to have global influence today. However, the long-term consequences of this exploitation were devastating for many colonized countries, which were left impoverished, underdeveloped, and politically unstable. There is an ancient philosophical truth that the universe tends toward balance — a concept echoed across spiritual traditions, political thought, and natural sciences. The statement that rich countries may face political unrest as knowledge and competence begin to spread evenly is not a curse nor a pessimistic forecast; rather, it reflects the deeper laws of equilibrium and justice that govern human systems just as they govern physical systems.

From a scientific perspective, nature abhors imbalances. In thermodynamics, for example, heat always flows from a region of higher temperature to a region of lower temperature until equilibrium is achieved. Water seeks its level, flowing from areas of abundance to areas of scarcity. This tendency is not just a property of physical elements, but a universal principle of distribution and entropy. Similarly, knowledge and human competence — once concentrated in a few geographies — are now spreading rapidly through technology, education, and communication.

In this diffusion, the monopolies of privilege and power are gradually dissolving. Just as in ecology, where the over-concentration of resources in one part of the system eventually destabilizes the whole, the extreme accumulation of wealth, power, and knowledge in a few nations inevitably creates pressure elsewhere. This is not driven by vengeance but by **natural systemic correction** — an equalizing force built into the very fabric of existence.

Philosophically, thinkers from Heraclitus to Hegel have posited that **conflict and change** are not anomalies but necessary components of progress. Heraclitus famously stated, *"Strife is justice"*, suggesting that oppositions and tensions are what bring balance and movement to the world. Hegel's dialectics — the triad of thesis, antithesis, and synthesis — illustrate how existing systems are challenged, opposed, and eventually transformed into new, more inclusive structures.

As marginalized societies gain access to knowledge and tools once reserved for the elite, the existing power hierarchies will no longer hold unchallenged sway. This does not inherently lead to chaos or destruction, but rather a rebalancing of global dynamics. The unrest that may follow is not the end, but a transition — a turbulent but necessary phase in the evolution of a more equitable global order.

Hence, your statement is rooted not in cynicism or pessimism but in the inevitable workings of natural law and moral truth. Just as the rivers do not choose to flow, but flow because of gravity and topography, knowledge and power, once unlocked, will move freely toward balance — and with it, will come a reshaping of societies, including those once thought untouchable by unrest or inequality.

"Humans can't rely on the brains alone to succeed at workplace-
Satya Nadella"

Job Market around the World

Between 1975 and 2010, the population doubled to 1.2 billion, reaching the billion mark in 2000. According to the UN's World Population dashboard, India's population now stands at slightly over 1.428 billion, edging past China's population of 1.425 billion people, as reported by the news agency Bloomberg. In 2015, India's population was predicted to reach 1.7 billion by 2050. In 2017 its population growth rate was 0.98%, ranking 112th in the world; in contrast, from 1972 to 1983, India's population grew by an annual rate of 2.3%.

In 2023, the median age of an Indian was 29.5 years, compared to 39.8 for China and 49.5 for Japan; and, by 2030; India's dependency ratio will be just over 0.4. However, the number of children in India peaked more than a decade ago and is now falling. The number of children under the age of five peaked in 2007, and since then the number has been falling. The number of Indians under 15 years old peaked slightly later (in 2011) and is now also declining.

The global Gross Enrolment Ratio (GER) in higher education was 40% in 2020. This represents a doubling of the GER from 19% in 2000. This means that 40% of the population of the relevant age group (typically 18-23) were enrolled in tertiary education globally in 2020.

In 2021-2022, India's Gross Enrolment Ratio (GER) in higher education was 28.4%. This means that 28.4% of the eligible population in the 18-23 age group were enrolled in higher education. The GER has shown a notable increase from 23.7% in 2014-15 to 28.4% in 2021-22. The goal is to increase the GER to 50%

by 2035. Unemployment rate in India was 6.0% in 2016-17 and dropped to 7.9% in 2024 and it is in the increasing trend while it is 4.2% in China for last 3-4 years. Even in the United Kingdom and USA, the unemployment rate ranges between 4.2% to 4.4%. even in the great economic countries like the U.S. unemployment rate in August 2025 was about 4.3%, up slightly from 4.2%. Some states have higher rates—California is about 5.5%, the District of Columbia about 6.0 %, and many others are in the 4–5% range.

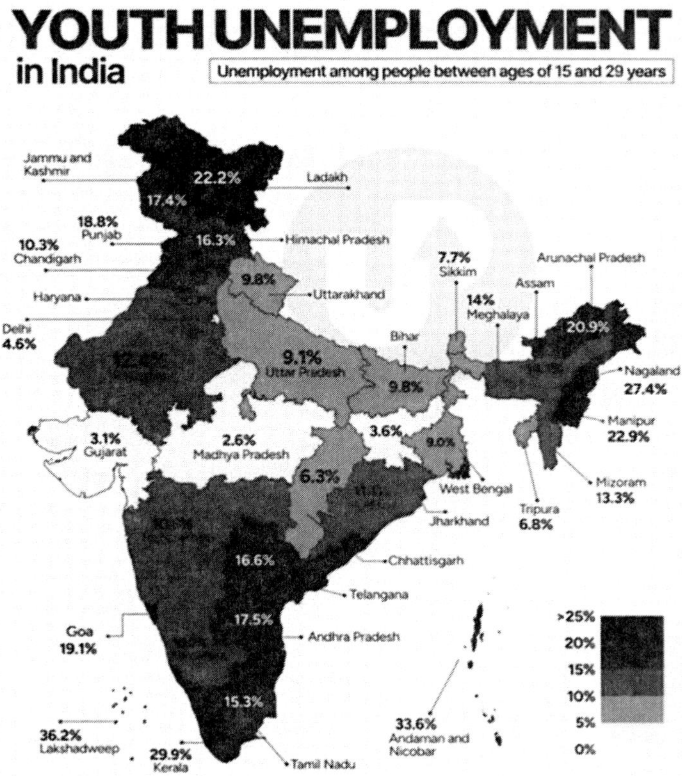

The U.S. federal government has entered a shutdown as of 1 October 2025 due to failure to pass funding legislation. This is forcing many regulatory agencies to furlough staff, including the SEC, which could impair market oversight, delays in IPOs or new product approvals, and reduce financial stability oversight.

This kind of fiscal uncertainty can erode business and investor confidence, and indirectly stress financial markets via liquidity, credit flows, and institutional trust. New U.S. tariffs on seafood, agricultural products, and a broad range of imports have unsettled markets and added uncertainty about trade policy. These moves can disrupt global supply chains, reduce export incomes, and feed into broader financial volatility. These current issues will surely hit the job markets and create instability in many countries.

Unemployment has emerged as a significant social challenge in China in recent years, marked by both a rise in overall numbers and uneven effects across various social and regional groups. Demographic factors like age and gender also influence unemployment trends. In particular, the status of women in the labour market has declined, reflected in a drop in labour force participation, higher unemployment rates, increased work demands, and a growing gender pay gap.

South Africa top the G20 in overall unemployment, but it also has a significant level of youth unemployment, as nearly half of the young population is unemployed. Thirty years after the end of Apartheid, The prominence of inequality in the country makes escaping unemployment and underemployment difficult.

Indian government is making its great efforts in imparting skills among youths, by introducing new 'Micro, Small and Medium Enterprises (MSME)' financial supports, subsidies and incentives through the developmental departments. MSMEs are the second-largest employer in India after agriculture, employing over 110 million people and contribute around 30% to India's GDP. They account for about 48% of the country's exports while promoting balanced regional development and reduce urban-rural disparities.

Although start-ups are increasingly contributing to job creation worldwide and playing a pivotal role in driving employment—especially in emerging sectors—their impact remains uneven and somewhat limited in pace. The job opportunities generated tend to be concentrated among individuals with specific, high-demand skill sets, particularly in areas like technology, digital marketing, and data analytics. As a result, large segments of the workforce, especially those with traditional or low-skill backgrounds, often find themselves excluded from these new opportunities. Furthermore, the overall rate of job creation by start-ups is relatively gradual when compared to the scale of global unemployment challenges, making it insufficient to absorb the rapidly growing labour force in many countries.

Opportunities in Disguise: A Call to Action for Aspiring Entrepreneurs

It is easy—and often habitual—for people to blame the government, the system, or society at large for their failures, delays, or missed opportunities. While some criticism may be valid, continuously pointing fingers only drains energy, fosters negativity, and keeps individuals locked in a cycle of inaction. Blame never built anything; action does.

India, with all its complexities, contradictions, and challenges, still stands as a land of immense possibilities. From its rich cultural diversity and vast natural resources to its youthful population and rapidly growing digital infrastructure, the nation is brimming with gaps waiting to be filled—problems waiting to be solved. And where there are problems, there are businesses to be built.

The entrepreneurial spirit doesn't seek perfect conditions; it thrives in imperfect ones. True entrepreneurs don't wait for ideal governance or flawless systems—they find opportunities amid chaos. Whether it's sustainable agriculture, renewable energy, digital education, rural healthcare, or local manufacturing, India provides countless avenues for those with vision and courage.

Success in India is not reserved for those with connections or capital, but for those who have clarity of purpose and a problem-solving mindset. Instead of cursing the darkness, be the one who lights a lamp. Let your energy be spent not on complaints but on creation. After all, the world remembers not the critics, but the builders.

Rather than wasting a lifetime waiting for change, be the change-maker. Nations are not shaped by governments alone—they are built by determined individuals who dare to dream, to act, and to persist. India is not a land of limitations—it is a land of layered opportunities, visible only to those who choose to look deeper.

While travelling extensively across the country, particularly through rural interiors, certain recurring patterns reveal deeper structural challenges confronting Indian villages. What appear on the surface as minor civic neglects are, in fact, indicators of institutional fatigue, social transition, and economic stagnation. It is a common scene even in some cities.

Village bus stops—once symbols of connectivity and aspiration—are often found in a state of neglect. Many are dilapidated, cluttered with debris, overgrown vegetation, and in some cases abandoned altogether, informally repurposed as dumping grounds or public toilets. This neglect reflects not merely a lack of maintenance, but the absence of ownership and accountability at the grassroots level, where public infrastructure exists without a clear custodian or incentive for upkeep.

Similarly, traditional open wells, which historically served as lifelines for drinking water, irrigation, and social interaction, are now choked with weeds and algae, showing clear signs of eutrophication. This ecological degradation signals more than environmental neglect; it points to a social shift away from community-managed resources. The youth no longer frequent these spaces, either because alternative water sources have emerged or because collective responsibility has weakened. What was once a shared asset has gradually become a forgotten liability.

A more concerning dimension is the condition of rural youth. In many villages, unemployed or underemployed young people are seen aligning themselves closely with local political actors. While such affiliations may provide short-term access to food, drinks, or minor favours, they rarely translate into sustainable livelihoods or meaningful economic contribution to their families. This phenomenon highlights a cycle of dependency rather than empowerment, where political proximity substitutes for productive engagement.

The underlying issue is not the absence of ambition, but the absence of viable rural economic pathways. Limited skill development, weak local enterprises, declining agricultural profitability, and poor linkage to markets leave young people with few credible alternatives. As a result, social energy that could have been channelled into entrepreneurship, community enterprises, or local governance is instead absorbed into informal political patronage systems.

From a management and policy perspective, these observations underscore the urgent need to reimagine rural development beyond subsidies and schemes. Villages require:

- Functional local institutions with accountability mechanisms,
- Youth-centric livelihood models rooted in local resources,
- Revival of community-managed assets such as water bodies and public spaces, and
- A shift from welfare dependence to enterprise-driven rural economies.

These visible signs of neglect—shabby bus stops, abandoned wells, idle youth—are not isolated failures. They are symptoms of a broader challenge: the erosion of community ownership and economic dignity. Addressing them requires integrated thinking that combines governance, entrepreneurship, environmental stewardship, and social leadership. Only then can villages transition from spaces of survival to ecosystems of opportunity.

The Will Power can create hundreds of jobs

If rural youth possess collective willpower and a sense of ownership, unemployment alone need not translate into social stagnation. Even in the absence of formal jobs, young people can emerge as custodians of their villages, taking responsibility for cleanliness, maintenance of public spaces, and revival of common resources. With organized effort, they can mobilize support from key stakeholders—local governments, line departments, CSR initiatives, and community leaders—to restore and rejuvenate open wells, desilt and deepen community tanks, and reclaim water bodies through systematic deweeding and maintenance.

Beyond infrastructure, youth-led initiatives can extend into economic organization. By forming commodity-based groups or producer collectives, villagers can aggregate their produce, improve bargaining power, and access markets that offer better price realization. Such collective action transforms individual vulnerability into shared strength, shifting the narrative from dependence to participation.

Encouragingly, these practices are visible in several regions of North-East India, where communities demonstrate high levels of cleanliness, discipline, and social organization despite limited employment opportunities. What distinguishes these regions is not the absence of hardship, but the presence of community cohesion, self-regulation, and contentment rooted in collective responsibility. People take pride in their surroundings, manage common resources effectively, and align individual behaviour with community well-being.

From a management perspective, this highlights a critical lesson: development is not solely a function of income or employment, but of mindset, leadership, and social capital. Where willpower, organization, and shared purpose exist, even resource-constrained communities can achieve order, dignity, and sustainability. Such models deserve closer study and replication, not as idealistic exceptions, but as practical frameworks for grassroots governance and rural transformation.

In the absence of willpower to create livelihoods, identify community-based services, or convert knowledge into enterprise, even highly educated youth can become trapped in a cycle of dependency and misplaced aspiration. Degrees such as MCA, PhD, and other postgraduate qualifications, which are meant to prepare individuals for innovation, problem-solving, and leadership, increasingly end up chasing roles that neither require nor reward such capabilities.

A striking illustration of this disconnect was recently witnessed in Odisha, where more than 8,000 candidates reportedly appeared for recruitment examinations conducted on public roads for just 180 Home Guard positions. What makes this episode deeply concerning is not merely the scale of competition, but the profile of the applicants—many of whom possessed advanced technical and academic qualifications. This is not a failure of the youth; it is a failure of the tertiary education ecosystem to align learning with employability, entrepreneurship, and societal needs. In the era of AI based knowledge system, the class rooms lectures are losing their relevance. The system appears to function largely as a mechanism to keep young people occupied, rather than meaningfully empowered.

From a management perspective, this phenomenon reflects a misalignment between education outcomes and economic realities.

Higher education has increasingly become credential-centric rather than capability-centric. Students are trained to clear examinations, not to identify problems, design solutions, or create value within their own communities. As a result, even well-educated individuals perceive security only in government-linked, low-paying, uniformed roles, rather than in self-created opportunities.

More critically, this mindset erodes local development potential. The same educated youth competing for Home Guard posts could have been mobilized to:

- Organize village-level service enterprises,
- Lead water resource rejuvenation projects,
- Form producer groups or rural start-ups,
- Deliver digital, educational, or technical services locally, or
- Act as intermediaries between government schemes and community implementation.

Instead, the absence of confidence, mentorship, and institutional encouragement pushes them toward job-seeking behaviour divorced from their skill sets.

The Odisha case should therefore be read as a warning signal. It underscores that unemployment is not merely a numerical problem, but a mindset problem shaped by education systems. When degrees fail to instil self-belief, adaptability, and entrepreneurial thinking, they inadvertently produce dependency rather than leadership.

Regions that demonstrate stronger community willpower—where youth engage in collective action, maintain public assets, and create informal yet productive economic roles—show that employment is not always a prerequisite for dignity or contribution. What is required is an education system that treats villages and communities as laboratories of opportunity, not as places to escape from.

Unless tertiary education is reoriented towards problem-solving, local enterprise creation, and societal engagement, such scenes will recur—not as isolated incidents, but as recurring symbols of systemic failure. The true measure of education must therefore be judged not by the number of degrees awarded, but by the confidence it builds to create value, even in constrained environments.

"The Wheels of justice turn slowly,
but they grind exceedingly fine- **Sextus Empiricus**"

The 'Bearings' of the Mind

The invention of the wheel during the Sumerian civilization marked a revolutionary leap in transportation, laying the foundation for mobility as we know it. However, the true transformation—an exponential leap—came much later with the creation of a seemingly simple yet powerful tool: the 'bearing'. While the wheel got us moving, it was the bearing that gave motion its grace, efficiency, and speed, reducing friction and opening doors to modern engineering marvels. This reminds us that even small innovations can turn revolutions into evolutions.

In the journey of life and achievement, every individual has ideas—some raw, some refined, and many waiting to be realized. But what truly transforms an idea from a spark into a blazing fire of success is not merely ambition or even effort. It is the presence of the right tool—the equivalent of a 'bearing'—that propels an idea forward smoothly, efficiently, and exponentially. This is what I want you to identify: the "bearing" in your journey that can take your idea or project to the next level.

Let me elaborate on this powerful metaphor. The invention of the wheel was a revolutionary milestone in human history. It enabled movement, trade, and transportation, thereby altering the course of civilizations. But the wheel had its limitations. As it moved, friction slowed it down, and the wear and tear it experienced created barriers to efficiency. It wasn't until the bearing was invented that the wheel—and in essence, all mechanisms relying on rotary motion—achieved a new dimension of functionality. The bearing reduced friction, enhanced durability, and allowed for speed and precision.

In modern terms, while the wheel started the journey, the bearing made it unstoppable.

So, what is the bearing in your life or in your project? It could be a mentor, a mindset shift, a key resource, or even a simple concept or method that unlocks momentum. Most people fail not because they lack ideas or ambition, but because they never identify or utilize their bearing. They keep pushing and pulling without realizing that the addition of a single component—a catalyst—could change everything.

Procrastination is often misunderstood as laziness or lack of discipline. But more often than not, it's the result of not realizing the missing bearing. People stall because something isn't clicking, the movement isn't smooth, or the friction is too high. When we can't identify what's slowing us down, we naturally avoid the task. But once the bearing is in place, resistance fades, and progress feels natural.

Over the years, I have met hundreds of young people—particularly unemployed youth—who come seeking direction. They knock on my door, asking for the 'right project' or the 'best idea' to start with. And yet, the irony is often striking. Many of them show up without a notepad or even a pen. But they do carry a costly smartphone, often more concerned with appearances than preparation.

This tells me something fundamental: they are not yet ready. Ideas are like seeds—they require a prepared soil to take root. When someone comes to me empty-handed, without the basic tools to note down thoughts, capture insights, or sketch ideas, it signals a lack of seriousness. And so, I've devised a simple method to filter out those who are merely enthusiastic from those who are genuinely committed.

I do not entertain unprepared visitors. I politely ask them to come on another day—a random date, not scheduled or guaranteed. If they are truly interested, if they see value in the interaction, they will return. This single act weeds out almost 90% of the crowd. Not because they are incapable, but because they are not invested enough to take the next step. The second visit is my litmus test.

And when they do return, I ensure they are given homework—not as a formality, but as a tool of engagement. The homework is not just about doing something for me; it's about them digging into their own capabilities, researching, reflecting, and coming back with something that reflects effort. This exercise alone begins to act as a bearing—it aligns their intent with action, their ideas with a framework, and their enthusiasm with accountability.

For those who stick around, something magical begins to happen. They start identifying their own bearings. Some discover that a particular online course unlocks their potential. Others find that joining a community, writing daily, or simply managing their time better becomes their turning point. A few realize that mentoring under someone, or shadowing a professional, is what propels their learning curve. Whatever it is, they find that progress accelerates once the bearing is in place.

And the bearing doesn't have to be grand or complex. It can be as simple as a notebook, a habit of reading 30 minutes a day, or committing to weekly brainstorming sessions with a peer. It's often not about money or access to expensive resources—it's about clarity, consistency, and commitment.

What many don't realize is that a bearing doesn't make the journey easier by removing obstacles—it makes it smoother by helping you navigate through them efficiently. Without the bearing, your idea might still move forward, but the drag, resistance, and risk of burnout are higher. With it, you conserve energy, increase precision, and build momentum.

In a world flooded with ideas and opportunities, what sets achievers apart is not just vision but the ability to execute. Execution demands structure, strategy, and support systems—your bearings. If you're stuck, reflect not on the magnitude of the challenge but on the absence of the right tool.

So, how do you identify your bearing?

Start by reflecting on your past projects or goals. When did you make the most progress? What support system or tool was in place then? Who were you interacting with? What habit made the biggest difference?

Then, examine your current state. What's missing? Is it clarity of direction? Time management? Technical skills? A sounding board for your ideas? A lack of discipline? Often, identifying what's missing is the first step to finding your bearing.

And remember, no one can find your bearing for you. Mentors and guides can orient you in the right direction, but the real discovery is deeply personal. It demands observation, experimentation, and persistence.

As someone who has interacted with a wide spectrum of aspirants—from students to seasoned professionals—I can assure you that everyone hits a wall. What matters is whether you stand there scratching your head or look around for a lever, a bearing, to push through.

If you're reading this and feel that you're stuck, don't rush to change your entire plan. Instead, focus on that one element that could make the system work better. It might be a person, a practice, a perspective, or a platform. Invest in that.

The bearing is a symbol of refinement, of quiet force, of subtle brilliance. Find yours—and you won't just move; you'll glide, accelerate, and perhaps even fly.

This is not merely about projects or professions. It's about life itself. Whether you're an artist, engineer, entrepreneur, teacher, or farmer—your wheel is turning. But is your bearing in place?

Find it, and you'll find your way.

Some people come to me for learning and end up teaching me what they know. Since we do not charge on hour basis like many consultants do, they pick up any subject and wander, laugh at loud and promise to come back with Himalayan hills and go back and don't return. Eventually, waste the time instead of using it.

In fact, I am not a person who suggest you the right project for you. Based on your intuition, knowledge, competence, capability, resource and the gut feeling, if you have any idea, I can shape it professionally and evaluate its potential and guide you to make appropriate decisions which enhances the winning probability.

"If you are going through hell,
keep going-**Winston Churchill**"

You are the Winner

In my view, the term 'beauty' should be erased from the dictionary altogether. It's a vague, overused, and deeply misunderstood word that has caused more confusion than clarity in the world. What exactly is 'beautiful'? According to many great thinkers and philosophers, beauty is merely a subjective perception—'in the eyes of the beholder'—and yet we've allowed it to become an absolute standard, often dictated by industries that profit from insecurity and imitation.

The cinema, fashion, and magazine industries have hijacked this term, shaping and reshaping its definition to suit their commercial agendas. Over time, we've blindly accepted these portrayals as truth. But can beauty really be packaged, marketed, and sold? And more importantly, should it?

Take nature, for instance. How do we define the magnificence of a forest, the mystery of a mountain range, or the serenity of a waterfall nestled between hills? Can we claim that this combination is 'beautiful' while ignoring the raw, untamed essence that defines it? These elements of nature don't strive to fit into a frame—they simply are. They exist in their own rhythm and grace, without any need for human validation or judgment.

We must learn to appreciate things as they are, not as we are told they should be. Nature doesn't conform to aesthetic norms, and neither should we. Every tree, cloud, rock, and river has its place in the tapestry of existence—not because it is beautiful, but because it is.

The same logic applies to language. Who authored grammar? No one, really. Grammar evolved from usage, from repeated patterns that communities accepted over time. Renowned grammarians like Wren & Martin or dictionaries like Webster's have compiled and structured it, but they didn't create it from thin air. It emerged naturally, collectively.

Likewise, the concept of beauty was never authored by a single mind. It evolved—or rather devolved—from cultural interpretations, commercial interests, poetic exaggerations, and societal expectations. From Shakespeare's sonnets to modern-day filters on social media, from Kalidasa to Monalisa of La Da Vinci and the latest social media sensation in India-the tribal girl 'Monalisa', we've been sold different versions of what 'beautiful' looks like. And we've internalized those versions without questioning their origin or their impact.

It's time we move beyond the superficial. True value lies not in appearances, but in essence, presence, character, and uniqueness. Let's stop chasing the illusion of beauty as defined by others and start embracing authenticity—unfiltered, unedited, and unapologetically real. Let 'beauty' be not a standard, but a celebration of diversity, of uniqueness, of being. Only then can we truly see the world—and ourselves—for what we are, not what we are told we should be."

The Commerce of Complexion:

It is both fascinating and deeply troubling to witness how certain industries have thrived for decades on a notion so shallow, yet so deeply ingrained: that fair skin is synonymous with beauty. For over half a century, companies have peddled fairness creams—small tubes of illusion—promising transformation in a matter of days. '*Become fair in seven days*,' they claim, as if fairness were a currency of worth, a ticket to success, or a passport to acceptance.

Yet, the truth behind their market dynamics tells a different story. These products, despite bold global aspirations, have not gained ground in many African nations where people, proudly rooted in their natural identity, do not fall prey to such manufactured ideals. Their skin is not a source of shame; it is a source of heritage, identity, and pride. The market didn't fail there because the product lacked merit—it failed because the people refused to subscribe to a fiction about themselves. I genuinely don't understand why these companies are so fixated on turning everyone fair-skinned. If their efforts had truly been effective, we'd be living in a world where every face looks the same—fair and uniform. Thankfully, nature doesn't yield so easily to marketing gimmicks.

Despite growing awareness about the harmful effects and ethical concerns surrounding skin fairness products, many brands have firmly entrenched themselves across several countries — especially in regions like Africa, India, and much of Asia, including nations with predominantly fair-skinned populations — all under the misleading guise of promoting 'healthy skin. This success is largely attributed to their persistent branding and aggressive marketing strategies, which skilfully tap into deep-rooted societal insecurities. I simply wish to remind readers that humanity has thrived for millions of years — enduring harsh climates, evolving through diverse environments, and sustaining healthy skin long before the advent of modern cosmetic products. The natural resilience of human skin, nurtured by traditional practices, balanced diets, and a connection with nature, was never in question until commercial industries began redefining beauty through artificial standards and synthetic solutions.

By capitalizing on long-standing notions of beauty that associate lighter skin with success, attractiveness, and social mobility, these companies have turned an emotional vulnerability into a profitable business model. The messaging subtly reinforces the idea that lighter skin equates to greater opportunity and desirability, thereby feeding into and sustaining the cycle of perceived inferiority.

The demand for skin lightening products in Africa is substantial. In Nigeria, for instance, over 77% of women have reportedly used skin whitening products, the highest rate in Africa . The Middle East & Africa skin lightening products market was valued at approximately USD 927.7 million in 2023 and is projected to reach USD 1.2 billion by 2030, growing at a CAGR of 3.8%

Now contrast this with India—a land of profound spiritual wisdom, ancient philosophies, and rich cultural diversity. And yet, paradoxically, it remains one of the largest consumers of fairness products. Why? Because generations have been conditioned to believe that lighter skin equates to beauty, status, and desirability. This belief is not born out of truth, but out of centuries of colonization, caste narratives, media influence, and internalized inferiority.

As of 2024, India's skincare market is valued at approximately USD 8.4 billion, with projections indicating growth to USD 17.1 billion by 2033, reflecting a compound annual growth rate (CAGR) of 7.8% during 2025–2033 . Another analysis estimates the market at USD 8.78 billion in 2024, anticipating an increase to USD 17.69 billion by 2033, with a CAGR of 8.43%

The tragedy is not the product itself; it is the psychology that fuels its demand. A psychology that suggests: "You are not enough as you are. Lighten your skin to brighten your future." This mindset is a spiritual ailment far worse than any physical imperfection. It speaks of a society that has not yet made peace with its own identity. A society that, instead of celebrating its brown, golden, and dusky hues—each one kissed by the sun—seeks to erase them in favour of a foreign ideal.

Philosophically, this is the ultimate alienation of the self. When one begins to dislike their skin, they are, in essence, rejecting their own essence. The skin is not just a surface; it is a symbol. To dislike it is to believe that one's birth, one's ancestry, and by extension, one's very being is somehow inadequate. And once this seed of inadequacy is planted, it spreads to every other part of life—eroding confidence, dimming potential, and stifling authenticity.

And who benefits from this mass delusion? Not the people. Not the youth. But the corporations that package insecurity into a cream and market it with dreams. They are not just selling a product; they are selling a prejudice. And worse, they are doing it in the garb of empowerment. All those chemicals and base materials eventually find their way into drains, ultimately polluting aquatic and other ecosystems — not just through the toxic substances themselves, but also through the packaging waste that accompanies them.

But beauty, if it exists at all, is not in fairness or in facial symmetry. It is in authenticity. It is in the fearless acceptance of oneself. The ancient Indian scriptures spoke not of light skin, but of tejas—an inner radiance that emanates from character, clarity, and conviction. True beauty is not a visual phenomenon; it is an existential presence. It is the integrity of being aligned with who you are, unapologetically.

So, when a society collectively begins to unlearn the lies it has inherited—when it stops looking in the mirror for worth, and instead turns inward—it takes the first step toward liberation. The youth of this nation deserve that liberation. They deserve to know that no cream can give them value; their value is inherent, eternal, and independent of any external approval.

Until then, as long as we continue to measure beauty by complexion, we will remain enslaved by our own ignorance, and companies will continue to profit by selling us cures for problems they themselves created.

Inferiority Complex Disorder (ICD)

Inferiority Complex Disorder (ICD) is, in many ways, one of the most insidious and underestimated psychological conditions affecting today's youth—particularly members of Generation Z. While not a physical illness in the traditional sense, its impact can be more devastating than some of the most feared infectious diseases, such as AIDS or Ebola. What makes ICD particularly dangerous is its invisibility; unlike physical ailments, its symptoms often go unnoticed by others—and sometimes even by the individuals suffering from it.

People affected by ICD typically appear physically healthy. They eat, walk, talk, and engage in daily routines just like anyone else. They may even participate in social gatherings, school, or work environments. However, beneath this facade of normalcy lies a turbulent internal world. These individuals often live in a constant state of mental detachment, emotionally disconnected from their surroundings. They interact, but do not engage. They smile, but feel hollow. They are surrounded by people, yet feel alone—trapped in an internal narrative dominated by self-doubt, comparison, and imagined inadequacy.

ICD does not manifest through fever, fatigue, or physical pain. Instead, its symptoms are psychological: persistent feelings of low self-esteem, chronic self-comparison, social withdrawal, and a tendency to retreat into an imagined world of personal shortcomings and failures. And because these signs are subtle and internalized, they are difficult to diagnose and even harder to treat.

In today's hyper-connected world—where social media often amplifies feelings of inadequacy and societal pressure—ICD has quietly become a psychological epidemic, and one that demands greater awareness and compassion.

The environment in which a child grows up plays a pivotal role in shaping their emotional and psychological well-being—and is often a major contributing factor to the development of Inferiority Complex Disorder (ICD). Among the various environmental influences, the home environment stands out as a critical source of either emotional nourishment or psychological void. Unfortunately, in today's fast-paced world, especially within micro and nuclear families, many children are growing up in emotionally imbalanced households.

In families where both parents are working professionals, the demands of career often overshadow the emotional needs of the child. While the intention might be to provide the best possible future, what is often overlooked is the present emotional void that is being created. The children, in the absence of attentive parenting, tend to form their emotional understanding through interactions with housemaids, caregivers, or grandparents. Though well-meaning, these substitutes may lack the emotional awareness, educational background, or time required to nurture a child's evolving psychological needs.

This leads to a significant communication gap. The emotional exchanges in such setups are often shallow, inconsistent, or even confusing. Children, in their formative years, require not just care, but meaningful conversation, validation, and the ability to observe and learn the full spectrum of human emotions in a healthy and structured way. When these interactions are either missing or mixed with emotionally unfiltered attitudes or outdated beliefs, children may grow up with a fragmented understanding of themselves and others.

As a result, when they step into broader society, they often find it difficult to interpret or navigate the emotional cues of diverse individuals. They become socially anxious, hesitant, or overly self-conscious. This inability to relate or adapt contributes to a state of internal confusion—a psychological fog where they feel misunderstood, inadequate, or even invisible.

Thus, the roots of ICD are not always in the child's own psyche, but rather in the emotional architecture of the environment they are raised in. A home lacking in emotional engagement becomes the silent incubator of a disorder that quietly grows, often without anyone noticing—until it's too late.

Dark and Lovely

Until 1988, I silently struggled with what I now recognize as an identity crisis. I was skinny, dark-skinned, and dressed in modest, often worn-out clothes. Forget speaking English—I wasn't even confident in expressing myself fluently in my own mother tongue—*Kannada*. I often felt invisible, overshadowed, and unsure of where I belonged.

In an attempt to break free from this sense of being unseen, unheard, and unremarkable, I made a conscious decision: to show up everywhere, in every way I could. I began participating in every possible activity, regardless of my skill level or prior experience. Whether it was a sport I barely knew how to play or a stage performance that demanded courage I didn't think I had—I jumped in with both feet.

I immersed myself in games, cultural programs, and artistic events. Singing, dancing, mime, cartooning, painting, pencil sketching, elocution, extempore speeches, mono-acting, drama, music, skits, dumb charades—you name it, I was there. I was driven not by mastery, but by the simple yet powerful desire to be noticed, to feel included, and to shape an identity of my own.

In retrospect, that restless energy was not just about recognition—it was a silent rebellion against the limitations imposed on me by my appearance, background, and lack of resources. It was my way of telling the world—and perhaps myself—that I was more than what met the eye.

Over the course of those four years, something remarkable happened—I ended up winning prizes in every single event I participated in. But let me be honest: it wasn't because I was the best, or even good, at all times. In fact, much of the journey was filled with awkwardness, failure, and public embarrassment. People laughed at my performances. I was mocked, even insulted, while standing on stage. Some labelled me a joker, a clown, someone who was just trying too hard. They didn't take me seriously.

But here's what they couldn't do: they couldn't 'Ignore Me.'

That became my quiet mission—not necessarily to win every time, but to ensure I was visible, present, and undeniably part of the process. I refused to remain invisible, to be just another face lost in the crowd. I wasn't content being a spectator to other people's success—I wanted to be in the arena, however bruised or flawed my performance might be.

And that's when I began to understand something deeper—life doesn't always reward perfection, but it does reward persistence. The world forgets those who sit quietly in the shadows, but it remembers those who dare to step into the light—even if they stumble.

There's a certain sacredness in the act of showing up, again and again, even after being laughed at. It's not about ego or attention. It's about reclaiming your place in the world when the world has told you don't have one. I may not have been the best speaker, or singer, or artist—but I was there. I was part of the narrative. I was on stage—not just physically, but metaphorically, participating in the unfolding of my own story.

I honestly don't remember sitting among the audience. Not because I was arrogant, but because I knew—even then—that the world rarely celebrates the spectators. It reserves its memory for the players. And I had decided, come what may, to be a player. People started noticing my talent and my complex faded away. I learnt the art of selling the 'Dark.' If you can learn this art, even you can do wonders irrespective of your educational qualifications.

Beauty is not yours; but Personality is yours

One of the fundamental truths of life is that we do not get to choose our parents. We are born into circumstances beyond our control—into a family, a lineage, and a genetic blueprint that shapes our early identity. The physical traits we inherit—such as the structure of our body, the colour of our skin, eyes, and hair—are part of the genetic lottery. Even certain predispositions like temperament or susceptibility to diseases may be passed down biologically.

But here's the liberating reality: beyond these inherited aspects, everything else is open to transformation.

Our character, our mindset, our skills, our worldview—all of these are shaped not by genetics, but by environment, experience, and choice. While our parents may gift us the biological scaffolding, it is the society we live in, the company we keep, the books we read, and the challenges we face that mould the person we become.

It's a common misconception that our potential is limited to our inheritance. In truth, inherited traits may set the stage, but it is our exposure to ideas, values, opportunities, and effort that writes the script of our lives. For example, your father may have been a strong-willed person—but unless you cultivate discipline in your environment, that strength may remain dormant in you. Similarly, even if no one in your family is artistic, you can still become an exceptional painter through training, exposure, and practice.

This concept is central to the science of epigenetics and the philosophy of self-development: while we cannot rewrite our DNA, we absolutely can redesign our destiny. And this isn't just idealistic—it's a well-observed phenomenon. Many of the world's most successful, creative, and impactful individuals come from humble or challenging backgrounds. They were not born with a silver spoon or exceptional lineage—but they acquired greatness through adaptation, exposure, and resilience.

So, rather than dwelling on what you inherited or didn't inherit, it's far more powerful to ask:

"What can I acquire? What can I become? What is your calling? What makes you happy?"

Ultimately, life is not just about the genes you carry, but the choices you make. You are not a prisoner of your biology; you are a product of your response to life.

Your parents poured their love, wisdom, and sacrifices into shaping you into the best version of yourself. It is now your responsibility—not merely to succeed—but to show the world that you are the living embodiment of their finest virtues. You carry within you the legacy of strong, noble genes, and your purpose is to ensure that this lineage of character, resilience, and excellence is not only continued but etched into the fabric of nature for generations to come.

The level of support you receive from your parents is deeply influenced by their financial capacity, the social environment they inhabit, and the culture that surrounds them. For most, this support extends through your formative years—typically until you complete your 10th or 12th grade. After that, life gently (or sometimes harshly) nudges you to make your own choices, to pick a path that aligns with your inner calling, and to pursue it with determination and clarity.

Throughout this book, I've made a conscious effort to steer away from the conventional idea that success is guaranteed if you simply 'study well.' Yes, without question, for those from modest or underprivileged backgrounds, education can be a powerful vehicle—it opens doors, levels playing fields, and builds confidence. But let us face a hard truth: the world is not equipped to absorb every educated individual into roles that match their qualifications. The system isn't designed to accommodate everyone who holds a degree with the same respect or opportunity.

We live in a time of relentless technological disruption—where new set of skills become obsolete overnight, and entirely new fields emerge from nowhere. In this reality, you must go beyond formal education. You must become a keen observer of the world, discover your unique strengths, and learn how to package, present, and position them in ways that create value—for yourself and for others. In essence, the future belongs not just to the most educated, but to the most adaptive, the most creative, and those who are willing to continuously evolve.

"Those who do not move do not notice their chains-**Rosa Luxemberg**"

Echoes of the Extraordinary Endure

The Story of Dolly Chaiwala and Beyond

Take a moment to observe the extraordinary journey of Dolly Chaiwala — a humble tea seller from Nagpur, Maharashtra, who turned into a national sensation. His rise to fame was not backed by academic degrees or corporate credentials, but rather by sheer individuality, authenticity, and self-belief. Known for his charismatic tea-making flair and distinctive persona, Dolly became a viral figure on social media. What followed was unprecedented — none other than Bill Gates, one of the world's richest and most influential individuals, sought him out and visited his roadside tea stall. Let that sink in: he didn't go to Bill Gates; Bill Gates came to him.

That moment wasn't just a photo opportunity — it was a powerful statement. The world doesn't necessarily follow those who imitate others; it follows those who create their own path. Dolly's uniqueness became his brand. He built an identity that people resonated with — and in doing so, he broke the norms of what success is supposed to look like. Post this encounter, Dolly became a sought-after guest at business schools, entrepreneurship summits, and high-profile events. Reports even suggest that he opened an office in Dubai and he is an ambassador for Starbucks in India— a far cry from the roadside stall where his journey began. He is all set to roll out his own brand, 'Dolly Ki Tapari,' in three unique formats: a mobile cart, a standard storefront, and a premium flagship model.

Sir Mokshagundam Visvesvaraya, renowned for his engineering prowess and statesmanship, held a profound belief in the dignity of labour and the importance of excellence in every task. One of his most inspiring statements encapsulates this ethos.

"Remember, your work may be only to sweep a railway crossing, but it is your duty to keep it so clean that no other crossing in the world is as clean as yours."

This quote emphasizes that no job is insignificant and that every role, when performed with dedication and excellence, contributes meaningfully to society. Sir Visvesvaraya's life was a testament to these principles; he was known for his discipline, integrity, and commitment to public service. His legacy continues to inspire individuals to uphold the dignity of their work, regardless of its nature, and to strive for excellence in all endeavours. The core message is clear: If you are authentic, committed, and believe in your own uniqueness — the world takes notice.

In 2023, my son Reshi Magada conducted a small but insightful social experiment in Mangalore. Along with his team, he set up a basic, no-frills tea stall in a crowded marketplace. The twist? While most of the other tea vendors operated in unclean surroundings, Reshi focused on hygiene, simplicity, and presentation — but charged the same price as the rest. The result? His stall saw a 42% increase in sales compared to others. This experiment proved a critical point: people value quality, hygiene, and experience — not just low prices.

India is a land full of paradoxes and possibilities. It's a country where someone pays ₹10 for a roadside chai and someone else happily spends ₹150- ₹780 for a cappuccino at a luxury café — in the same city. The key takeaway is this: value creation is not always about undercutting prices. Sometimes, your Unique Selling Proposition (USP) can be your integrity, your hygiene, your style, your story — or simply your unwavering commitment to being different.

In today's social media age, where everyone is trying to follow trends, those who stand out — by staying true to themselves — are the ones who truly rise. Dolly Chaiwala didn't follow the so called heroes. He led his own way and he became the hero. That is not just a business lesson — it's a life lesson.

Khabane Khaby Lame

He is a Senegalese-born social media personality and content creator, best known for his humorous and wordless reaction videos on TikTok. Born on March 9, 2000, in Senegal, he moved to Italy with his family at a young age.

Khaby rose to global fame by silently mocking overly complicated life hack videos—often responding with a simple, logical solution and his signature deadpan expression and hand gesture. What made him unique and widely relatable is that he rarely speaks in his videos, transcending language barriers and reaching a global audience.

Some quick highlights about him:

- As of 2022, he became the most-followed person on TikTok, overtaking Charli D'Amelio.
- He is known for embracing simplicity and authenticity in a digital world full of filters and exaggeration.
- Despite his fame, he often emphasizes humility, family values, and humour without hate. According to Alessandro Riggio, the social media manager who signed Lame when he had only 1,000 Instagram followers, the TikToker was earning up to $750,000 per post and was on track to make $10 million by the end of 2022.
- Lame was a juror for the Cannes Festival alongside Rithy Panh in 2022, where he judged TikTok short films.
- Since 2023, Lame has served as a judge on the television show Italia's Got Talent.
- In August 2023, Lame was added as a cosmetic outfit in the 2017 video game Fortnite Battle Royale, as part of the "Last Resort" Battle Pass.

Taylor Lorenz and Jason Horowitz of *The New York Times* attribute Khaby Lame's success to his "universal exasperated everyman quality," noting that his rise stands out from typical TikTok stars due to its "entirely organic" nature. Samir Chaudry, founder of *The Publish Press,* highlights Lame's appeal as rooted in his focus on "authenticity over production" and his effortless style, emphasizing that he succeeds by "not trying too hard." Christina Ferraz, founder of the marketing agency *Thirty6Five,* adds that Lame's expressions of frustration resonate widely, stating, "His exasperation is relatable, and feelings are universal." Lame himself credits his global popularity to his expressive facial reactions and deliberate silence, describing it as "a way to reach as many people as possible

"Never trust a man who speaks well of everybody
-John Churton Collins"

Effective Communication

Needless to say, communication is not just a supplementary tool—it is the lifeblood of any successful business or institution. Whether it's a small enterprise, a multinational corporation, or a public institution, the ability to convey ideas, share information, and build understanding is foundational to its growth and stability.

Clear, honest, and timely communication fosters trust, enhances collaboration, reduces misunderstandings, and builds a healthy organizational culture. It aligns teams with a common purpose, empowers leadership to inspire action, and enables institutions to connect meaningfully with stakeholders, clients, and the community at large.

In the absence of effective communication, even the best strategies fail, the most talented teams crumble, and valuable opportunities are lost. On the other hand, institutions that prioritize communication—both internal and external—become adaptive, resilient, and trusted in the long run. In essence, success doesn't depend only on what you do, but also on how well you communicate it.

Every species on this planet, from the tiniest insect to the largest mammal, has evolved its own unique method of communication — a set of signals, sounds, or gestures designed to convey intent, emotion, or warning. This ability to connect with others is fundamental to survival. Fortunately, among the estimated 8.7 million species that inhabit the Earth, human beings stand out as the most advanced in their capacity for complex, nuanced communication.

Our words, language systems, technologies, and emotional intelligence give us an unmatched edge in expressing thoughts, building societies, and driving progress. Recognizing this, even institutions like the National Productivity Council highlight the immense value of effective communication — estimating that enhancing communication alone could boost national productivity by up to 27%. That's not just a statistic; it's a powerful reminder of how much efficiency, innovation, and collaboration hinges on our ability to share information meaningfully.

Yet, in many government and office systems, this potential is often squandered. Simple matters that could be communicated instantly through digital tools are still routed through layers of paperwork, unnecessary physical meetings, and outdated protocols. This not only consumes valuable time and energy, but also drains resources — from fuel and manpower to public funds.

In an era where technology offers seamless, real-time interaction, clinging to archaic modes of communication is not just inefficient — it's regressive. We must evolve, not just as individuals, but as systems, by embracing smarter communication practices that reflect the intelligence and capabilities we pride ourselves on as a species.

Even today, when most professions demand a practical demonstration of skills, the teaching profession—ironically one of the most critical pillars of society—often lacks such evaluation. Teachers are still largely selected based on academic qualifications, such as university marks and published research papers. While these indicators reflect a certain level of knowledge, they do not necessarily translate into effective communication, real-world relevance, or classroom engagement. I have personally come across educators who struggle to write a coherent page or speak confidently for even three minutes without reading from a script.

In stark contrast, we are witnessing a revolution driven by the power of digital platforms and social media. Thousands of young minds, without traditional degrees or academic accolades, are passionately creating videos and reels on subjects they love—be it history, science, technology, fitness, or even philosophy. With authenticity, clarity, and creativity, they are connecting with millions, educating, entertaining, and inspiring. Many of these creators are now earning monthly incomes in the range of lakhs and even crores—an amount that might take decades or may not possible to achieve through conventional career ladders, including teaching roles in government institutions.

This shift compels us to rethink what truly defines a good teacher in today's world. Is it merely certificates and publications, or is it the ability to engage, inspire, and educate in meaningful ways? The digital age is blurring the boundaries of traditional professions, and perhaps it's time our education systems catch up. Practical aptitude, communication skills, and the capacity to connect with students—online or offline—must become essential criteria in the selection and growth of educators. After all, education is not just about delivering content; it's about awakening curiosity and transforming lives.

Within the framework of technical university education systems, particularly at the postgraduate and doctoral levels, there exist structured components known as 'Credit Seminars' and 'Research Seminars'. These platforms are designed not only for students to present their ongoing or completed research, but also to nurture academic dialogue, peer review, and inter-disciplinary learning. Ideally, these forums should foster a vibrant intellectual ecosystem where students, faculty members, and research scholars critically engage with each other's ideas, offer constructive feedback, and refine their scholarly pursuits.

However, what is observed in many institutions today is a disappointing dilution of this vision. Major advisors and committee members often restrict their participation to seminars delivered solely by their assigned students. They attend, make a few comments—often formalities—and leave, disengaging themselves from the broader academic discourse unfolding within the department or faculty. This practice, in my opinion, is not just a missed opportunity—it is a dangerous trend.

By not attending seminars of other students, faculty members lose the chance to benchmark the performance of their own mentees. They miss out on observing varying presentation styles, understanding emerging research areas, and—most importantly—recognizing where their students stand in relation to others. Comparative evaluation is an essential part of academic growth, not to create unhealthy competition, but to encourage improvement and excellence.

As someone who makes it a point to regularly attend research seminars—whether or not I am officially involved—I can confidently say that there is immense learning to be gained from these young researchers. Today's students are working at a level of depth and breadth that reflects the changing times. No surprise here—they *should* be better. I studied science three decades ago, when access to information was limited to libraries, hard-bound journals, and long correspondence with experts. These students are growing in the information age, where access to knowledge is not just easy—it's instantaneous. They are exposed to global research, collaborative tools, and the latest technologies that allow them to model, simulate, and test ideas in ways we never imagined.

Moreover, active faculty involvement in all seminars helps maintain academic standards. It sets a culture of seriousness, accountability, and mutual respect. When students see that their professors are genuinely interested—not just as evaluators, but as learners—they develop confidence, purpose, and a greater sense of value in their own work.

In essence, seminars should not be viewed as academic obligations but as opportunities for collective growth. The moment we stop learning—from anyone, especially the younger generation—we stop growing. True academic maturity is when a teacher sits among students not to teach, but to learn. And I have found that, more often than not, the most profound insights come from the voices we least expect—those who are still discovering their own.

In many instances, it may appear on the surface that I am teaching students — delivering lectures, guiding projects, or leading academic discussions. But in reality, the process is far more reciprocal than it seems. Every academic exercise I engage in, every question a student asks, and every perspective they bring to the table offers me an opportunity to learn.

Teaching is often mistaken as a one-way transaction, where knowledge flows solely from the teacher to the taught. But genuine education — the kind that transforms minds — is a dialogue. When I prepare a lesson, I dive deeper into the subject than I ever did not do as a student. When a student challenges a concept, or connects it with something new, it pushes me to think differently. Their curiosity becomes contagious, their insights refreshing, and their interpretations sometimes surprising.

In fact, students today are not just recipients of information; they are explorers of knowledge. With access to global resources, current research, and interdisciplinary tools, they bring new dimensions to familiar ideas. Engaging with them compels me to stay updated, humble, and open-minded.

Over time, I have realized that the classroom — or any academic setting — is not merely a platform for instruction; it is a shared space for intellectual evolution. I may hold the role of a teacher, but I am a student too — constantly learning, evolving, and being shaped by the very minds I am supposed to shape. And in that exchange lies the true beauty of education.

Across the country — and indeed around the world — There is no shortage of institutions and training centres claiming to teach communication skills. Most of these programs, however, focus almost exclusively on speaking — how to speak fluently, confidently, and persuasively. Their curriculum revolves around vocabulary building, pronunciation, public speaking, and sometimes even body language. But amid all this emphasis on how to speak, one crucial element of communication is often entirely neglected: "The art of listening.'

Ironically, true communication begins not with speaking, but with listening. As you know "The deaf kid definitely become dumb." And yet, I've rarely come across a single institute or course that teaches people ***how to listen*** — actively, empathetically, and without judgment. Listening is not a passive act. It requires patience, presence, emotional intelligence, and a genuine interest in the speaker's thoughts. In fact, a good listener often communicates more than a good speaker.

We live in a world where everyone is eager to be heard, but very few are willing to listen. This imbalance creates noise, not dialogue — argument, not understanding. In personal relationships, professional settings, and public life, the inability to truly listen is at the root of many misunderstandings and conflicts.

Effective communication is a two-way process, and if we keep polishing only one side — our speaking skills — while ignoring the other, we are not truly becoming better communicators. We are merely becoming louder.

It's high time we recognize that listening is a powerful skill, one that deserves equal — if not greater — attention in our education and training systems. A person who knows how to listen can learn faster, empathize deeper, lead better, and respond more wisely. Let us not forget: the greatest minds in history were not just brilliant speakers, but also patient, attentive listeners.

So, while learning to speak well has its place, let us not underestimate the quiet strength of a listening ear. Because sometimes, in listening, we say more than words ever could.

Some charge exorbitant fees, capitalizing on the societal perception that effective communication, particularly in English, is the key to personality development. You can often spot advertisements shouting slogans like "Join Our English-Speaking Course – Transform Your Personality!" This narrative, while well-meaning, is deeply flawed and misleading. There is a dangerous misconception at play here — the idea that merely learning a foreign language, especially English, can automatically enhance one's personality. This assumption reduces personality to mere linguistic ability, overlooking the deeper, more meaningful components that truly define a person's character.

Personality is not about fluency in a particular language. It is rooted in attitude, self-awareness, confidence, integrity, and the way one interacts with others. A person's values, empathy, resilience, and sense of purpose shape their personality far more than their vocabulary or accent. If English alone were the measure of personality, then what should we infer about people who are mute or speech-impaired? Or about those who speak eloquently, yet display arrogance, dishonesty, or apathy? Do we dare say that those who cannot see, speak, or hear are void of personality? That would not only be false but deeply unjust.

Communication is undeniably important — it is the bridge between minds and the thread that binds relationships. But communication is much more than language. It includes your body language, your listening skills, your ability to connect emotionally, and your intention behind every word you speak. Even a person who cannot speak a word can communicate volumes through gestures, presence, and authenticity.

The obsession with English is largely a colonial hangover, reinforced by globalization. It has created an unfortunate class divide, where linguistic ability is mistaken for intelligence or worth. This needs to change. While learning English, or any new language, can certainly open doors and offer practical advantages — especially in a global context — it must not be mistaken as the sole or primary ingredient of one's personality.

If we truly want to develop ourselves, we must begin by nurturing confidence in our mother tongue, clarity in our thoughts, kindness in our actions, and responsibility in our words. These are the true markers of a strong, admirable personality — not the language you speak, but the values you stand for.

"To be a fool at the right time is also an art
-**Giacomo Casanova**"

Writing skills

In this section, I am not focusing on essay writing or scientific writing skills — which are, of course, important in academic and professional circles. Instead, I am drawing attention to a fundamental, often overlooked practice: the art and discipline of 'noting down.'

It may sound simple, even trivial, but it is astonishing how this basic habit is gradually disappearing. In 2024, I had the privilege of addressing a distinguished group — more than 32 officers from the Indian Administrative Service (IAS), representing all 30 districts of Karnataka. These individuals had cleared one of the most competitive and challenging examinations in the world, which tests not only intellect but also endurance, awareness, and general aptitude. By the very nature of their positions, they are among the highest decision-makers in the administrative machinery of our nation.

However, during my session, something deeply troubling caught my attention — not a single one of them was taking notes. All of them were given a good pen and a pad. But, no one had opened them. It may seem like a small detail, but to me, it revealed a profound lapse in learning culture. While they had certainly proven their merit in the past, the moment you stop learning, especially in such roles, you begin to stagnate — and in public service, stagnation doesn't affect just the individual; it affects the people and country they serve.

There is a dangerous myth that once you reach a certain rank or designation, the process of learning becomes optional. But knowledge is not a one-time acquisition; it is a lifelong process. And leadership, especially in governance, demands the humility to listen, reflect, and evolve continuously. Power without evolving wisdom turns into mere control — mechanical administration without soul.

Yes, they are managing the machinery of the state. Yes, they are implementing programs, allocating budgets, and appearing at press briefings. But are they truly learning from the grassroots? Are they genuinely adapting to the changing dynamics of society, technology, and citizen expectations? Are they actively trying to improve themselves and the systems they govern? If they were, we would have seen more inclusive policies, deeper empathy, and faster progress. But the outcomes we witness — the gaps in governance, the sluggish development, the continued social disparities — speak volumes.

Taking notes is symbolic. It reflects an open mind — a willingness to absorb, to question, and to grow. When a leader stops carrying a pen, they risk carrying only their pride. And in public service, that pride can come at the cost of public good.

I have personally witnessed that in more than 90% of conferences, workshops, and academic gatherings — even among scholars and students — participants arrive without a pen or notebook. They rely entirely on the organisers to provide writing materials. While it is a courteous and professional gesture for event hosts to offer these items, it is not their obligation. It is the participant's responsibility to come prepared.

Carrying a pen and notebook is not just about being ready to jot something down — it reflects one's attitude toward learning. It shows humility, preparedness, and respect for knowledge. It signifies that the individual values the opportunity to learn and wants to retain what they hear.

During my tenure as the head of an academic institution, I made it a point to stress this habit. I instructed both faculty and students to carry their own writing materials to every meeting, seminar, and discussion — no exceptions. Initially, there was some resistance. Some found it unnecessary, others even mocked the idea. But gradually, the culture shifted. Now, everyone come equipped, and over time, they started to appreciate the power of that small, deliberate act.

In an era where digital distractions are everywhere and attention spans are shrinking, the act of noting down — physically writing something by hand — becomes even more important. It helps encode knowledge in the brain more effectively, triggers reflection, and fosters deeper understanding.

Let us not forget: civilizations were built on recorded ideas, philosophies were preserved through written manuscripts, and revolutions began with handwritten notes. The simple pen remains a timeless tool of transformation — and those who carry it are often those who lead, learn, and remember

Learn to Speak at a Right Time

There was a mime selection trial going on, and it was no ordinary event t my college. The seniors, a bunch of seasoned seniors—Madhu Nanjappa, Vijay Anand, Suman Cariappa, Poonacha, Sanju, Rajeev Chopra, and the graceful Yamuna Yermal and Huda Ahmed—were already there, deeply engrossed in rehearsing. These folks had everything: fluency in Hindi, English, and an air of experience that made them seem untouchable. Meanwhile, Swamy and I, the underdogs, waited in the side wings for hours, eagerly anticipating our turn. Little did we know, the selection process was more of a staged "drama" than an actual trial. The team had already been handpicked by Dr. Radhakrishnan— *a teacher who in-charge of student activities* based on his special connections with the students.

The theme of the mime? 'Eve teasing.' Now, let me tell you, I didn't even know such a term existed in the English language. The practice session began, and Dr. Radhakrishnan, with his stylish English and flair for drama, took command of the stage. There was Yamuna, standing gracefully in the middle of the stage, with Suman—this almost tall, handsome guy—coming up to her, giving her "the look." And there she was, acting all irritated and pretending to be totally uninterested, like some old Bollywood scene.

I was confused, standing there trying to make sense of it all. So, in my usual clueless way, I leaned over towards Dr Radhakrishna and asked in Kannada, "Sir…Enidu—what's this?"

Dr. Radhakrishnan looked at me as if I'd just asked him to explain quantum physics. "You don't understand," he said, waving me off and continuing to direct the mime actors, his English rolling off his tongue in a grandiose fashion.

But I couldn't hold back. Something about the scene didn't sit right with me, so I asked again, "Why is the girl rejecting him, even though he's handsome?"

The entire room erupted into laughter. It was like someone had hit the comedy jackpot. Dr. Radhakrishnan looked at me with disbelief, then said, "Hey, look at this funny guy! Can you believe him?"

And I wasn't done yet. With my signature deadpan delivery, I added, "If the girl's going to reject someone, shouldn't the guy be ugly? I mean, I could play that role perfectly!"

That was it. Everyone burst into uncontrollable laughter, literally rolling on the floor. Even the seniors who had been so serious moments ago were doubled over, clutching their stomachs. Dr. Radhakrishnan shook his head, still laughing, but I knew I'd made my mark that day— as a mime actor. The mime theme might have been "eve teasing," but that day, the real show was the humour I brought to the stage.

Suman—a stocky, thick-necked guy was shocked the I way changed the entire situation. I was asked to take on his role, and I did it so well that I ended up replacing him as the lead. Though Suman still stayed on the team, playing a different part, I had stolen the spotlight with the lead role.

We went to the Youth Festival in Bangalore, where we took first place. This win earned us the chance to compete at the zonal level which was held at Mysore where universities from all four states participated.

The core message I wish to share is this: Learn to speak up—especially when it matters the most. Timing and courage go hand in hand. There are moments in life when silence might feel like the safer option, but it can also cost you opportunities that may never come again.

Looking back, had I chosen to stay quiet and simply accept the situation as it was—out of fear, doubt, or discomfort—I would have missed a crucial turning point in my journey. I may never have made it into the team, never found my place, and certainly wouldn't have come this far.

Speaking up doesn't mean being loud or confrontational. It means standing up for your truth, asserting your worth, and letting the world know you are ready—not just to be seen, but to be counted.

Sometimes, all it takes is one voice—your own—to change the direction of your life. Don't let hesitation hold you back. That one decisive moment can open doors you didn't even know existed.

"You live most of your life inside your head. Make Sure it's a nice place to be-**Unknown**"

English: Just another language

The Japanese and Chinese can confidently assert that language is merely a tool—not a barrier to knowledge or progress. They have every reason to make such a claim. Their entire educational journey—from primary school to advanced studies in science and technology—is conducted in their native languages. They have successfully internalized and innovated within complex fields like engineering, artificial intelligence, and robotics without relying on English. Their mastery of science and technology has come through culturally rooted systems of learning, enabling them to build world-class industries and institutions.

However, the situation in India is far more complex and nuanced. We are at a linguistic crossroads. While early education in many parts of the country is conducted in regional languages, the medium of instruction in higher education—particularly in science, medicine, and engineering—is predominantly English. This creates a significant disconnect. Students who transition from local language schooling to English-medium universities often find themselves struggling—not with concepts, but with comprehension and communication.

As a result, we cannot simplistically say "English is just a language" in the Indian context. For millions of Indian students, English is not only a language—it is an unofficial gatekeeper to opportunity. Fluency in English often determines access to prestigious institutions, well-paying jobs, and career advancement, especially in sectors like IT, corporate services, international research, and government administration.

In my experience, I have seen talented, knowledgeable students being denied job opportunities—not due to a lack of skill or intellect—but solely because of their inability to communicate fluently in English. Their academic qualifications and technical abilities were sound, yet their confidence faltered during interviews or group discussions. In many cases, the problem wasn't a lack of knowledge, but a lack of linguistic fluency in the language of the evaluator.

This is a harsh reality that our education system must reckon with. While we take pride in our cultural and linguistic diversity, the dominance of English in higher education and the job market cannot be ignored. It has created a duality where language proficiency often overshadows competence, and where bright minds are left behind simply because they weren't trained in a particular tongue.

The real challenge, then, is not to choose between English and Indian languages, but to bridge the gap. We need to develop models that allow students to think in their own languages while expressing fluently in English—especially in the sciences and professional spheres. This is where soft skills training, language support, and communication workshops should become an essential part of our curriculum.

In the spirit of *Management Beyond Academics*, this situation underscores a broader truth: success in the modern world is not determined by knowledge alone, but by one's ability to convey it, share it, and lead with it. Communication, especially in a global language like English, is no longer a soft skill—it's a core competency.

To truly empower our youth, we must acknowledge the complexity of India's linguistic reality and respond with compassion, innovation, and reform. We must teach our students to own their ideas in any language—but also to express them in the one that opens doors.

It took me several years to truly understand that there is absolutely no direct link between one's ability to speak English and their intellect or personality. For the longest time, I too held the false belief that fluency in English equated to superior knowledge or status. But in reality, English is simply one of over 7,000 languages spoken across the globe — no more, no less. Its prominence today is largely a result of the colonial past, especially in countries like India and many others that were under Western rule. Because of that history, English became a necessary medium for administration, education, and even social mobility. Over time, this necessity was mistaken for superiority.

Unfortunately, this mindset seeped deep into our own communities. We began to judge people based on how accurately they spoke or wrote in English, often mocking or belittling those who made mistakes. But errors are natural when learning or using any foreign language — just as native English speakers struggle with our languages, we too may stumble with theirs.

It is essential that we begin to shed the remnants of our colonial mindset, particularly the deep-rooted belief that fluency in English equates to superiority in intellect or status. We must remind ourselves—and our students—that language is fundamentally a medium of communication, not a reflection of one's intelligence, integrity, or value as a person. It is a tool, not a yardstick.

That being said, we cannot turn a blind eye to the entrenched dominance of the English language in our educational and professional systems. Over time, English has evolved from being a colonial legacy to becoming a socio-economic filter—a symbol of privilege that often dictates who gets access to better opportunities and who gets left behind. The reality is that while language shouldn't define one's potential, in practice, it still often does.

Language, Power, and Self-Esteem: A Reflection on Communication and Identity

In many national television broadcasts in India, it's a common sight — journalists questioning Members of Parliament (MP) or public figures in Hindi or English, expecting crisp, articulate responses on complex national issues. What's even more disheartening is how our own politicians often struggle to respond fluently in those languages. When they falter — be it a slip of tongue, a mispronunciation, or a grammatical error — it becomes fodder for social media. The clips go viral, and millions indulge in ridicule, turning language into a weapon of mockery.

But who is truly at fault here? Is it the speaker, or the system that expects linguistic perfection in a non-native language?

It is unfortunate that many journalists — who are supposed to be the torchbearers of truth and inclusivity — forget one of the foundational tenets of journalism: accessibility. Their implicit assumption that everyone should speak their language, whether Hindi or English, reflects a dangerous arrogance. Would you expect a Miss World from Venezuela, China or Japan to speak impeccable English? Of course not. Yet their voice is understood and respected worldwide, because communication is not just about language — it is about message, authenticity, and presence. It is the *duty of the journalist* to understand and convey that, not the other way around.

My experience at Shanghai Ocean University in 2017 remains a striking contrast. The Vice-Chancellor of the university, hosting an international conference, delivered his speech entirely in Mandarin — his native tongue. Not for a moment did he attempt to apologize for it, nor did anyone in the room expect him to. Every foreign delegate was provided with a printed English version of his speech, and as he spoke, a professional translator conveyed his words in real time. The dignity of his expression remained intact, and everyone understood him — perhaps even better, because he spoke in the language of his heart.

The Irony of Linguistic Elitism in India

In India, even our Prime Minister — Mr. Narendra Modi and former Prime Minister Mr. H. D. Deve Gowda — have not been spared from public ridicule when they spoke in English. The criticism didn't arise from their lack of clarity in policy or vision, but from the very fact that their fluency in English wasn't polished enough. What a tragedy — not theirs, but ours.

In a world increasingly driven by innovation, vision, and leadership, one would expect the focus to remain on ideas and their impact. However, in India, the yardstick by which public figures are judged often hinges disproportionately on their fluency in English — rather than the substance of their message.

A striking example of this irony occurred when Prime Minister Narendra Modi delivered a compelling and well-structured speech on Artificial Intelligence. His address — forward-thinking, articulate, and relevant — touched upon the future of technology and its implications for society. Yet, rather than engaging with the vision he presented, sections of the media and public discourse were quick to dismiss the speech as "AI-assisted." The insinuation was clear — that it was too polished to have come from him, or that his delivery in English couldn't have been authentic. Instead of celebrating a leader attempting to bridge the gap between policy and technological progress, the focus shifted to trivial mockery.

Contrast this with the cultural landscape of countries like China or Japan. There, it is not only acceptable but expected for their leaders to communicate in their native languages — even on international platforms. Presidents, Prime Ministers, and other high-ranking officials routinely deliver important addresses in Mandarin or Japanese, with professional translators bridging the linguistic gap for global audiences. You will seldom, if ever, find a Chinese citizen mocking their President for not speaking English fluently. Nor will you find Japanese citizens belittling their leaders for not switching to a foreign language in order to impress the West. The priority in these nations remains firmly rooted in *what* is being said — not *how* it's said in English.

This stark difference reveals a deep-rooted issue within Indian society: our obsession with English as a status symbol. While it is undeniably a powerful tool for global communication, it should never become a measure of one's intellect, patriotism, or leadership capability. The very fact that we ridicule our leaders for not being fluent in English — rather than engage critically with the content of their message — reflects a lingering colonial mindset that still hasn't been shed.

Language is a medium, not a merit. Ideas are what change the world — not accents or grammar. When we, as a society, learn to respect the substance over style, we'll begin to elevate not only our discourse but our collective confidence as a nation.

The damage done by the English language in India isn't the language's fault, but our own collective perception of it. English, instead of being a tool of communication, has been turned into a measure of intelligence and status. An entire generation has grown up with an embedded inferiority complex — not because they lacked talent, but because they didn't speak the "right" language in the "right" way. Ironically, the harm was inflicted not by colonizers, but by fellow Indians who continue to worship this linguistic elitism.

A personal incident from 2004 remains etched in my memory. Two young women from Goethe University, Germany, visited our institute as part of a cultural and academic promotion. They had come to introduce their university and promote the German language. The hall was unusually packed — not for what they had to say, but because they were foreigners. They spoke with great pride about their culture, their language, and their institution — and the audience listened in reverent silence.

After their presentation, I went on stage and handed them a copy of a Kannada drama I had authored. The reaction from the audience was disappointing — there was spontaneous laughter, as though what I had done was either comical or unimportant. But the visitors were genuinely delighted to receive the book. I simply asked them to place it in their university library. A few months later, I received a formal email from Goethe University. My book had been catalogued and assigned an accession number in their library — an official space of respect.

That small gesture taught me a big lesson: it revealed the self-esteem and cultural confidence of the Germans, and the contrasting insecurity we, as Indians, often carry. We still measure worth through a foreign lens, forgetting the value of our own voices.

In the end, communication is about content and clarity — not colonial hangovers. Let us teach our children that the ability to think, feel, and express is far more important than the accent they use. And let us build a society where no one feels small for speaking the language they were born into.

"If you are free, you are not predictable and you are not controllable-**June Jordon**"

All are Ordinary People

At some point in my journey of self-discovery, I began studying successful people—not to imitate them, but to understand what sets them apart. And here's what I found: apart from their talent, there's nothing extraordinarily different about them. They're human, just like the rest of us—with fears, flaws, setbacks, and scars. But what makes them shine is not merely how they look—it's what they've become through relentless pursuit of their craft. The kids of these people will be natural advantages and I don't comment on anything on the people who have established or trying to establish based on the privilege of their parents. However, some people, though initially takes the advantage of their parents, they soon establish their personality and identity.

Take any name—Charles Chaplin, Jim Carry, Will Smith, Dr Rajkumar, Amitabh Bachchan, Shah Rukh Khan, Aamir Khan, Sachin Tendulkar, M.S. Dhoni, Virat Kohli, Hrithik Roshan, Priyanka Chopra, Anushka Sharma, Nana Patekar, Rajinikanth, Yash, Mohanlal—the list goes on. At first glance, they seem extraordinarily attractive, charismatic, almost magnetic. But if you strip away the fame, what remains? The same ordinary human being, but one who has built themselves from the ground up with grit, consistency, and clarity of purpose.

Fame has a strange cosmetic power. It can turn a face into a brand, a voice into a legend, and a name into a legacy. In truth, it is not beauty that brings fame—it is often fame that bestows the aura of beauty. Success enhances appearance, not the other way around.

This observation led me to a liberating conclusion: Stop trying to fit into the box of societal definitions of 'looking good'. The obsession with appearance is a distraction. Instead, invest your energy in refining your inner assets—your strengths, your skills, your potential. The world is always drawn to excellence, not cosmetics.

Just ask yourself—would brands run after Sachin Tendulkar or P.V. Sindhu if they hadn't proven themselves through extraordinary talent and relentless effort? Their skill makes them desirable, their success makes them radiant. And it's not just them—this principle applies to every one of us.

So if you truly want to be noticed, don't worry about impressing the world with appearances. Impress the world with your substance. Hone your talent. Discover your core strengths. Work quietly and persistently to master your chosen path. Because when you become excellent, people will begin to see beauty in you—not because you changed how you look, but because you changed how you live.

And one more thing—don't get trapped idolizing these stars. Respect their journey, admire their discipline, learn from their focus, but always remember: they are entertainers. They are there to make their fortunes. Let them inspire you, not distract you. Take the spark of their success and ignite your own fire. Keep your eyes on your own race track.

Do not get carried away with their ads on Kesar Pan Masala, Betting Apps, fairness products or soft drinks etc. If the products are good, they get noticed without these ambassadors.

Because ultimately, personality isn't built by imitation—it's built by introspection, perseverance, and purpose. When you find that, the world doesn't just follow you—it celebrates you.

"An idiot with a plan can beat the genius without a plan-
Warren Buffet"

Consequential Yield

All results are merely the products or by-products of your actions. 'Good' or 'bad' are labels shaped by personal or societal judgment. To achieve better outcomes, actions must change. When we fixate on results, we often overlook the root problems and their origins. In many situations, simply identifying the root of a problem can bring us halfway to a solution. Often, we tend to search for remedies without truly understanding what is causing the issue in the first place. It's like trying to treat a disease without diagnosing it. Instead of introspection, people frequently turn to rituals and symbolic acts in hopes of influencing their fate.

They go to temples, not necessarily for spiritual growth, but often to strike deals with God — offering a sort of divine barter. "If my wish is fulfilled, I will donate this much," or "I will perform this ritual every year." Some even make lifestyle promises, like abstaining from non-vegetarian food on certain days or observing fasts for a period. These practices are often less about devotion and more about expectation management — an attempt to 'negotiate' with the divine.

What's more concerning is the mindset behind it. I've heard people say, "I have done nothing wrong to anyone. Why is God testing good people like us?" It reflects a limited understanding of life's complexities. Goodness, while noble, doesn't guarantee a life free of trials. Pain and challenges aren't always punishments — sometimes they are part of the larger fabric of existence, shaped by choices, circumstances, or simply the natural order of cause and effect.

In the first place, the very notion of labelling someone as a "good person" is, in itself, a flawed premise. Goodness is not a static identity

— it is subjective, situational, and often complex. When we brand someone as "good," we tend to idealize them, forgetting that every human being is a blend of strengths and weaknesses, virtues and shortcomings. No one is entirely virtuous or without fault — not even those we hold in the highest regard.

The second, and perhaps even greater misconception, is the belief that good people are somehow shielded from suffering — as if morality comes with an immunity badge against life's hardships. This assumption has caused more disillusionment than we realize. Life doesn't operate on a transactional model where good deeds are always rewarded with comfort, and bad actions punished with pain — at least, not in the immediate, visible sense.

Suffering is an inevitable part of the human experience. It does not discriminate based on one's moral compass. In fact, history and personal lives are replete with examples of kind, compassionate, ethical individuals facing intense struggles — sometimes even more than others. Their suffering isn't proof of the world's unfairness; it's a reminder that pain is not a punishment, and virtue is not an insurance policy. Instead of asking, "Why do bad things happen to good people?" — perhaps the better question is, "What can all people — good or otherwise — learn from suffering?" Because in the end, suffering has a strange way of refining the soul, deepening empathy, and expanding understanding. The worth of a person is not determined by the absence of pain in their life, but by how they respond to it.

Without identifying the real 'causative agents' — whether emotional, psychological, social, or physical — we keep circling around the problem, assigning blame to fate, God, or others. True resolution begins when we look within and understand the pattern, instead of outsourcing accountability to the cosmos.

Arthur Ashe: A Gentle Warrior Who Asked No Favours

In the glittering world of sports where applause often drowns depth, Arthur Ashe stood out — not for his aggression, but for his astonishing grace. He wasn't merely the first Black man to lift Grand Slam trophies like the US Open, Wimbledon, and the Australian Open — he was the first to teach the world that dignity can be louder than triumph.

Born in 1943 in segregated Richmond, Virginia, Ashe entered a world where colour defined one's worth. But through relentless discipline and a quiet defiance, he carved his name into history — not just on tennis courts, but in the hearts of people worldwide. Yet, his greatness was never about how many matches he won; it was about how he lived, how he stood, and more importantly, how he fell — with his spine straight and his voice still meaningful.

After heart surgery in the early 1980s, Ashe received a blood transfusion — one that, unknown at the time, was contaminated with HIV. The news of his infection didn't break from his own mouth; it leaked through a journalist's pen. And even then, he didn't react with bitterness. Instead, he owned it — not for sympathy, but to use his suffering to educate others.

In a world still ashamed to speak of AIDS, Arthur Ashe did the unthinkable: he humanized it.

He founded a foundation, gave talks, wrote, and stood beside others who suffered — not behind a curtain of fame, but shoulder to shoulder. And when someone once asked him, "Do you ever ask, *Why me?*" his reply was soaked in rare wisdom:

"If I were to say, 'God, why me?' about the bad things, then I should have said, 'God, why me?' about the good things that happened in my life."

This — from a man who had already endured racial slurs on the court, exclusion from clubs, and medical negligence that led to his death. This — from a man who had every right to be angry, to demand answers, to collapse under the unfairness of it all. But Arthur Ashe never believed that being *good* exempted one from *grief*.

He passed away in 1993, not as a broken man, but as a gentle warrior — whose final lesson was this: The purpose of life isn't to avoid suffering, but to carry it without losing your purpose.

In the age of loud victories and viral voices, Arthur Ashe remains a whisper — the kind that stays in your conscience longer than any shout.

The Poets of Kannada Language

The following story is an earnest attempt to help you grasp the consequences of our diminishing sense of ownership toward our land, literature and our tendency to overlook the unique strengths and resources it holds. It seeks to highlight how a lack of possessiveness and awareness can gradually erode both identity and opportunity. Before the world went digital, we were rich in stillness and stories. I consider myself truly fortunate to have lived the first thirty years of my life without a cell phone. It was a time of quiet mornings, where the rustling of a newspaper was the most awaited sound; where the radio was not noise, but a companion; and where weekly magazines, novels, and handwritten letters carried the fragrance of knowledge, art, and human connection. That era gave us something the modern world often misses — depth over distraction.

But while we basked in those simpler times, the shadows of colonialism continued to linger — not just in the political ruins they left behind, but in the invisible prisons of our collective self-esteem. The colonial rulers not only plundered our lands and looted our wealth, but also executed a far more insidious theft — the looting of our cultural pride, our language, our identity and our self-esteem.

They made us believe that William Shakespeare and William Wordsworth were the ultimate literary icons. Yes, they were remarkable poets of their time — the 16th to 18th centuries — Yet, the global spotlight has rarely been directed toward our own literary legends, who not only lived few centuries earlier but also wrote with even greater brilliance and depth.

Pampa and Ranna, the titans of Kannada literature, crafted poetic marvels in the 9th and 10th centuries. Yet, they remain largely unknown beyond regional borders. Kalidasa, the jewel of classical Sanskrit literature from the 4th–5th century, is often ironically described as "the Shakespeare of India" — when in fact, Shakespeare should be known as the 'Kalidasa of England.'

This narrative was not just imposed upon us; we internalized it. We failed not only to tell our stories, but to sell our stories to the world. We allowed the brilliance of our poets, authors, and visionaries to be buried under the dust of foreign textbooks and English accolades.

It pains me deeply that our own Kannada literary giants — Kuvempu, the visionary who gave us the concept of *Vishwamanava* (Universal Human); Masti Venkatesh Iyengar, the storyteller of simplicity and depth; Bendre, whose verses held the pulse of the soil; Dr. K. S. Narasimha Swamy- a great poet who gave us *'Mysore Mallige'* a collection of poems celebrated for its romanticism, lyrical beauty, and emotional depth. Dr. N. S. Lakshminarayana Bhatta, Dr. G. S. Shivarudrappa, Dr. K. S. Nissar Ahmed, Dr. Dodda Rangegowda, and Prof. H. S. Venkatesha Murthy — all poets of substance, struggle, and spiritual richness — remain mere names assigned to layouts and roads in our cities.

These are not just poets; they are mirrors of our soul, our language, and our spirit. They gave rhythm to resistance and beauty to belonging. Yet, their legacies are not enshrined in global consciousness the way Shakespeare is. Why? Because we, as a nation, have often failed to cherish, preserve, and promote what is inherently ours.

It's time we break free from this inherited inferiority complex. Let us reclaim our narratives, restore our cultural confidence, and tell the world — not with arrogance, but with rightful pride — that we too have a literary lineage worth celebrating.

We must market ourselves

We must tell our stories to the world — because if we don't, the world will never truly know who we are. History remembers what is documented and shared, not what remains in silence.

One such lesser-known story takes us back to the final days of World War II. It is said that the two atomic bombs, codenamed *Little Boy* and *Fat Man*, were originally intended to be dropped on Tokyo — the heart of imperial Japan. However, according to some historical interpretations and lesser-discussed narratives, the plan was altered. The then-president of the United States had once visited Tokyo and was captivated by its beauty, culture, and vibrance. Perhaps that personal impression, that emotional connection, played a role in sparing Tokyo from destruction. Instead, the bombs were dropped on Hiroshima and Nagasaki — cities that paid the price for decisions shaped far from their borders. It was also portrayed in a 2023 Hollywood movie 'Oppenheimer.'

This story, whether fully factual or part of the many complex layers of war history, reminds us of the power of narratives and relationships. It reminds us that if we want to shape how the world sees us — our cities, our people, our culture — we need to speak up, document, and share. Silence may be graceful, but it often leaves our fate in the hands of those who speak louder.

The Architecture Marvellous

Sometimes, in our fascination with foreign wonders, we overlook the extraordinary marvels that stand quietly in our own backyard. Take, for instance, the Rathneshwar Mahadev Temple in Varanasi, India — a structure that leans at an incredible 9 degrees, more than double the tilt of the globally celebrated Leaning Tower of Pisa, which tilts at around 4 degrees. Not only is the temple more dramatically inclined, but it is also taller, standing silently near the sacred Manikarnika Ghat, almost forgotten in the noise of global tourism.

Likewise, the Brihadisvara Temple in Thanjavur, Tamil Nadu, is a masterpiece of ancient engineering. Its towering vimana and the majestic Kumbam — a single stone weighing nearly 80 tons — are testaments to the architectural brilliance of the Chola dynasty. Yet, despite its scale and historical significance, this monumental structure often fails to receive the global recognition it so richly deserves.

These are not just structures; they are stories carved in stone — stories of vision, devotion, and skill. By neglecting them, we are not just ignoring monuments; we are ignoring our own identity, our legacy, and the silent treasures that define who we are.

The Echo of the Self: Becoming a Story the World Cannot Forget

We live in an age overflowing with stories — stories told through books, films, social media, and coffee shop conversations. And yet, somewhere in the rush to keep up with others, we often forget to tell our most important story: our own. In much the same way that we celebrate grand monuments while ignoring the ancient marvels in our own land, we overlook the value of our individual journey. We forget that personal legacy does not begin on a global stage, but rather in the quiet corners of our everyday life — among family, peers, and the communities we touch.

The metaphor here is simple but profound: *If you don't tell your story, the world will never know you existed.*

This isn't a call for vanity or self-promotion. It is a reminder that each human being is born with a unique voice, shaped by circumstances, values, struggles, and small triumphs. When that voice is hidden, silenced, or simply neglected, we lose a chance to inspire, influence, and immortalize something meaningful. The world remembers those who chose to stand out — not by being louder, but by being *clearer* about who they are and what they represent.

Your Personal Story is Your Identity

Just as civilizations are remembered by the pyramids they built or the philosophies they passed down, individuals are remembered by the character they displayed, the values they upheld, and the impact they left behind. Your story is your silent monument. Every decision you make, every kindness you offer, every failure you rise from — these become the bricks and mortar of your legacy.

You don't have to be a celebrity, scholar, or saint to be remembered. You only need to be someone worth remembering in the context of your life. The child you taught to read, the neighbour you stood by during a crisis, the colleague you encouraged during a rough patch — they are all parts of your story, and through them, you are remembered.

Becoming Unforgettable Starts Small

You do not need to change the world overnight. Rather, start by becoming someone unforgettable in your micro-society — the small circle that includes your family, friends, co-workers, and local community.

How do you do that? Begin with *excellence*. Not in the abstract, perfectionist sense, but by consistently doing ordinary things with sincerity and purpose. Speak with clarity. Work with intention. Listen with empathy. Make yourself reliable, respectful, and real. When you excel in character, contribution, and competence, people begin to associate your name with trust — and that is the foundation of being remembered.

Your micro-society is your training ground. As you build influence and integrity there, your reach will organically expand. One day, your actions may resonate far beyond the people you know. But for that to happen, you must first own your space and define your presence within it.

Expand Your Horizon, Not Just Your Reputation

Once you establish a strong foundation within your immediate circle, it's time to push your boundaries. Growth doesn't come by settling for the comfort zone. Ask yourself:

- Can I mentor someone beyond my team?
- Can I write, speak, or share knowledge that helps others in my field?
- Can I participate in initiatives that benefit society at large?

Each new step widens your horizon. You are no longer just known; you are felt. Your influence begins to ripple outward, like concentric circles in a still pond. And the beauty is, this journey is not powered by ambition alone — it is fuelled by purpose.

This is how personalities are remembered — not by shouting into the void, but by leaving footprints of value wherever they go.

The Simplicity of Immortality

The notion of being remembered often feels tied to monumental achievements or dramatic events. But legacy is not always carved into stone — sometimes, it's woven into conversations, habits, traditions, or even the way someone else smiles because of you.

Being unforgettable doesn't require you to change the world. It only requires you to change *your* world — and keep expanding it, one circle at a time.

The formula is simple:

1. Know your story.

2. Live it with intention.
3. Share it when it matters.
4. Inspire others to begin their own.

So, do not wait for the world to ask who you are. Begin by knowing who you are. Be someone that your micro-society respects, someone whose values echo in your work, your words, and your way of life. Keep growing. Keep giving. Keep being *you* — because, when done well, that is more than enough.

And one day, without trying too hard, you'll realize that you have become a story the world cannot forget.

Why These Stories Belong Here?

I am writing these reflections in a book on *Management Beyond Academics* deliberately—because universities and academic institutions, while temples of knowledge, often create invisible boundaries around what can be discussed, debated, or challenged. These boundaries are typically set by dominant ideologies, majority perceptions, or governmental narratives. As a result, voices that speak beyond the prescribed syllabus or offer uncomfortable truths are often silenced or ignored.

Management, in its true essence, goes far beyond textbooks, boardrooms, or business models. It involves self-awareness, cultural rootedness, and a strong sense of identity—without which no leader can authentically manage people, processes, or systems. The neglect of our own literary and philosophical heritage is not merely a cultural concern; it is a management crisis of a deeper kind—where we fail to manage narratives, history, and national esteem.

How can we expect our future managers and leaders to think independently if they are not even encouraged to question why Shakespeare is known worldwide but Kalidasa is footnoted in our own country? Why is the idea of "Personality" still linked to fluency in English rather than clarity of thought or strength of character?

These stories are not digressions. They are necessary disruptions—attempts to reframe what we define as education, leadership, and intellectual freedom. The failure to promote our own heroes, our poets, our thinkers, and our values is a failure of management at a civilizational level. If we do not reclaim our narrative, we will remain excellent at importing theories, but poor at inspiring action rooted in our soil.

Hence, *Management Beyond Academics* must also mean redefining what deserves academic attention, and having the courage to say things that classrooms often avoid. That is why these pages carry not just strategies and theories, but soul-stirring reminders of what we've forgotten to celebrate.

"Judge a man by his questions rather than by his answers-
Voltaire"

Self-Awareness

In the intricate and rapidly evolving framework of modern society, it is important to recognize that our social norms and value systems are not arbitrary—they are deeply rooted in the legacies passed down through generations. Historically, in closely-knit communal or joint family structures, a significant portion of values, etiquette, and social formalities were adopted and practiced unquestioningly. These behaviours, often transmitted through observation and imitation rather than formal instruction, became embedded within cultural consciousness and have persisted even in highly developed, technologically advanced societies.

However, societal advancement invariably brings transformation—not only in infrastructure and knowledge, but more crucially, in the collective psyche. As modernization accelerates, traditional values, belief systems, and behavioural practices undergo recalibration. This shift profoundly affects individual identity, emotional orientation, and interpersonal dynamics. One's personality, in essence, becomes a living reflection of the evolving societal fabric they inhabit.

Furthermore, with the marked decline in the size of nuclear and extended families, the foundational community interactions that once nurtured shared behaviours have significantly diminished. This contraction of familial and communal structures has led to a more individualized, and often fragmented, social experience. Consequently, the social behaviour of an individual today is not merely a product of inherited customs, but a complex interplay of contemporary influences, personal choices, and residual cultural memory.

In this context, every individual stands as a representative microcosm of their societal environment—a dynamic embodiment of its values, transitions, and tensions. Understanding this continuum is crucial for any serious inquiry into human behaviour and cultural evolution.

Self-Awareness

Before attempting to comprehend the broader society or make sense of the complex world around us, it is essential that we first turn inward and strive to understand ourselves. Self-awareness forms the foundation for meaningful engagement with others and with society at large. Without a clear grasp of who we are—our values, beliefs, strengths, and limitations—our interpretations of the world can easily become clouded or misguided. Each of us is uniquely positioned to evaluate our own thoughts, emotions, and behaviours. We are, in fact, the most qualified individuals to assess our perspectives, motivations, and responses. While intuition often guides us in recognizing what we like or dislike, what brings us joy or discomfort, relying solely on instinct may offer only a surface-level understanding.

To delve deeper and gain a more structured, objective insight into our personality and behaviour, the use of established psychological tools and self-assessment exercises becomes invaluable. These methods help translate abstract concepts like temperament, emotional intelligence, and communication styles into measurable traits. By quantifying such attributes, we not only enhance our understanding but also create a roadmap for personal growth.

This process allows us to identify areas that may need attention or improvement, empowering us to make conscious changes rather than relying on vague introspection. In essence, self-assessment bridges the gap between knowing ourselves intuitively and understanding ourselves analytically—enabling us to evolve with purpose and clarity.

Exercise #01: Self-Assessment

SWOT Analysis

In this exercise, you are invited to engage in a process of honest self-reflection by conducting a personal **SWOT analysis**—an introspective look at your **Strengths**, **Weaknesses**, **Opportunities**, and **Threats**. This is not just a routine task; it is a meaningful exploration meant to uncover the real 'you' behind the layers of everyday roles, expectations, and societal masks.

To make this exercise truly effective, you must approach it with complete honesty and zero bias. This is your moment to pause, look within, and evaluate yourself—not as the world sees you, but as you *truly* are. Write your thoughts freely and fearlessly. You are not here to impress anyone. This is not a report card for others to grade—it's a mirror held up to your inner self.

Take your time before you fill in each section. Reflect deeply. Ask yourself the tough questions. Are you really as confident as you appear? Are you holding back your talents due to fear or doubt? Are there hidden opportunities you're ignoring? Are there unspoken fears or habits that are silently sabotaging your growth?

Be bold enough to acknowledge both your strengths and your flaws. Admitting weaknesses is not a sign of failure—it's a crucial step toward self-improvement. Similarly, recognizing your strengths reinforces your self-belief and reminds you of your capabilities.

One of the biggest risks in this exercise is self-deception. If you lie to yourself—by overstating your strengths, hiding your weaknesses, or ignoring your threats—you'll end up building a false image. That illusion may bring temporary comfort, but in the long run, it will keep you stuck in cycles of dissatisfaction, confusion, and underperformance. Self-cheating leads to misplaced efforts, missed opportunities, and prolonged struggles with the very issues you could have resolved with awareness and courage.

Remember, clarity is the first step to change. This SWOT analysis can become a powerful tool—**if** you treat it with sincerity and maturity. When you are honest with yourself, you give yourself the chance to grow, evolve, and take charge of your own development. That is the ultimate empowerment.

Attributes	Your Answers	Remarks if any
Strength		
Weakness		
Opportunity		
Threat		

*There need not be only one answer. You may write as many as possible, preferably the most critical ones you feel.

Many individuals tend to focus primarily on their strengths, which is indeed a positive and encouraging approach. Recognizing what you are good at builds confidence, motivates progress, and helps you make the most of your abilities. However, it's important to remember that strength alone doesn't guarantee stability or success in the long run. Imagine a rope that is 99% strong. It may appear reliable and capable of bearing a heavy load, and most people might be content with that. But what if just 1% of that rope—the tiniest section—is weak or frayed? That single weak point becomes the most vulnerable spot, and under pressure, that's exactly where the rope will snap. All the strength in the rest of the rope becomes irrelevant if that one small flaw is ignored.

The same principle applies to personal development. Ignoring or avoiding your weaknesses doesn't make them disappear. In fact, they often become the hidden cracks that eventually lead to breakdowns—in relationships, careers, health, or mental well-being. Addressing your weaknesses is not a sign of negativity; it's a smart, proactive strategy. It shows maturity, self-awareness, and a willingness to grow.

In the context of personal or professional growth, focusing on your vulnerabilities is actually a core management principle. Just as engineers reinforce the weakest part of a structure to ensure its overall integrity, individuals must identify and strengthen their weak spots to build resilience and prevent future setbacks.

So, don't shy away from confronting the areas where you struggle. Doing so doesn't make you pessimistic or self-critical—it makes you responsible, strategic, and empowered. True growth happens not just when we play to our strengths, but when we fortify our weaknesses and turn them into future strengths.

About opportunities, students find it difficult to identify their own opportunities. It is very simple. It is your unknown alternative strength that you might have ignored consciously or because of the societal or family compulsions. By careful examining, instead of going in a wrong direction for a long time and be unhappy, if your calling is somewhere in the other streams other than what you are pursuing, you must take a sound call at a right time and make bold decisions. Otherwise, you cannot walk for a long distance with someone's shoes.

You might currently be pursuing a degree in engineering, medicine, law, or even working on a doctoral program—perhaps not entirely out of passion, but due to external pressures or expectations. It could be the influence of parents, societal norms, or simply the fear of uncertainty that led you down this path. While academic qualifications are valuable and can open doors, it's important to ask yourself: *Is this truly what I want?*

Deep within, you may have a different calling—a genuine interest in singing, painting, acting, sports, or any other creative or physical pursuit that sets your soul on fire. Maybe you've always loved music, but you've silenced your voice out of fear of judgment. Maybe you've been a natural on the field but were told that sports don't guarantee stability. Or perhaps your tall frame draws attention and could open doors in modelling or athletics, yet you've never explored it seriously. Often, our unique traits—our voice, our energy, our sense of rhythm, or even our artistic sensitivity—are quiet indicators of paths we were meant to walk.

It's time to reflect, not with regret, but with clarity and courage. Listen to your inner voice—not the one conditioned by fear, but the one that quietly urges you to follow your true interests. Don't ignore the artist, athlete, or performer sleeping inside you. Talents that go unexplored often become sources of lifelong dissatisfaction.

If something keeps pulling at your heart, don't suppress it. Take a bold decision—at least start nurturing it alongside your current path. You don't necessarily have to abandon your degree or career overnight. But give yourself permission to pursue what you truly love. Even small, consistent efforts in that direction can awaken something powerful and fulfilling.

Timing is key. Recognizing your passion and acting on it at the right time can change the course of your life. Remember, greatness doesn't always come from doing what the world expects—it often comes from doing what *you* were truly meant to do. Let the artist, the dreamer, the sportsperson, or the singer inside you come alive. Set them free—and watch how life starts to feel more purposeful, more joyful, and more *yours*.

Identifying threats in a personal SWOT analysis can be a bit tricky because, unlike weaknesses (which are internal), threats come from external sources—factors or situations outside of your control that may hinder your progress, damage your confidence, or block your path toward your goals.

Don't confuse ***weaknesses*** with ***threats***:

- Weakness: "I'm not good at time management"

- Threat: "My degree program doesn't allow flexibility, limiting my personal growth time"

Threats are external like for a student threat may be following factors:

- **Financial:** Fear of supporting your higher education
- **Ethical:** You want to do organoleptic tests with fish; but you may be a strict vegetarian
- **Cultural Barriers**: A student may be interested in acting. Because none of their family members were not in fashion or cinema, there will be natural inhibition to take up such careers.
- **Social:** Some of the castes are not supposed to take up certain jobs
- **Emotional:** Some students do not wish see the blood or cut the animal for dissection
- **Environment:** Though one is willing to work in Military services, they will not choose they cannot manage extreme weather
- **Unknown**

So, when you sit down to fill out your personal SWOT table, do it consciously, thoughtfully, and without haste. This is not just a formality—it's a powerful tool for self-discovery and personal development. Every strength, weakness, opportunity, and threat you identify is a mirror reflecting a deeper aspect of who you are and where you're heading.

Once you've written down your strengths, you can begin to build on them. But more importantly, when you identify the traits, habits, or circumstances that are hindering your professional growth—whether they fall under weaknesses or external threats—you must take them seriously. These are the roadblocks standing between you and your fullest potential.

Rather than brushing them aside or rationalizing them away, use this awareness as a starting point to develop actionable strategies to minimize or eliminate their negative impact. For example:

- If procrastination is a weakness, set up structured schedules or accountability systems.
- If public speaking is a fear, enrol in a speaking course or start practicing in small groups.
- If a lack of networking is limiting your exposure, make a conscious effort to attend professional events or connect with mentors.

This kind of self-awareness is incredibly empowering. It helps you see beyond the surface and understand *why* certain patterns keep repeating in your life. It shifts you from a passive observer of your circumstances to an active designer of your future.

By working on your weak areas and preparing for external threats, you begin to build a more resilient, confident, and focused version of yourself. Ultimately, this clarity doesn't just help you grow professionally—it strengthens your self-esteem, sharpens your decision-making, and helps you move forward with purpose and direction.

In essence, your SWOT analysis becomes more than just a self-assessment—it becomes your personal roadmap to transformation.

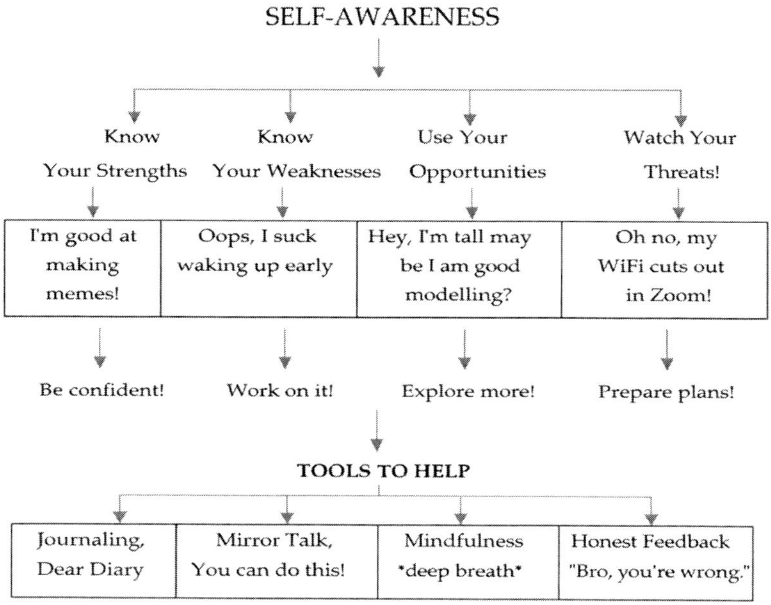

NEXT STEPS

- Accept yourself, but level up!
- Make better choices with self-clarity
- Fix what needs fixing, with love
- Be the best YOU!

"Inside every cynical person,
there is a disappointed idealist-**George Carlin**"

Self-Esteem

In the earlier chapter, we focused on the concept of self-awareness, which is essentially the ability to understand *yourself* in relation to the *external world*. This includes being conscious of your thoughts, emotions, actions, strengths, weaknesses, and how others perceive you. It's like holding up a mirror not just to your inner self, but also to how you fit into your surroundings—socially, emotionally, and professionally. Self-awareness helps you evaluate where you stand, what drives you, and how you react to various situations.

Now, moving beyond that, self-esteem is a deeper, more personal journey. It's not just about knowing yourself—it's about how you feel about who you are. It is the emotional outcome or result that often emerges from the process of self-awareness. If self-awareness gives you the data, self-esteem is your emotional response to that data.

For example:

- If you are aware that you're good at public speaking and people appreciate it, your self-esteem may improve.
- On the other hand, if you recognize certain flaws or past failures but learn to accept and grow from them, your self-esteem still strengthens—not because you're perfect, but because you accept yourself.

In short:

- **Self-awareness** = Knowing yourself through a lens that includes the world around you.

- **Self-esteem** = Valuing and accepting yourself based on that awareness.

One is the map; the other is the confidence with which you walk the terrain. Self-esteem is not just a feeling; it's a deep-seated belief about your self-worth and capabilities. However, it doesn't always come from balanced or rational thinking—it can be shaped by many external and internal factors. Broadly speaking, self-esteem can fall into three categories

1. Low Self-Esteem **(Inferior)**
2. Rational Self Esteem **(healthy)**
3. High Self-Esteem **(Superior)**

Low Self-Esteem: This often develops over time and is shaped by:

- **Your background** – upbringing, childhood experiences, or trauma
- **Financial condition** – persistent struggle or poverty can make one feel inferior. You might have observed the body language of Kids of rich people and the poor people.
- **Genetic make-up** – traits like shyness, anxiety, or learning difficulties may affect confidence. Not only physique carried from your parents, you also carry diseases as well as behavioural traits. Most of your behaviour has the genetic basis. Only 5% will be influenced by the environment. However, with conscious efforts, one can change, modulate the personal traits.
- **Social environment** – being raised in a critical or unsupportive atmosphere
- **Cultural or societal pressures** – constantly being compared or judged

A person with low self-esteem tends to:

- **Undervalue their abilities:** When you switch-off the main switch in your mind, nothing moves further.

- **Constantly seek validation:** Dependable on societies view point and endorsement by the peers is weak strategy. Such people will not take any initiation independently. They can even camouflage stating that it is a team work and they value the people the most and get cheated.
- **Avoid challenges due to fear of failure:** Such individuals are often easy to recognize. They tend to remain on the side-lines, quietly observing others' efforts. Instead of taking action themselves, they comment from a distance—often saying things like, *"If I were in their place, I would've done it differently."* These statements usually mask their hesitation or fear of stepping out of their comfort zone.
- **Blame themselves unnecessarily:** Some individuals struggle to appreciate what they have and constantly dwell on what went wrong in their past. They often blame their family, educational institutions, or even their country for their current situation. Instead of confronting the world with courage and openly expressing what they're experiencing, they find comfort in blaming fate or fortune. This becomes a psychological shield—it gives them a sense of safety, as if they're protected from judgment or failure by shifting responsibility away from themselves and they feel that they are guarded.

Effect: This mindset becomes a mental block that can severely limit growth, performance, and happiness. It can affect anyone, regardless of their age or nationality.

Rational (Healthy) Self-Esteem: This is the **ideal** form of self-esteem. It is:

- **Balanced and realistic**
- **Grounded in facts**, not fantasies
- **Rooted in self-awareness**, acceptance, and continual improvement

- **Responsive to feedback**, yet emotionally stable

People with rational self-esteem:

- Recognize their strengths without arrogance
- Acknowledge their flaws and work on them
- Take pride in achievements but remain humble
- Accept failures as learning opportunities

Effect: This type of self-esteem fosters resilience, healthy relationships, good decision-making, and consistent performance.

Inflated or Ego-Driven (High) Self-Esteem

This kind may **look like confidence**, but it's often built on shaky foundations:

- **Family status or wealth**: A person may feel superior because of their background
- **Unrealistic comparisons**: They may think they're better than others without actual merit
- **Superiority complex**: Believing others are beneath them without logical basis
- **Denial of flaws**: Inability to accept criticism or failure

Such individuals:

- **Overestimate** their abilities
- **Disregard** feedback
- Can be arrogant or **dismissive**
- Often **blame others** for their shortcomings

Effect: Just like low self-esteem, this inflated version can **ruin** performance and damage relationships, because it disconnects people from reality and growth. It leads to poor decisions, conflict, and eventual decline in performance—no matter how successful they seem on the outside.

Both low self-esteem and ego-driven high self-esteem can be damaging. Whether you feel inferior or superior, you lose the balance needed for personal and professional development. Only rational self-esteem, which comes from honest self-awareness and realistic self-evaluation, leads to sustained success and inner peace—regardless of your field, age, or country.

Strategies to Boost our Rational Self-Esteem

Understanding how others perceive you is a vital part of self-awareness. Once you've taken the time to reflect inwardly and understand yourself, the next step is to view yourself through the eyes of others—particularly your peers, friends, or colleagues. This helps you align your self-image with how you're actually perceived in the real world.

A useful exercise in this process is to gather honest feedback from your peer group. Ask them to share their opinions about your behaviour, habits, strengths, and especially your areas for improvement. You may request them to note down your perceived weaknesses or negative traits.

However, be prepared:

- Some people might express themselves **sarcastically**,
- Others might **exaggerate or sugar coat**,
- A few might give **raw and honest feedback**,
- And some might even offer **random or unrelated observations**.

Don't immediately dismiss or reject any feedback—even if it feels uncomfortable or unfair. Remember, society is diverse, and so are the ways people express themselves. Sometimes, what you see as sarcasm may contain a hidden truth. What's important is to look for patterns. If multiple people point out the same issue or behaviour, that's a strong signal that it's worth working on.

Also, there may be times when certain traits you've developed—such as being assertive or disciplined—are misunderstood or seen negatively by others. If you've consciously cultivated a quality and believe it aligns with your values and goals, stand by it. But don't just defend it—own it confidently and communicate it wisely. Over time, consistently expressing and living that trait can lead to it being accepted, respected, and even admired by the larger community.

In essence, use peer feedback as a mirror—not a verdict. Reflect on it, learn from it, and use it to grow into a more aware and authentic version of yourself.

Improvement Strategies

- **Choose your company wisely:** You become a reflection of the people you spend the most time with. Surround yourself with positive, uplifting, and inspiring individuals. Avoid people with negative thoughts, they will find problems for every solutions.
- **Adopt healthy habits:** Maintain a routine that supports your physical, mental, and emotional well-being—eat well, sleep enough, and stay active by choosing any outdoor/indoor sports or games.
- **Cultivate a reading habit:** Books are powerful tools for personal transformation. Great leaders are attributed to their great reading behaviour. Read regularly to expand your knowledge, perspective, and critical thinking. Avoid reading in tabs and mobiles unless it is inevitable.
- **Observe and learn from your surroundings:** Pay attention to the world around you—society, people, and nature are rich sources of wisdom and insight.
- **Dream big and pursue it fearlessly:** Let your vision be bold. Set meaningful goals and take consistent action to turn your dreams into reality.

After collecting the feedback from your peers about your negative traits — frame it and hang it on your wall as a reminder. Use it as a compass to steer away from those behaviours. At the same time, write down a statement that reflects the person or professional you aspire to be. Look at it ten times a day, and let it guide your journey forward.

"Invest in good friendship,
there are no market risks-**R K Lakshman**"

The Habits

We are the outcome of our own habits. If you study the most successful individuals across the globe, you'll notice one thing they all share: a disciplined routine rooted in positive, intentional habits. Whether it's waking up early, practicing focus, continuous learning, or cultivating gratitude — it's the habits that build the person, not just the goals they pursue.

Personality is not a gift we're simply born with — it is a dynamic construction, shaped day by day by our actions, thoughts, and especially our habits. In essence, your personality is the visible outcome of your invisible routines.

Habits are the small decisions and actions we repeat consistently. Over time, these repetitions sculpt our mindset, behaviour, character, and ultimately, how we are perceived by the world. Whether it's the way we greet others, manage stress, respond to failure, or commit to learning — every consistent behaviour contributes to our personal identity.

How Habits Influence Personality:

1. **Consistency Builds Trust:** People who show up on time, deliver what they promise, and maintain a steady attitude are often seen as reliable and trustworthy. These are not accidental traits — they are cultivated through habitual discipline.
2. **Habits Shape Thought Patterns:** The habit of journaling, for example, helps develop self-awareness. Reading regularly fosters empathy, critical thinking, and open-mindedness.

Thought patterns driven by habits eventually mold emotional intelligence and interpersonal skills.

3. **Confidence is a Habitual Outcome:** Confidence isn't a switch — it grows when we repeatedly step out of our comfort zones, achieve small wins, and reinforce positive self-belief through actions.
4. **Values are Reinforced by Habits:** Compassion, honesty, gratitude, and patience may be taught, but they are truly developed when practiced regularly. Our moral compass is maintained and strengthened through habitual alignment with our values.
5. **Breaking Bad Habits is Part of Growth:** Personality development is not only about adopting good habits but also about consciously identifying and shedding the ones that hold us back — procrastination, negativity, comparison, or self-doubt.

I recently completed reading the book *Atomic Habits* by James Clear, and it left a profound impact on my understanding of personal growth and behaviour change. The central theme of the book revolves around the power of small, consistent habits and how these seemingly minor routines, when practiced regularly, have the potential to shape our identity and influence long-term success. Clear masterfully illustrates that lasting transformation doesn't come from sudden, dramatic changes but from the gradual accumulation of small improvements over time. The book offers practical strategies rooted in psychology and neuroscience, making it both insightful and actionable for anyone seeking to build better habits and break unproductive ones.

Fundamentally, the human body tends to seek comfort and avoid exertion—it is, by nature, inclined toward laziness. This inherent desire for ease doesn't originate in the body alone but is deeply rooted in the mind. The mind plays a central role in shaping our motivations, decisions, and behaviours. When the mind is untrained or lacks discipline, it often gravitates toward choices that provide immediate pleasure or relief, rather than long-term benefits.

However, the good news is that the mind is highly adaptable. With conscious effort and practice, you can train your mind to overcome this laziness. The key lies in developing discipline and building consistent routines. By creating a structured schedule and committing to it—even when it feels uncomfortable—you gradually form habits that align with your goals. In the beginning, this process requires deliberate mental effort and self-control. It may feel unnatural or forced. But over time, with repetition and persistence, these habits begin to transform into automatic behaviours—things you do without needing to push yourself every time.

Until that transformation happens, your mind must be guided, conditioned, and reminded of the purpose behind your actions. Only through this conscious mental training can laziness be replaced with drive, and comfort-seeking behaviours be substituted with productive routines.

"Delete that old version of me in your head, it expired." Keep sending this message to your enemies.

Opportunities

Though the principles of personality development are universal, there may be variations while adopting them across region and religion, but the principles remains the same. One of the greatest cricketers of all time, Mr. Jonty Rhodes, once made a profound statement: *"We don't get catches; we have to create them."* This insight goes beyond cricket — it holds true for life, career, and entrepreneurship. In today's fast-paced and highly competitive world, opportunities are not handed over; they are discovered, shaped, and created by those who are observant, persistent, and visionary.

If you simply observe the world as it is, you may only gather surface-level information — facts and realities that are already known. But when you begin to observe critically, with a mind trained to question, connect, and improve, you unlock a different kind of vision. This is where creativity begins — the ability to see beyond what is, and imagine what could be.

It is through critical thinking and thoughtful analysis that one identifies gaps, inefficiencies, and possibilities for innovation. When you identify ways to save time, reduce effort, or minimize costs — even in the smallest tasks — you are not just solving problems, you are adding value. And value creation is the first step to building relevance in any field.

Moreover, when you assess the magnitude and commonality of a problem, you gain insight into the potential market size and the scalability of your solution. A problem that affects many people, across regions or demographics, indicates a wider demand and greater scope for impact — whether through a start-up, a service, or a product.

In essence, success lies in your ability to move from being a passive observer to an active creator. Don't wait for perfect conditions or invitations to contribute. Observe deeply, think critically, and act decisively. Opportunities may be rare, but your ability to create them can be limitless.

The redBus Journey: From a Simple Idea to a Nationwide Revolution

The redBus story began when three young engineers decided to step out of their comfortable and well-paying jobs in search of something more meaningful. In January 2006, they began working on a software solution with the intention of selling it, but their initial attempts did not yield the expected results.

Their breakthrough came when they discovered the TiE Entrepreneurship Acceleration Program in Bangalore. After connecting with the TiE team and presenting their ideas, they were assigned three experienced mentors. These mentors encouraged them to start their own venture and provided them with valuable assignments to help refine their business concept. One of their first tasks was an extensive survey—to study the industry from the ground up.

Diligently, the trio gathered detailed insights on the bus travel ecosystem: the number of buses and routes, ticket pricing, how people purchased tickets, customer profiles, and the revenue model of bus operators and agents. Their meticulous groundwork laid the foundation for a disruptive idea.

In August 2006, with just one bus operator, five available seats, and a modest capital of ₹5 lakh, they officially launched redBus. They created a user-friendly website, redbus.in, that aimed to digitize and simplify the traditional bus ticket booking process. The journey was far from easy—they faced several obstacles and setbacks—but their perseverance carried them through the tough times.

Today, redBus stands as a shining example of entrepreneurial success in India. It has transformed into a leading online bus ticketing platform, featuring over 10,000 buses and more than 700 operators across 15 states. The company now sells over 5,000 tickets every day.

RedBus has since expanded its services beyond bus ticketing to include hotel bookings, bus rentals, and pilgrimage packages. With its headquarters in Bangalore, redBus serves as a central hub for bus operators not only across India but also in countries like Malaysia, marking its global footprint.

"If you feel pain, you are alive, if you feel other people's pain, you are a human being-**Leo Tolstoy**"

The Big Data

The success of any business, whether traditional or modern, can largely be attributed to the quality of its leadership—particularly the leader's ability to understand and leverage data effectively. In today's fast-paced and competitive landscape, data has become the backbone of decision-making, enabling businesses to identify trends, optimize operations, and tailor services to customer needs.

This data-driven approach is especially crucial in technology-led companies, where innovation and speed are key. Technology doesn't just support business growth—it accelerates it, often disrupting entire industries in the process. Consider, for instance, the iconic Indian snack brand Haldiram's. Despite its massive popularity and legacy, it took nearly 90 years to build a business valued at $10 billion. In stark contrast, Zomato, a tech-powered food delivery and restaurant aggregation platform, achieved a similar scale in just seven years.

This striking difference highlights the transformative power of technology and data. While traditional businesses often rely on steady, incremental growth, tech-driven companies can harness real-time insights, scale rapidly, and meet evolving consumer demands with agility. It's this dynamic combination of visionary leadership and data intelligence that sets the most successful modern enterprises apart from the rest.

The take away message from the above story is 'Haldiram's long-standing success can be credited to its strong and consistent leadership, which guided the brand through decades of growth in the traditional food and snack industry. On the other hand, Zomato's rapid rise to prominence is a testament to the power of data-driven management. Unlike conventional models, Zomato harnessed real-time data and consumer insights to make strategic decisions, optimize user experience, and scale at an unprecedented pace. Of course, at the heart of Zomato's model lies technology—not just as a supporting tool, but as a core driver of innovation and growth. While leadership remains vital in both cases, Zomato's success story underlines how the integration of data and technology can dramatically accelerate a company's journey.

Ola and Uber: Redefining Ownership, Reinventing Management

In traditional business thinking, ownership equalled power. A transport company needed to own a fleet of vehicles, employ drivers, and manage logistics hands-on to thrive in the car rental business. But the advent of companies like Ola and Uber shattered that paradigm. These companies do not own a single car, yet they've become giants in the global mobility and transportation industry. Their success challenges conventional management wisdom and symbolizes what we explore in *Management Beyond Academics*—the idea that leadership, innovation, and strategic thinking cannot be confined within textbook definitions.

1. The Asset-Light Revolution: Owning the Model, Not the Means

At its core, Uber and Ola operate on an asset-light model. This means they focus not on owning the vehicles but on creating a platform that connects vehicle owners with users. It's a powerful shift from capital-intensive ownership to network-enabled coordination.

Instead of investing billions in car purchases, insurance, and maintenance, they invest in:

- Technology infrastructure (apps, maps, payment gateways)

- Data analytics
- Driver and customer onboarding
- Brand trust and user experience

From a management lens, this is a genius move. It eliminates the headaches of depreciating assets while retaining control over value creation. It's not about what you own; it's about what you control. This concept alone stretches far beyond what academic syllabi traditionally cover—and highlights why adaptive, modern management education must look outward, not just inward.

2. Platforms: The New Age Enterprises

Uber and Ola are not car rental businesses in the traditional sense. They are technology platforms, connecting two sets of users—riders and drivers. This is known as the platform business model, where value is created not by producing a product but by facilitating interactions.

The power of this model lies in scalability and minimal marginal costs. Once the app is built, adding another driver or customer costs next to nothing. Compare this with the traditional model, where every customer demands proportional infrastructure (cars, employees, maintenance). The platform model decouples growth from physical expansion, enabling exponential scaling.

In management terms, this is a disruption—an idea borrowed from Clayton Christensen's innovation theory. Uber and Ola did not just improve the taxi service; they reinvented the definition of mobility. Their innovation wasn't a better car—it was a better system.

3. Management Beyond Assets: Managing Stakeholders, Data, and Ecosystems

What do Ola and Uber manage if they don't own cars? They manage:

- **Driver ecosystems**: recruitment, onboarding, incentivization

- **Customer expectations**: quality, safety, pricing, loyalty
- **Technological infrastructure**: app performance, map integration, GPS accuracy
- **Regulatory environments**: city-specific laws, taxes, permits
- **Brand perception**: trust, public relations, crisis handling

This tells us something vital—modern management is not about managing things; it's about managing systems. This is a key pillar of *Management Beyond Academics.* Ownership of assets becomes secondary when you are the orchestrator of relationships, data, and decisions.

4. Learning from Real-World Application: Why Academics Alone Isn't Enough

If we look through the lens of traditional business education, many of Uber and Ola's early decisions may seem risky or even impractical:

- Launching without owning inventory
- Entering price wars with competitors
- Subsidizing rides to attract users
- Trusting strangers (drivers) to represent the brand

Yet, these were calculated risks rooted in customer-centric innovation and strategic market capture. These models weren't taught in business schools before—they were written through real-world trial and iteration. This reinforces the idea that management excellence comes not only from knowledge but from bold experimentation and agile thinking.

5. The Gig Economy: Managing People Without Employing Them

Another layer of this model is its dependence on the gig economy. Uber and Ola drivers are not employees; they are independent contractors. This gives them flexibility and independence, but also shifts accountability and benefits away from the platform.

From a managerial standpoint, this introduces new complexities:

- How do you build loyalty in a non-employee workforce?
- How do you maintain quality without control?
- How do you create a sense of community among freelancers?

These are questions that traditional HR models may not fully answer. Managing the gig workforce demands empathy, transparency, and new-age incentive structures. It's a fresh chapter in the story of leadership.

6. Technology as a Leadership Tool

While Uber and Ola do not own physical assets, they own technology—and that's what gives them power. Through real-time data, algorithms, dynamic pricing, and behavioural tracking, they manage demand, supply, and service quality.

Let's break this down in terms of managerial skills:

- **Forecasting**: Predicting high-demand hours and positioning cars in advance
- **Optimization**: Reducing customer wait time and maximizing driver availability
- **Personalization**: Recommending rides, offering discounts based on behaviour
- **Risk management**: Verifying drivers, tracking rides, responding to emergencies

In this model, code is king, and data is the compass. **A** modern manager must now be digitally literate—not just in tools, but in mindset. *Management Beyond Academics* insists that leaders learn to manage both people and platforms.

7. Ethics and Regulation: Power without Ownership Needs Responsibility

With great innovation comes great scrutiny. Ola and Uber have faced global backlash over:

- Surge pricing during emergencies
- Driver exploitation and low wages
- Gender safety issues
- Regulatory evasion

These issues teach us that ownership of influence comes with responsibility. As platform leaders, they don't own the cars, but they shape public transportation habits. That influence must be wielded ethically.

Management today must go beyond P&L sheets to think about values, inclusivity, and justice. A leader must be accountable not only to shareholders but to society. This too is rarely found in textbooks—but is central to *Management Beyond Academics*.

8. User-Centric Models: Redefining Customer Experience

Uber and Ola succeeded because they understood a fundamental truth: convenience is king. Their user interfaces are seamless, feedback systems are instant, and support is largely automated. They removed friction from the user journey, a key component of modern business design.

Traditional management may teach customer service from the lens of call centres, complaints, and satisfaction scores. But today, UX (User Experience) is the new frontier. Every touchpoint—from app login to drop-off—shapes perception.

Managers must now work with designers, coders, behavioural psychologists, and community managers—not just marketers and MBAs. Cross-functional leadership is the new normal.

9. Resilience and Reinvention: Learning from Setbacks

The road has not been smooth. Uber faced global bans, lawsuits, leadership crises, and protests. Ola had to pivot multiple times, including launching food delivery (Ola Foods), electric mobility (Ola Electric), and financial services.

Their journey shows us that innovation isn't just about launching something new—it's about learning fast, failing forward, and bouncing back stronger. They teach us that disruption also demands discipline—the ability to reinvent culture, improve systems, and rebuild trust.

Resilience, adaptability, and humility are real-world management lessons far more valuable than theoretical perfection.

10. The Bigger Lesson: You Don't Need to Own to Lead

Ultimately, Ola and Uber symbolize a new truth: leadership is not about ownership; it is about orchestration. They've shown the world that you don't have to own the physical means of production to lead an industry. You only need to design, enable, and guide the ecosystem.

This concept stretches far beyond transportation. Airbnb doesn't own hotels. Swiggy doesn't own restaurants. BYJU'S doesn't own schools. These are all platform orchestrators—a new breed of enterprise that challenges traditional management frameworks.

This evolution demands a new mindset. One that blends:

- Strategic thinking
- Technological intuition
- Empathy and ethics
- Systems design
- Stakeholder alignment

This is the soul of Management Beyond Academics.

The Road Ahead Is Asset-Light but Insight-Heavy. Ola and Uber didn't redefine transportation by buying more cars. They did it by **redefining what transportation meant**. They made access more important than ownership, experience more important than possession, and coordination more powerful than control.

In doing so, they gave the world not just a mobility solution—but a management lesson.

In a world that's increasingly digital, decentralized, and dynamic, the managers of tomorrow must evolve beyond academic knowledge. They must learn to lead without owning, to influence without authority, and to build ecosystems instead of empires.

Just as Ola and Uber don't own cars but run car businesses, the leaders of the future may not "own" anything in the traditional sense—but they'll own the narrative, the network, and the impact. And that, indeed, is Management Beyond Academics.

From Three Decades to Three Years: The Changing Arc of Wealth Creation

Mr. Shah Rukh Khan, one of India's most iconic film personalities, has taken more than three decades of relentless work, creativity, and resilience to build his empire. His success story is a classic example of perseverance — a journey shaped by time, experience, and the gradual building of value through consistent effort and personal branding.

In contrast, Mr. Aravind Srinivas, the Co-founder and CEO of *Perplexity AI,* represents a new paradigm in wealth creation. According to the *Hurun India Rich List 2025,* he has emerged as India's youngest billionaire with an astonishing net worth of ₹21,000 crores. What took a generation of traditional achievers several decades to accumulate, the digital-era innovators are accomplishing in a fraction of that time.

This contrast is not merely about money — it reflects the transformation in how value is created and perceived in today's world. Mr. Khan's wealth was built on emotional capital — the admiration of millions — while Mr. Srinivas's wealth is built on intellectual capital — the power of algorithms, innovation, and technological disruption.

In essence, the timelines of success have compressed dramatically. What once demanded thirty years of visibility, discipline, and reputation-building can now be achieved within a few intense years of innovation, risk-taking, and scaling. The world is no longer rewarding longevity alone; it is celebrating relevance, speed, and the ability to see what others miss.

The lesson for managers and leaders is profound — time is no longer the only currency of success; adaptability, vision, and agility are. Those who understand the pulse of transformation can create in a decade what once took a lifetime.

"Happiness come from what we do;
Fulfilment comes from why we do it"

The Re(a)el Truth

In 2022, Mrs Sudha Murthy, chairman, Infosys foundation says studies have shown that 85% of fresh engineering graduates are not immediately employable and need to improve quality of education. It is even applicable for many other degree programs as well. In one of the LinkedIn posts by NEWS9 in the month of April 2025 says one Ms Bisma Fareed, a first year English (Hons) student at Delhi University's Hansraj College did not get any internship program in spite of being topper with over 50 certificates and 10 medals. She admitted it took to realise that skills and practical experience hold mare value than marks.

While working on this book, I also had the responsibility of coordinating a newly introduced course titled "Personality Development"—a thoughtful addition to the curriculum for students of Fisheries Science. This course was designed to go beyond technical education, aiming to shape well-rounded individuals equipped with life skills, self-awareness, and the confidence to engage meaningfully with the world around them.

During one of my sessions, I decided to understand my students better—not through tests or assignments, but through simple, spontaneous conversation. There were 52 students present that day. I asked a few informal questions to get a glimpse into their personal interests and passions, thinking it might help us build better connections throughout the course.

I began by asking, *"How many of you love music?"* Around 40% of the students raised their hands—an encouraging number, showing a collective inclination toward creativity and rhythm. Next, I asked,

"How many of you are passionate about sports or play regularly?" This time, about 25% of them responded positively. Again, it was good to see some engagement with physical activity and team spirit.

- Then I asked, *"And how many of you enjoy reading books?"* To my surprise, not a single hand went up. The room fell into a momentary silence.
- This unexpected response lingered in my mind long after the class ended. It was not just about the absence of a reading habit—it hinted at a deeper issue. In an academic setting where textbooks and manuals dominate the learning landscape, the joy of reading for leisure, for self-growth, or simply for curiosity, seemed lost or perhaps never awakened in the first place. Though they appear bright in their appearance and attire, they noticeably lack the confidence to ask questions or engage in discussions during class.

I must admit, there was a part of me that felt genuinely glad that the students did not try to impress me with rehearsed or superficial answers. They were honest and unfiltered in expressing their opinions—something that is rare and refreshing in today's world of appearances and pretense. However, as much as I appreciated their candour, the truth they revealed was disheartening. The more I learn about the mindset and priorities of today's youth, the more it troubles me.

What I observed is not just an individual lapse in ambition or engagement—it is the cumulative outcome of a shifting social fabric. We are witnessing a generation growing up in a world where distraction has replaced depth, and instant gratification has taken precedence over meaningful growth.

One of the most telling symbols of this shift is the cell phone, which has now evolved from being a useful gadget to what seems like a permanent extension of the human body. It is no longer just a tool for communication; it has become a portal of escape, entertainment, and validation. In many ways, it dictates attention, influences emotions, and silently robs people of time and focus—two invaluable resources for learning and self-development.

This transformation of societal priorities reminds me of a popular slogan once championed by the Indian Government: "Roti, Kapda aur Makaan"—food, clothing, and shelter—the three basic necessities of life. But if we were to revisit that slogan in the context of today's generation, perhaps a more accurate version would be: "Mobile, Kapda, Roti aur Makaan." The cell phone, in many ways, has leapfrogged food in terms of emotional necessity and attention.

This isn't merely a humorous observation—it is a profound indicator of how priorities have changed. The hierarchy of needs has been reordered, not by choice, but by the overwhelming influence of technology, consumerism, and social conditioning.

As an educator and mentor, this realization is both challenging and sobering. It forces me to ask: *What are we preparing our youth for? What kind of future are we equipping them to face, if the fundamental building blocks of character, curiosity, and communication are being overshadowed by passive consumption?*

This is exactly why a book like *Management Beyond Academics* becomes essential. Academic success alone cannot prepare students for life. We must nurture awareness, emotional intelligence, discipline, and digital balance. We must guide them to reclaim their time, rebuild their focus, and redefine what truly matters.

The cell phone, while powerful, should not be the centre of their universe. That place should belong to purpose, learning, and meaningful interaction—all of which can only grow when we teach them to look beyond the screen, and within themselves.

That moment became a powerful reminder of why this book and this course matter. The students I work with are intelligent, capable, and full of potential. But their development—as professionals and as human beings—cannot rely solely on technical expertise. They need exposure to thought, expression, philosophy, and creativity. Reading cultivates perspective. It expands vocabulary, sharpens critical thinking, and most importantly, fosters empathy and imagination—qualities essential for anyone who wishes to lead or manage effectively in any field.

The incident underscored a growing gap between academic learning and personal enrichment—a gap that courses like Personality Development, and indeed Management Beyond Academics, seek to bridge. It revealed the urgency of introducing students not just to skills, but to a culture of curiosity, reflection, and lifelong learning.

In order to understand their mindset, the same day in the afternoon, I went to the boys hostel and randomly visited few rooms. They were so shabby and unorganized. No things were in their place, dust, unorganised cupboards, table and cot. Shabbily hanged clothes.

The very next week, I found myself in Mysore, a city that holds a special place in my heart. As I was driving past one of the old student hostels, a wave of nostalgia washed over me. This was not just any building—it was a hostel I used to frequent nearly four decades ago during my early student life. Built by the Maharajas of Mysore, the hostel was an architectural gem—its grandeur understated yet graceful. With high ceilings, wide staircases, sprawling gardens, and intricately carved wooden windows, it resembled a mini-palace crafted for the welfare of poor students. It was a place that once nurtured dreams and inspired dignity in those who had very little material wealth.

Curious and sentimental, I decided to step inside and revisit the room I once stayed in. As I approached the staircase, I was met with a deeply unsettling sight. The once-pristine passageway had been misused in the most disrespectful way—students, perhaps too lethargic to walk a few steps to the restroom, had begun using the hallway as an open urinal. The air was heavy with stench and neglect. My heart sank.

Climbing the familiar stairs to the first floor, I reached my old room—once a place of study, friendship, and quiet resilience. But what I found was a scene of total disarray. The room looked more like a garbage dump than a living space. Chairs were scattered on top of cots, dust and cobwebs hung from the corners like neglected memories. Clothes lay muddied and crumpled on the floor, and plates with uneaten, rotting food were left out in the open, releasing an unbearable stench. It was a sad testimony to how far the spirit of the place had fallen.

A few boys were sprawled out lazily on the floor, eyes glued to their mobile phones. Others sat in the corridor, similarly disengaged, lost in the virtual world. There was no life, no energy, no curiosity—only a quiet apathy that echoed through the space.

I couldn't hold back. I stepped in and introduced myself, mentioning that I had once stayed in the very room they now occupied. But to my surprise, they showed little reaction—no curiosity, no spark of interest. It was as though the past meant nothing, and the future even less.

Trying to start a meaningful conversation, I asked them about their aspirations and future plans. A few mumbled responses—some said they were preparing for police recruitment exams, others mentioned attempting competitive exams, but their voices lacked conviction. There was no sense of purpose in their eyes.

With a heavy heart, I urged them to clean their room and take care of their surroundings. I told them how the space they now take for granted was once maintained with pride by students who had very little but dreamt very big. I reminded them that self-respect begins with the way we live—the cleanliness of our environment is often a reflection of the clarity of our minds.

As I walked out of the building, the contrast between the hostel of my time and the one I had just seen felt symbolic of something larger. It wasn't just about a messy room—it was about the erosion of discipline, values, and vision. The physical decay mirrored a deeper neglect—a disconnection from purpose.

This incident made me reflect deeply on youth leadership, accountability, and self-management. In a world full of digital distractions and short-term goals, many young minds are losing sight of the big picture. What we desperately need in today's academic institutions is not just subject knowledge, but a revival of dignity, discipline, and purpose.

This experience reaffirmed my belief in the importance of courses like Personality Development and in writing this book—*Management Beyond Academics*. Because real education must go beyond classrooms, marks, and placements. It must build character, shape habits, and ignite self-worth. A clean room, a well-made bed, and a purposeful mind are perhaps small things—but they are the foundations of leadership and personal growth.

What can we expect from these youths? A lot—if only we begin to expect more from our educational system, our institutions, and from ourselves as mentors and educators. Because change doesn't happen in grand gestures. It starts with a broom, a conversation, a choice—and the courage to see things differently.

"When the time comes to act,
let action lead and planning step aside -**Magada**"

Business Planning

As long as you serve people and charge fairly for your products or services, there is nothing indecent about any business you do. In a few developing countries, professions still carry status labels, but in most developed nations, every job is just that — a job, respected equally. To succeed in business, more than money, ideas, or technology, you need a burning passion and the willpower to take on any venture. After the COVID-19 crisis, I saw many workers and youth return to their hometowns — because, in the end, life matters more.

Many of these vulnerable youths, in their urgency to survive and support their families, hastily started small businesses upon returning to their native places. With limited guidance, inadequate planning, and little understanding of market dynamics, their ventures were often driven more by necessity than strategy. As a result, a large number of these businesses shut down within a short time. Some continue to operate, but without sustainable models or proper financial oversight, they are slowly turning into hidden economic burdens — draining resources, time, and energy, rather than contributing to growth. Eventually, the realization sets in that, despite their efforts, they may be facing a significant cumulative economic loss.

Highway Dhaba

Across many parts of the country, roadside hotels have shut down due to a sharp decline in foot traffic. At the same time, a new wave of businesses—particularly restaurants and food stalls—have sprung up along these main roads. However, most of these ventures were started without proper market research or planning. Entrepreneurs often overlook crucial factors such as the average daily traffic, types of vehicles passing through, the nature of local businesses, proximity to major cities, the purchasing power of commuters, existing competitors, pricing trends, and even seasonal weather patterns. Without this foundational data, they set up operations based on assumptions or hope rather than informed decisions. Consequently, many of these ventures struggle to sustain themselves and eventually incur losses, becoming yet another example of failed opportunity due to inadequate groundwork.

How to nurture the idea into business

Not every idea is destined to evolve into a successful business. For an idea to truly stand out and have the potential for success, it must undergo rigorous scrutiny and be tested under a variety of extreme conditions. It should be challenged, evaluated from multiple perspectives, and exposed to real-world pressures that reveal its strengths and weaknesses. Only after surviving these trials — refining its purpose, validating its market fit, proving its feasibility, and demonstrating resilience — can an idea transform into a strong, sustainable foundation for a business. Success is not just about having a creative thought; it is about shaping, testing, and fortifying that idea until it is ready to thrive in a competitive and ever-changing marketplace.

Small businesses should not be founded merely because raw materials or other resources are abundantly available. Instead, their establishment must be driven by a clear understanding of local demand. Before launching any venture, it is crucial to thoroughly study and assess the market — analysing not just whether there is a need, but also the size of the demand, seasonal fluctuations, customer preferences, and competitive gaps. Entrepreneurs must identify a strong Unique Selling Point (USP) that sets their business apart, while also carefully considering factors such as the cost of production, the durability or shelf-life of their products or services (keeping quality), and the potential for long-term sustainability. A business built on strategic insights into demand, rather than just resource abundance, is far more likely to thrive and adapt in a dynamic marketplace.

Big Stories of Small Businesses

Ideal Ice Creams

Ideal Ice Creams of Mangalore has become a beloved and iconic brand, a household name across Karnataka. For anyone visiting Mangalore — the vibrant coastal city known for its rich culture and cuisine — savouring a treat at Ideal Ice Creams is almost a tradition, an experience not to be missed. Personally, I have been indulging in their delicious offerings for over three decades. Though in recent years I have scaled back my consumption for health reasons, I still find it hard to resist their tempting creations, especially when hosting guests. On those occasions, the joy of sharing a classic Mangalorean delight often outweighs my usual restraint.

Mr Mukund Kamath-the present CEO of the Ideal Ice Creams Pvt. Ltd., Mangalore says that they are running this business for last 50 years. His father Mr Prabhakar Kamath started this business on 1 May 1975 and is the biggest ice cream manufacturer in Mangalore with an 80% market share.

It has several outlets in and around Mangalore and supply chains across Goa, Karnataka and northern Kerala. The brand's signature dish is the 'Gadbad,' a tall glass with layers of ice-cream, jelly, dry-fruits and fresh fruits. The brand has won several accolades through the years.

In and around Mangalore, only a select few outlets have accomplished the extraordinary — building businesses valued at over 300 crores while securing numerous prestigious awards, standing shoulder to shoulder with some of the world's most renowned brands. Having travelled extensively across various countries, I can affirm that such passionate enthusiasm is truly rare. It is uncommon to see people willingly wait in long queues, often for hours, just to step into these establishments and savour their offerings. This phenomenon speaks volumes, not only about the exceptional quality of their products but also about the deep-rooted pride and emotional bond the people have with these homegrown icons.

The Bindu

From the humble village of Bellare in Dakshina Kannada District, Karnataka, a rickshaw driver — a man who had not even completed his 12th grade — embarked on an extraordinary journey. With nothing more than a simple jeera-flavoured soft drink in the name of 'Bindu,' he laid the foundation for what would eventually become a business empire. Starting from one of the remotest corners of the region, his sheer determination, entrepreneurial spirit, and unwavering belief transformed a modest idea into a thriving enterprise. Today, that once-small venture has grown into a colossal business valued at over 1000 crores, serving as a powerful reminder that success is born not from privilege, but from vision, perseverance, and relentless hard work.

In both the businesses, the success is attributed to their commitment to the consistence in quality and the unique taste. They never invested on the advertisement. It was a people movement in promoting these brands.

From One Paisa to 250 Crores: Ramakrishna Achar

Ram Krishna Achar is a self-made man — a pioneer of the paddy processing industry whose journey from poverty to prominence is a testament to sheer grit and vision. From earning just one paisa as a child to building a business empire worth ₹250 crores, his life is a true story of rising from rags to riches.

Born in 1963 in the small village of Goodangadi, nestled in Karnataka's Kundapura taluk, Udupi District. Ram Krishna grew up amidst struggle. He was the son of Gangolli Srinivas Achar, a carpenter, and Bhavani Achar. One among seven children, his family often didn't have enough food for even a single meal. Getting to school was a miracle in itself. At just seven years old, he began helping support his family. He would fill his stomach with wild fruits from the hillside on the way to school and wore hand-me-down clothes from relatives.

While most children played, Ram Krishna worked. He started by pushing fishermen's bicycles uphill — his first earning was one paisa. That coin was more than just money; it was the seed of self-worth. As a teenager, he worked with a blacksmith for ₹30 a month, and by 14, he spent nearly three years learning on the job. Between 1977 and 1980, his curiosity led him to the world of automobiles, where he began work at Adarsh Garage in Kundapura.

At 16, his journey took a new turn. He joined Vinod Engineering Company, where his exposure to rice mill machinery sparked a lifelong fascination. The company's owner, Ram Achar of Vinod Engineering, recognized his talent and sent him to study grain processing at CFTRI, Mysore. For Ram Krishna, it was the first encounter with quality education. To pay his fees, he worked night shifts at Naidu's Workshop from 6:00 p.m. to 2:00 a.m., earning ₹400 a month.

Constantly hungry for growth, he travelled often for work. During a trip to Moodabidri, he met Vishwanath Prabhu of Balaji Industries — the man who would catalyse his entrepreneurial journey. Impressed by his capabilities, Prabhu gave him a project worth ₹18,000, with an advance of ₹2,000. Ram Krishna used ₹1,000 to purchase a defunct welding shop, thus giving birth to Sri Kalikamba Fabrications.

From that modest beginning, there was no looking back. He toiled day and night to expand his small enterprise across Karnataka. By 1994, the company evolved into SKF (Sri Kalikamba Fabrications) and began making waves in Andhra Pradesh. With increasing success, he invested ₹35 lakhs to build a larger facility in Bhatkal. Soon, SKF was turning over ₹19 crores.

But life brought challenges. In 2001, a government ban on rice exports collapsed the market. Prices plummeted, and millers were hit hard — SKF included. Amidst the downturn, Ram Krishna didn't give up. He founded an ITI (Industrial Training Institute) to skill 150 students annually, reflecting his belief in giving back.

In 2003, he bounced back by introducing Hot Air Technology and Aged Rice Technology, revolutionizing rice processing by enhancing grain quality while saving time and costs. His innovations attracted international attention. Demand surged, and SKF became India's top seller of hot air tech, achieving a turnover of ₹48 crores.

Despite his growing stature, money was never his end goal. Ram Krishna sought to solve emerging societal problems. In 2014, seeing the urgent need for pure drinking water and effective wastewater management, he founded Elixir — a company manufacturing advanced mineral water and treatment plants. He invested ₹45 crores, and the first order came from Dr. Mohan Alva, chairman of Alva's Foundation.

Soon, SKF Elixir India Pvt. Ltd. became the only Indian company offering a complete range of mineral water plants. But Ram Krishna was already looking ahead. Disturbed by rising depression, climate change, and farmer distress, he launched "Godama", a desi cow breeding and organic farming centre in Muniyal village. Spanning 30 acres, Godama focuses on youth training, organic agriculture, and restoring chemical-free fertile land. It shelters 85 desi cows across six breeds and reintroduces India's lost farming wisdom.

Over 25 years, Ram Krishna Achar's contributions have been monumental — from transforming India's paddy industry to pioneering water purification and reviving traditional agriculture. Through SKF and its subsidiaries, he has empowered nearly 1,000 families.

In recognition of his work in agriculture, education, and service, Mangalore University conferred upon him an honorary doctorate. Today, Dr. Ram Krishna Achar — with no formal engineering degree or certificate — commands respect as a master of rice processing, STP/ETP plants, and mineral water systems. He is an inventor, an entrepreneur, and a visionary.

From a single paisa to ₹250 crores — his life is not just a journey, but a legacy.

The remarkable success of this journey can be fully credited to the keen identification of industry gaps, unwavering perseverance, and the consistent honing and application of practical skills.

Cashew Castle-Leadership Vignette

From Survival to Strategic Advantage: The Kalbavi Cashews Story

Leadership often reveals itself not in moments of comfort, but in periods of uncertainty, loss, and reinvention. The entrepreneurial journey of Mr. Prakash Kalbavi, Managing Director of Kalbavi Consumers Foods Pvt Ltd., Mangaluru, offers a compelling illustration of how resilience, continuous learning, and strategic collaboration can transform adversity into long-term competitive advantage.

The encounter was incidental yet instructive. During a live television appearance on *Business Tonic,* a long-running business programme hosted by CA S. S. Nayak, a simple observation—exceptionally good cashews served during a commercial break—sparked a deeper inquiry. The product traced back to Kalbavi Cashews, and coincidentally, Mr. Prakash Kalbavi joined the programme live through an online platform. His articulation of business decisions, export strategy, and operational challenges stood out not as rehearsed success stories, but as lived managerial lessons. Although the manuscript of *Management Beyond Academics* was nearing completion, this narrative demanded inclusion.

The Entrepreneurial Leap

Mr. Kalbavi's background was modest yet grounded in trade. His father was an areca merchant—financially stable but far removed from industrial-scale processing. Armed with a bachelor degree in Mechanical Engineering from Manipal and driven by a desire to build an independent enterprise, Mr. Kalbavi entered the cashew processing industry on 1 May 1987, investing ₹5 lakh of borrowed family capital supplemented by limited external sources.

The timing could not have been worse. The year 1987 was devastating for the cashew processing sector. Market volatility, operational inefficiencies, and widespread closures wiped out capital across the industry. Mr. Kalbavi lost his entire initial investment. For many, this would have been an exit point. For him, it became a classroom.

Leadership, at this stage, was not about expansion—it was about survival with dignity and learning with intent.

Human Capital as the First Turning Point

The first strategic inflection came not from technology, but from people. At a critical juncture, Mrs. Baby, an experienced employee cashew processing professional from Moodabidri, joined the enterprise. Her contribution went beyond routine supervision. She systematized operations—training workers in peeling, grading, boiling, cooling, value addition, and packaging. Each processing unit was optimized to function with eight workers (six women and two men), ensuring efficiency, consistency, and quality control.

This focus on process discipline and skill development laid the foundation for market credibility. The company soon entered the export market, particularly Japan, while maintaining a domestic presence. Trust from the Japanese buyer translated into advance payments, stabilizing cash flows and reducing working capital stress. Operational stability, however, did not dilute Mr. Kalbavi's appetite for improvement.

Incremental Innovation and Productivity Leadership

Unlike many entrepreneurs who accept operational routines once stability is achieved, Mr. Kalbavi remained restless. He questioned everyday inefficiencies. One such intervention came through an innovative knife design developed by a local mechanic, Mr. Venkappa of Bunder, Mangaluru. This small but powerful innovation doubled labour productivity—from 6 kg per worker per day to 14 kg.

The lesson here is profound: innovation need not always be capital-intensive or imported. Sometimes, it emerges from local ingenuity, when leadership remains open to ideas regardless of their source.

Strategic Risk-Taking and Collective Confidence

As a mechanical engineer, Mr. Kalbavi had an inherent inclination towards automation. When a newly designed automatic cashew processing machine entered the market at a cost of ₹9 lakh, the industry response was sceptical. High capital cost, uncertain returns, and fear of failure discouraged adoption.

Mr. Kalbavi viewed the decision differently. For a continuous learner, even failure is a management lesson. He proceeded with the purchase. His decision altered industry sentiment. Inspired by his confidence, fellow processors collectively placed orders for 16 machines. Through **collective bargaining**, the price was negotiated down to ₹7.5 lakh per unit, reducing capital burden while accelerating modernization.

This episode highlights a critical leadership trait: the courage to be the first mover, not merely for personal gain, but to build collective momentum.

Institutionalizing Collective Power

Recognizing the limitations of operating in isolation, Mr. Kalbavi and his peers formalized their collaboration by forming the **Karnataka Cashew Manufacturers Association**. This institutional platform transformed individual enterprises into a negotiating bloc. Exports expanded to Europe, Japan, Vietnam, China, and the Middle East.

One of the association's most impactful interventions was in logistics risk management. Export insurance costs, charged at ₹12–14 per tin box, significantly eroded margins. Through collective negotiation with banks, the association reduced this cost to 60 paise per tin box—a dramatic improvement in profitability. This was not merely cost reduction; it was strategic leverage through unity.

Leadership Beyond Balance Sheets

Mr. Prakash Kalbavi's journey underscores that leadership is not defined by uninterrupted success, but by the ability to absorb shocks, learn rapidly, and convert individual insight into collective advantage. His story demonstrates that:

- Failure can be a powerful management teacher
- Human capital is often the first lever of turnaround
- Incremental innovations can outperform expensive disruptions
- Strategic risk-taking inspires collective confidence
- Institutions amplify individual leadership into systemic impact

In a world obsessed with unicorns and rapid scaling, this narrative reminds us that sustainable leadership is built patiently—through resilience, learning, and collaboration. Mr. Kalbavi's enterprise did not merely survive; it evolved into a benchmark of adaptive entrepreneurship, offering enduring lessons for MSMEs, start-ups, and policymakers alike.

An Interruption and a One-Line MBA

While I was deeply engaged in a serious boardroom discussion with Mr. Prakash Kalbavi—surrounded by polished tables, business charts, and the unmistakable aura of "decisions being made"—the door opened quietly. In walked his son, Mr. Adeeth Kalbavi, an engineer and an MBA from the Indian Institute of Management, Mumbai. Without much ceremony, he took a seat right in front of us.

He did not look like someone who had come to seek blessings or casual advice. He looked like a man who had already scheduled three meetings in his head, cancelled two, and optimized the third. A well-oiled machine, running silently but efficiently.

Mr. Prakash introduced him to me. I could sense that Adeeth was already deeply involved in the business. Since this enterprise was not built by him from scratch—and because I am old enough to know that second-generation entrepreneurs don't enjoy pop quizzes from visiting professors—I avoided asking any serious questions.

But curiosity is a dangerous thing in a boardroom.

So, with the innocence of a casual query and the mischief of a management teacher, I asked him,
"What is your mantra for a successful business?"

He did not pause. He did not blink. He did not consult his MBA notes.

He replied, calmly and confidently:
"Don't chase scale. Chase sustainability and profitability."

That was it. No PowerPoint. No jargon. No footnotes. Just one clean sentence—delivered like a quarterly result.

At that moment, I realized something important. Some people don't chase success. Success chases them, probably because they are too busy minding their margins and systems to notice.

Adeeth sat there, serious, composed, and disturbingly efficient—exactly how balance sheets like their owners. The father built the foundation with sweat and resilience; the son is a well-oiled machine and oiling the machine with precision and restraint.

And if you ever doubt that philosophy, do one simple experiment: Taste Kalbavi Cashews in your town. You won't just taste the crunch—you will taste discipline, patience, and profitability.

CA SS Nayak

From a management perspective, this book draws largely from first-hand experiences and observed leadership practices. The preference for writing about people I have closely interacted with is deliberate, not personal. First-hand narratives offer authenticity, contextual accuracy, and managerial realism—qualities often missing in abstract models and borrowed case studies. While a few stories in this book are drawn from secondary observations, its core strength lies in lived experiences, where decisions, failures, discipline, and persistence can be examined without embellishment.

One such example is Mr. S. S. Nayak, a Chartered Accountant who was already professionally successful when I first encountered him. He is a well-recognized figure in the coastal region, known not only for his professional excellence but also for his sustained social engagement. What warranted his inclusion in this book, however, is not his success, but his approach to continuous value creation beyond his primary profession. His office has produced hundreds of Charted Accountants who are practising working in various companies with flying colours. He is an instrumental person in establishing one of the leading education centre in the state that is "Expert Coaching Centre."

Mr. Nayak conceptualized and continues to host a weekly television programme titled "Business Tonic" on the local channel "Namma Kudla"—a term that signifies our Mangaluru in the local idiom. Remarkably, the programme has crossed 350 episodes over seven years, reflecting consistency, relevance, and audience trust. Every week, he curates discussions by inviting experts from diverse domains such as agribusiness, fisheries, banking, investment, Union and State Budget, taxation, automobiles, healthcare, industry, economy, education, and development—areas that intersect directly with managerial decision-making.

What distinguishes his leadership practice is the discipline of preparation and learning. For each episode, he prepares 30–40 pages of structured notes, even today. At an age when many professionals choose consolidation over curiosity, he continues to learn, synthesize information, and deliver insights with clarity. His ability to recall data, contextual examples, and even Sanskrit aphorisms reflects not just memory, but intellectual engagement and cognitive discipline. He is a motivational speaker par excellent.

From a management standpoint, his journey underscores an important lesson: professional sustainability comes from relevance, not designation. Even if he were to disengage from his accounting practice, his knowledge capital, communication skills, and credibility would allow him to remain economically and intellectually productive.

He has been bestowed with numerous Awards and accolades and the recent one Vietnam – India International Award as "MSME Start-up, Mentor and Business Coach" is the most best suited for his achievements. Through his regular Union budget talk in various forum over the last two decades has made him to earn the name and fame as "Nani Palkiwala" of Mangalore. He has mentored countless

MSME's, Start-ups and Entrepreneurs to set up and scale up their business ventures. As a prolific speaker he has delivered lectures in India and Abroad. While philosophy often advocates contentment, management demands a certain degree of constructive dissatisfaction—a persistent urge to improve, to explore new platforms, and to move to the next level of value creation. Mr. Nayak exemplifies this balance, making his story a relevant leadership vignette for students and practitioners alike. He has authorised four books of quotes "Words of the wise", "More words of the wise", "Wise words of the wise" and "Voices of the wise" consisting of pragmatic wisdom for ease of living and ease of doing business.

He always believes in "Desire changes Nothing, Decision changes something and Dedication changes everything."

"The invisible winds inspire us;
the visible waves compete with us -**Magada**"[1]

Unknown Success Stories

When we seek inspiration in any field, our eyes often go straight to the extraordinary — those rare, shining stories of exceptional success. These stories are remarkable, but they represent exceptions, not the norm. More often than not, such achievements are difficult to replicate, as they are shaped by unique circumstances, timing, or resources that cannot be reproduced on a large scale. While it is certainly valuable to draw motivation from these big stories, one must be cautious not to lose excessive time or energy attempting to copy them step by step.

Equally, if not more, meaningful are the countless success stories that exist within the ordinary population. These examples may not make headlines, but they are grounded, replicable, and accessible to many. Their impact is no less significant than the so-called "big" stories, because success, at its essence, is not defined by grandeur but by achievement and progress. In fact, these relatable stories often provide more practical lessons, showing us that sustainable success can be built on replicable paths rather than rare miracles.

The Rise of the Ashoka

One evening, while I was deeply absorbed in my writing, my wife, Rekha, came up to me and asked, almost out of the blue, what I was working on. She rarely interrupts me in such moments, and almost never with such a question. But that day, something moved her to ask.

---

[1] Inspiration comes from the unknown people and competition comes from the known people.

I replied that I was writing about success stories worth emulating. She listened carefully and, in her usual casual way, remarked, "We have all studied such stories — of Subhash Chandra Bose, Rani of Jhansi, Sir M. Visvesvaraya, Abdul Kalam, and many more. They are inspiring, no doubt, but for an ordinary person, they are too distant to imitate. They belong to extraordinary times, extraordinary circumstances."

Then she paused for a while, as if searching within herself, and added softly, "Why don't you write about common success stories instead?"

I was curious. "Common stories? Like what?" I asked her.

For a few moments she remained silent, lost in thought. Then, almost suddenly, she said, "Write about Ashoka — the carpenter who lives next door to my house."

Her answer made me laugh, and I said nothing further. Yet, her words lingered with me. Sometimes wisdom arrives in such unassuming ways — reminding us that greatness is not only found in history books and monuments, but also in the unnoticed lives lived right beside us.

Then I began collecting details about Ashok, the carpenter whom my wife had mentioned. He must have studied 7th class. At first glance, he appeared to be just another hardworking artisan, but the more I learned, the more I realised that his story was anything but ordinary. His financial management, in particular, was truly remarkable.

He lived in a modest 900-square-foot house. For many, such a home would have been just enough for shelter and little more. But Ashok saw beyond walls and space; he saw possibilities. Adjacent to his house, there was a little extra land. Instead of letting it remain idle, he invested his effort and savings to construct four small shops. Of these, he rented out three, while he himself continued his carpentry work in the fourth. This not only gave him a steady stream of rental income but also kept his profession alive.

In time, Ashok expanded his vision. He even put the rooftop of his house to productive use, leasing it out to a telecom company for a mobile tower. Every corner of his property was turned into an asset, a silent contributor to his family's income.

Yet, as the years passed, he grew weary of the physically demanding labour carpentry required. With foresight, he decided to shift towards a less strenuous but more rewarding venture. He took back two of the rented shops and, together with his family, started a mini supermarket. What made it special was that it was not just his business — it was a family enterprise. Ashok, his wife, and their two daughters all became active participants in running it. Their combined effort turned it into a thriving business that now earns them not less than two lakhs every month.

What began as the story of a simple carpenter slowly unfolded into a lesson in vision, discipline, and financial wisdom. Ashok's success was not sudden, nor accidental; it was built patiently, step by step, on the foundations of resourcefulness and family unity. His life proves that true entrepreneurship is not about huge capital or extraordinary background, but about the ability to see opportunities in the ordinary and to make the most of them.

From Mr. Ashok's life, one can draw several invaluable lessons. His journey reflects the power of hard work, the importance of discipline, and the wisdom of sound financial management. He teaches us that setting clear goals and pursuing them with consistency can transform even modest beginnings into remarkable achievements. Above all, his story reminds us that true happiness does not come merely from wealth, but from living with purpose, unity, and contentment as a family.

Lesson from a Lineman's family

There once lived a small and poor farmer's family. They owned only two buffaloes and worked as daily wage labourers during the planting season. The husband also found work as a daily wager in the Electricity Board. With five children to raise, they still managed to live happily with what little they had.

Their modest house stood just a few meters away from the railway station. From there, they often saw tourists and film actors stopping at the famous Maddur Hotel to enjoy its vadas. Watching them stirred dreams in the parents' hearts — dreams of seeing their own children one day in modern clothes, working as officers.

Every evening, they made their children sit and study. The irony was that even if their children hold their books upside down, they were unable to make it out. Yet, the parents were strict about discipline. If any child refused to study, they were punished by being sent to stand in the cowshed, where the mosquitoes bit them mercilessly.

The parents decided to send their sons to Government Boarding Schools in Bangalore. At that time, some four decades ago, the passing rate was barely 10–12%. Yet, against all odds, their children performed well. The eldest was a daughter; she studied up to the 9th standard before being married. The four sons, however, continued their studies diligently and eventually graduated in diverse fields — Commerce, Veterinary Science, Engineering, and Fisheries. Each of them went on to build an independent life of their own.

For a family that once had almost nothing, these achievements marked a transformation. With perseverance and sacrifice, they even managed to purchase a modest house through a Government Housing Scheme and another small plot at the district headquarters.

What made this journey possible was a combination of unwavering dreams and strict discipline. Education was never easy to afford. Every time college fees were due, they borrowed money from neighbours, never once hesitating if it meant their children could continue studying. The mother, too, contributed in her quiet, steadfast way. By selling milk, she would save whatever little she could, dropping coins into a simple earthen piggy pot.

Many times, when the son studying Veterinary Science returned home during holidays, the parents would break open that pot before he left, handing him the coins they had painstakingly saved. The boy, embarrassed to carry such a heap of coins to college, would stop at a nearby bakery, exchange them for currency notes, and only then travel back. Those coins, though humble, carried the weight of sacrifice and the fragrance of dreams — small in appearance, but priceless in meaning.

I consider this to be one of the greatest success stories of building and establishing a family. What made it extraordinary was not wealth, nor status, but the courage to dream beyond their circumstances. They dared to envision a brighter future, they sowed that dream deep into the hearts of their children, and they nurtured it with relentless discipline and sacrifice. Step by step, they turned hope into reality, and their children into independent, educated individuals.

The true measure of success lies here — not in material riches, but in raising a family with values, resilience, and dignity. The father, who once struggled as a daily wage worker, left this world free of debt, his life a testament to honest labour and perseverance. The mother, my mother, continues to live with unyielding spirit even today. At 85 years of age, she embodies the strength, simplicity, and grace that sustained our family through hardship and lifted us towards success.

Reshi's U-turn in a straight road

He was a bright student throughout his schooling, studying diligently up to the 12th standard. Like many parents with high aspirations, his mother and father enrolled him in NEET coaching, dreaming of seeing their son become a doctor. But destiny had something unusual in store. Just three months before the final exam, in an act that surprised everyone, he shifted his focus completely. Instead of NEET, he began preparing for the Joint Entrance Examination (JEE), one of the toughest exams in India, the gateway to the prestigious IITs.

Against all odds, and to the astonishment of his parents, he scored an impressive 96.8 percentile. His success earned him admissions in IIIT Jabalpur and NITK Suratkal. His parents, eager to support him, even paid fees at both colleges. Eventually, he joined NITK, just 20 km from his home, opting for Chemical Engineering.

But he was restless. He wanted independence, to live life on his own terms, away from the familiar environment of home. So he left the safety of NITK and chose RV Engineering College in Bangalore, one of the country's top-rated institutions, where he enrolled in Mechanical Engineering. The shift was bold, but not easy. He struggled with some subjects, managed to scrape through others, and then came the global disruption — the Corona pandemic.

Back at home in Mangalore during the lockdown, his life took a sharp turn. Like most youngsters, he spent a lot of time on his mobile phone. But unlike many, his curiosity led him into the world of finance, investments, and cryptocurrency. He was particularly drawn to Bitcoin and the emerging financial ecosystem around it. Driven by self-learning, he began creating reels and short videos on finance and investment. To his surprise, these caught attention, and soon opportunities began to open up.

With growing confidence, he launched his own company — **ROB Media** — starting with a team of 15–20 young people. However, balancing academics with entrepreneurship proved difficult. After much inner struggle, he finally decided to discontinue his studies. It took him 20 long days to prepare himself to break this news to his parents. He feared disappointment, for his father was a senior academician, deeply rooted in the world of education. To his surprise, his parents, already familiar with his passion and unpredictability, accepted his decision with grace. Their casual acceptance gave him strength, and he was overjoyed to follow his own path.

With newfound freedom, he set up a grand office in Indira Nagar, one of Bangalore's most expensive localities. He travelled across major cities, meeting people, building networks, and investing in his brand. Life became a whirlwind of energy and excitement. He spent generously — partly to celebrate his journey, and partly to show the world that he was not just surviving, but thriving.

He grew up with a quiet fear of money. As a child, he had witnessed the silent struggles of his family — the constant worry of expenses, the burden of loans, the delicate balance of survival. That early impression stayed with him. Strangely, even when he began spending money lavishly in his youth, a part of him retained the instinct to save. It was as though he carried within him both the shadow of fear and the spark of wisdom.

His life was not just about changing careers or chasing fleeting trends. It was, at its core, a story of courage — the courage to step beyond the prescribed paths, to risk failure, and to follow the stirrings of his own passion. Success, as his journey shows, is never a straight line dictated by societal expectations. It is a winding road, marked by dreams, discipline, failures, and the willingness to walk into the unknown.

But the unknown often carries its own storms. One day, his Instagram account, which had gathered more than five lakh followers, was suddenly blocked for a passing reference he made to a drug dealer in one of his reels. Panic gripped him, and he nearly broke under the weight of fear. By fortune, the account was restored — but the incident left a deep scar. He realised then the fragility of fame and the risks hidden beneath easy income.

Meanwhile, his parents, with patience and gentle persistence, urged him to complete his degree. For a long time, he resisted, but one day, a spark of determination arose in him. He decided he would finish his backlogs and even prepare for the civil services. He purchased heaps of books for the Indian Administrative Service (IAS), as though building a fortress of knowledge around himself.

Fate, however, had another twist waiting. While passing by the National Law School (NLS) in Bangalore, he was captivated by its serene and beautiful campus. A simple visit turned into a new direction for his life. He decided, almost impulsively, to pursue law. His parents, who accompanied him, encouraged this choice warmly. What he did not realise then was that they had been quietly observing his restless spirit, guiding him with patience while allowing him to feel free. The very next day, he filled his room with stacks of law books — a new dream taking root.

Yet, his personal habits weighed heavily on him. Sleep was erratic, food habits careless, and he had gained excessive weight. His parents, out of love, teased and body-shamed him gently, but their words pricked his pride. Feeling insulted, he enrolled in one of the best gyms in Bangalore. The effort was sincere but strenuous, and soon he fell ill, confined to bed for days.

NAS Company Calling

And then, when he least expected, opportunity knocked again. One fine day, the global media platform NAS Daily reached out to him, offering a chance to work with them. Ironically, his phone was switched off for a few days, and the message went unnoticed. When he finally saw it, he responded, and within a short time, he was on board with them, working with great enthusiasm. His performance was outstanding, and he quickly rose to higher positions, proving his worth.

Through all this, he never forgot the promise he made to his parents — to complete his degree within six months. Life seemed to be finally falling into rhythm.

The lesson his story offers is simple, yet profound: the path to success is never straight, never certain. It is carved through risks, wrong turns, unexpected breaks, and the courage to walk uncharted roads. Sometimes, what looks like chaos is just life rearranging itself to reveal hidden possibilities. Success, then, is not about reaching a fixed destination, but about daring to travel the unknown with faith, resilience, and hope.

Today, he is earning several times more than many who followed the traditional path of systematic study and secured jobs through campus placements. This highlights an important truth: true capability lies in being able to succeed with or without a formal degree. Beyond academics, success often comes from trusting one's intuition and having the courage to act on it.

Self-Respect as a Career

Many visit the beach to admire the sea—its waves, its vastness, its sunsets that pause time for a moment. It is a place of beauty and escape. Yet, every evening she stands there without looking for the sunset or counting the waves. The shore erases every footprint as new waves arrive, reminding us how fleeting marks can be. But she is not there to watch what disappears. She is there to stand firm, to leave a different kind of imprint—one not on the sand, but in resolve. That is Ms. Chetana. I met Ms. Chetana Rao, a graduate who once worked with hospital groups but chose to step away when professional ethics were compromised. With limited safety nets and no guarantees about the future, she made a deliberate choice—to protect her self-respect rather than cling to a title. She began selling tea and snacks at Someshwara Beach, Mangaluru, earning just enough to live with dignity.

What left a lasting impression was not the nature of her work, but the strength of her will. In a situation where many would feel defeated or ashamed, she stood composed, confident, and unbroken. Her resilience was quiet, her confidence unannounced, yet unmistakable. She did not see herself as vulnerable; she saw herself as capable.

Her journey is a reminder that vulnerability does not imply weakness, and that self-esteem can be a powerful form of resistance. When circumstances change abruptly, it is not ambition that sustains us, but inner resolve. This narrative finds its place in my forthcoming book, Management Beyond Academics, as a reflection on courage that emerges not from institutions, but from character.

Case Study: Nuseir Yassin – Redefining Success in a Connected World

In the modern world, where success is often defined by titles, salaries, and possessions, very few dare to question the purpose of their journey. Nuseir Yassin, an Israeli-Palestinian graduate from Harvard University, did just that. His story is not only about entrepreneurship but also about self-management — the art of managing one's time, passion, and purpose before managing money or people.

From Harvard to Humility

Born in the small Arab town of Arraba in Israel, Nuseir grew up in an ordinary family that valued education as a way out of limitation. His parents, a psychologist and a teacher, ensured that their children saw the world through the lens of possibility. When Nuseir earned a scholarship to study at Harvard, majoring in Economics and Computer Science, it seemed that the traditional arc of success was already scripted for him.

After graduation, he joined *Venmo* in New York — one of the dream destinations for many young professionals. Yet, the glossy skyscrapers, the stable income, and the social prestige failed to fill an inner void. He realized he was living someone else's definition of success. He was rich in opportunities but poor in fulfilment.

This internal dissonance became the seed of his transformation. Many management books speak of "innovation," but Nuseir's innovation began not in technology but in thought — questioning the very system that celebrates overwork and under-living.

The Birth of NAS Daily

In 2016, at the age of 24, Nuseir quit his high-paying job, gathered his savings, and embarked on a global journey to tell stories. He set himself a radical challenge — to make one video every single day for 1,000 days. These would be short, one-minute videos about people, cultures, ideas, and the extraordinary moments hidden in ordinary lives.

This idea became *NAS Daily* ("NAS" meaning *people* in Arabic). It was not merely a content project — it was an experiment in consistency, curiosity, and connection. For three years, Nuseir travelled to more than 70 countries, carrying a small camera and an open heart.

He told stories of the uncelebrated — from an Indian man who plants trees on a barren island to a Filipino mother raising a family on a floating house. His videos were not scripted advertisements for optimism; they were human mirrors reflecting kindness, resilience, and creativity. Within a year, his Facebook page attracted millions of followers.

The Manager of His Own Time

Behind those one-minute videos were hours of filming, editing, scripting, and traveling. Yet, he never missed a single day for 1,000 days. In a world obsessed with shortcuts, his discipline stood out.

This commitment offers a lesson for management professionals: leadership begins with self-leadership. Managing a team or an organization is secondary to managing one's emotions, motivation, and attention. Nuseir's "one-minute rule" was simple — consistency over complexity. The focus was not on perfection but on progress.

His success illustrates a profound management principle: when passion meets discipline, persistence becomes effortless. The invisible management of self is what sustains visible success.

Purpose Over Profit

By the time he completed his 1,000th video, *NAS Daily* had become a global phenomenon. He had built a community of more than 20 million followers, with billions of video views. Yet, Nuseir was never chasing numbers. His mission was to bridge divides — between East and West, between privilege and poverty, between technology and humanity.

He realized that stories have the power to manage human perception better than any corporate campaign. Governments, businesses, and NGOs began inviting him to tell their stories. But instead of turning into a celebrity influencer, he decided to turn his storytelling movement into an educational platform.

NAS Company — Turning Stories into Systems

In 2020, he founded *NAS Company*, an organization that helps creators, brands, and governments tell meaningful stories at scale. The idea was to institutionalize storytelling — to make it teachable, replicable, and impactful.

Under *NAS Company*, Nuseir launched *NAS Academy* (an online learning platform for creators) and *Nas.io* (a community-management tool). His philosophy was simple: teach others what you've learned and empower them to create better narratives for the world.

Today, these ventures employ hundreds of people across Singapore, Dubai, and the Philippines, and their content reaches over 300 million people each month.

From an individual storyteller, Nuseir evolved into a management visionary who understood that the most powerful organizations are those built on stories, not hierarchies.

The Economics of Meaning

What makes Nuseir's journey remarkable is that it embodies a new kind of economics — the economics of meaning. Traditional business education teaches us how to create profit; Nuseir teaches us how to create purpose.

He transformed intangible human stories into a tangible business model. His company's revenue streams include educational courses, content partnerships, and software tools — all rooted in one principle: *authentic human connection is the best marketing strategy.*

In a world where AI threatens to automate creativity, Nuseir shows that genuine storytelling remains irreplaceable. Algorithms may amplify content, but only authenticity sustains engagement.

Leadership Lessons from NAS Daily

1. **Purpose Is the New Profit:** The success of *NAS Daily* was never measured in revenue alone but in resonance. When an idea resonates emotionally, it builds trust — the currency of the digital era.
2. **Consistency Beats Talent:** His 1,000-day discipline shows that persistence creates visibility. Management is not about managing people; it's about managing persistence.
3. **Storytelling as Management Tool:** Great leaders are not those who give orders but those who tell compelling stories that align people toward a common goal.
4. **Global Perspective, Local Relevance:** Nuseir's videos celebrate both diversity and unity, showing that global thinking starts with respect for local realities — a lesson for multinational organizations.

5. **Minimalism and Clarity:** Each one-minute video forced him to focus only on the essence. Similarly, great managers cut complexity and focus on clarity.

Philosophy of Simple Living

Though Nuseir built a multimillion-dollar company, his lifestyle remained minimal. He travels light, values experiences over possessions, and promotes conscious living. His simplicity is not a lack of ambition but a refusal to be enslaved by consumption.

He once said, "I don't want to own things; I want to own my time." That statement is a management manifesto in itself. In the 21st century, the most valuable asset is not money or property but freedom — the freedom to choose one's work, one's values, and one's impact.

His journey resonates with ancient wisdom too. Philosophers have long said that the ultimate management is the management of desires. By choosing purpose over possessions, Nuseir demonstrated how simplicity leads to sustainability — both personal and professional.

Conclusion: A New Model of Management

Nuseir Yassin's story is a living case study for modern management thought. He teaches that the next generation of leaders will not emerge from corner offices but from communities. They will not build companies first but audiences. They will not chase quarterly profits but lifelong purpose.

His journey reflects the evolution of management from command-and-control to connect-and-care. It shows how authenticity, discipline, and empathy can coexist with innovation and entrepreneurship.

In the end, Nuseir's message to aspiring managers is timeless:

"Don't manage people. Manage meaning."

When organizations learn to manage meaning, they no longer need to motivate employees — people motivate themselves because they see significance in their work.

Thus, from a Harvard graduate searching for purpose to a global storyteller shaping purpose, Nuseir Yassin proves that the greatest success stories begin not in boardrooms but in moments of personal honesty.

He reminds us that the real management begins within.

"Not every failure becomes a stepping stone
-Magada"

Failure Stories

Case Study: Strategic Misalignment in Areca Plate Manufacturing

Background:

An entrepreneur launched an areca leaf plate manufacturing unit in Mysuru, Karnataka—a region that does not have native areca palm cultivation. This fundamental location mismatch resulted in a critical supply chain vulnerability from the outset.

Challenge:

Due to the absence of local raw material availability, the unit relied on sourcing areca sheaths from distant regions, spanning 120 to 250 kilometres. This significantly escalated transportation costs, which adversely impacted profit margins. Despite the rising input costs, the market price for areca plates remained flat, as customers showed little regard for sourcing distance or production sustainability—price competitiveness was their only concern.

Strategic Oversight:

The promoter presumed the existence of a robust export market based on anecdotal input and general assumptions, without conducting a formal market study or demand validation. Initial exports were facilitated through third-party exporters, but in the absence of binding trade agreements, such as contracts or letters of credit, there was no assurance of payment or repeat business.

Outcome: The business was ultimately rendered unsustainable due to high operational costs, lack of pricing power, unverified market assumptions, and poor risk mitigation. The absence of formal trade frameworks and direct buyer relationships further compounded the challenges. The unit was eventually shut down, highlighting a classic case of misaligned location strategy and inadequate market due diligence.

Key Learnings for Investors & Entrepreneurs:

- Conduct thorough feasibility studies before setting up location-sensitive enterprises.
- Never substitute assumptions for market research—validate demand and buyer behaviour through formal channels.
- Establish secure and formalized trade agreements in international transactions to mitigate financial risk.
- Align raw material proximity, operational cost structure, and customer expectations before entering competitive markets.
- Understand the Minimum Scale of Economy (MSE)

Failure story from a Lineman's Family

In the success stories, while it is important to acknowledge the remarkable efforts of the lineman's family in shaping a brighter future for their children, the journey of the first two children, unfortunately, took a different course. Despite the foundation laid for them, they were unable to establish themselves meaningfully even after completing their service and retiring from their respective government jobs.

Unlike their parents, who dreamed big and sacrificed deeply, these two lacked a vision for their own lives. Instead of striving forward, they often complained about their circumstances, relying on others for support whenever they faced financial difficulties.

Responsibilities were neglected, and opportunities were allowed to slip by.

Neither did they build financial security nor did they safeguard their health, two essentials that sustain a person in later years. At one time, they enjoyed respect and a good standing in society, but over the years, that reputation slowly withered away. Their story stands in contrast to the legacy of sacrifice and discipline that once lifted the family upward — a reminder that success requires not only opportunities given, but also responsibility, foresight, and effort sustained.

In contrast, the younger two children chose a different path. Life tested them as well, with its share of struggles and uncertainties, yet they did not falter. Unlike their elder siblings, they held firmly to their core principles, refusing to let circumstances bend their spirit. It was this quiet steadfastness — the discipline to stay true to values even in the face of hardship — that became the compass guiding their journey.

Success, for them, was not an accident of chance but the outcome of perseverance and integrity. By any measure that values meaning over mere appearance, they can be called truly successful. And it is from the heart of that lived experience that one of them now writes these very words, offering not just a story, but a testament — that resilience and principle can shape a life worth remembering.

The contrast between the two paths teaches us a profound lesson. The human mind is much like fertile soil: it yields according to what is sown in it. If one sows complaints, negligence, and dependence, life offers little in return. But if one sows discipline, dreams, and values, then, despite storms and uncertainties, the harvest will be rich.

Situations may vary, fortunes may fluctuate, yet one must never abandon core principles. They are the compass that keeps us aligned with our purpose. Ultimately, success is not to be confused with the mere accumulation of wealth or possessions. In the spirit of this book, success means realizing a dream that holds worth — a goal shaped with integrity and recognised by society as meaningful. True success is not measured in gold, but in the value of a life lived with purpose and acceptance.

Success grows from failure's roots.

From Two Failures to a ₹2,300 Crore Success: The Wakefit Story

Every entrepreneur's journey begins with uncertainty, and few embody resilience as powerfully as Chaitanya Ramalingegowda.

Born into a middle-class family in Karnataka, India Chaitanya's early life was shaped by ambition and curiosity. He pursued Computer Science at Visvesvaraya Technological University, followed by an MBA at the Indian School of Business (ISB), Hyderabad—a combination that reflected both logic and leadership. Yet, despite his academic excellence, success didn't come easily.

His first venture, a dating-meetup app called *TwolyMadlyDeeply*, struggled to survive due to poor monetisation. His second, a media-based start-up, also collapsed after failing to achieve a product–market fit. Two failures in a row would have disheartened many—but not Chaitanya. Instead, he saw them as lessons in value creation, customer behaviour, and market reality.

Fate intervened when he met Ankit, a friend suffering from chronic back pain. They realised that India's mattress market was outdated—dominated by legacy brands, arbitrary pricing, and poor consumer education. The opportunity was clear: *to democratise good sleep.*

With personal savings of ₹13 lakh, Chaitanya set up a small foam-cutting and mattress-assembly unit in the Hosur–Mysuru industrial belt near Bengaluru. That modest beginning in 2016 gave birth to Wakefit — a company that would soon redefine how India sleeps.

In the early days, Chaitanya played multiple roles — product tester by day, delivery agent by night. To build credibility, he introduced a radical 100-night free trial policy, unheard of in the Indian market. Initially, it brought logistical chaos, delayed deliveries, and countless customer complaints — but he handled every call personally. That commitment turned frustration into faith.

By 2018, Wakefit had crossed ₹80 crore in revenue, powered purely by word-of-mouth. Selling directly to customers made their products nearly 40% cheaper than traditional brands. For the first time, legacy players like *Kurlon* and *Sleepwell* were forced to wake up and take notice.

The momentum drew investor attention. In 2018, Sequoia Surge invested ₹65 crore, enabling Wakefit to expand its manufacturing footprint to Sonipat (Haryana) and Hosur (Tamil Nadu). By 2019, the company's revenue had surged to ₹197 crore.

Wakefit then evolved beyond mattresses — expanding into sofas, beds, wardrobes, and study tables, positioning itself as a complete home solutions brand. Its customer-centricity, pricing innovation, and operational discipline helped it race past ₹400 crore in sales, outpacing even the most established competitors.

To reinforce its leadership, Wakefit invested in India's first sleep research lab, scientifically testing foam quality and orthopaedic claims. Its creative "Sleep Internship" campaign went viral, bringing science, humour, and brand recall together brilliantly. By 2022, the company had reached 19,000 pin codes and doubled revenue to ₹820 crore, backed by a ₹200 crore investment from Investcorp.

By 2024, Wakefit had served over two million customers, with mattresses still contributing 70% of its sales. It became one of India's fastest-growing consumer brands, crossing the ₹1,000 crore revenue mark and continuing its upward climb.

Today, Wakefit stands tall with ₹1,017 crore in revenue and ₹65.85 crore in profit, operating five manufacturing hubs and 98 stores across 35 cities. What began as a response to a friend's backache became a ₹2,300 crore enterprise — built not on luck, but on learning, perseverance, and a relentless focus on solving real problems.

Chaitanya Ramalingegowda's story is a masterclass in entrepreneurial resilience — proof that two failures are often just the training ground for one great success.

"Education prepares the mind;
action shapes the destiny-**Magada**"

Why Beyond Academics Now?

In times when opportunities seem abundant and resources were more freely available, education has long been considered the primary ladder to success. For many in the middle class, it has been a sacred belief: get your degree, secure your job, and you will rise.

Yet when you look at where many billionaires derive their wealth—finance, investment, technology, entertainment, media, fashion—you realize a different pattern. Quite often, it is not merely formal credentials that elevate people, but rather the ability to think beyond the rigid frames of convention. Relying exclusively on a government job, no matter how secure, can sometimes be just a step away from stagnation or poverty, especially if one's thinking remains bounded by old models.

Truly, education's highest purpose is not confined to preparing someone for a job. It must be to expand the horizon of what a person can imagine and achieve. Education gives knowledge—facts, theory, frameworks—and guidance. But beyond that, one must have the courage, the ingenuity, to use that knowledge, to trust one's intuition, to experiment, to solve real problems. It is this mix of learning, boldness, and action that enables a person to create work—not simply seek it—both for themselves and for others.

Success, then, is not merely a certificate or a score; it is a state of being, a constant becoming: using what you know, what you feel, what you believe, to fashion something worthwhile—something that resonates, something that contributes.

Artificial Intelligence and Machine Learning

We are living in an era where artificial intelligence (AI) and machine learning (ML) are reshaping the very foundations of work and industry. While these technologies hold the promise of efficiency, innovation, and progress, they also raise deep concerns about employment.

According to the International Monetary Fund (IMF), nearly 40% of jobs worldwide may be affected by AI in some form—positively or negatively. But it is important to understand the nuance: "affected" does not necessarily mean "eliminated." Many jobs will not vanish overnight; instead, they will be transformed. The way tasks are performed, the skills required, and the value employees bring to the table will evolve.

Similarly, the OECD (Organisation for Economic Co-operation and Development) reports that about 27% of jobs in OECD countries are in occupations at the highest risk of automation or AI disruption. Yet again, "risk" is not the same as "certainty." Technology disrupts, but it also creates. Alongside the fading of certain roles, entirely new opportunities arise—roles that didn't exist even a decade ago.

However, there lies the challenge: the jobs created by AI and ML are often not immediately accessible to everyone. They demand new skills, adaptability, and a mindset willing to embrace continuous learning. Those who remain rigid or rely solely on outdated knowledge may find themselves left behind.

This reality sends a clear message, especially to the youth: in a rapidly shifting world where traditional career paths no longer guarantee stability, one must look toward new avenues, emerging fields, and entrepreneurial opportunities. Upskilling—whether in digital literacy, critical thinking, or creative problem-solving—is no longer optional; it is the very foundation of survival and growth.

Thus, the age of AI is not just about machines replacing humans—it is about humans redefining themselves. Those who adapt, learn, and innovate will not only remain relevant but also thrive in ways never before imagined. It is the time where you have to prove to the computer that you are a human.

Disruptive Businesses

The rise of apps like Amazon, Flipkart, Swiggy, Zomato, Instamart, and Blinkit have transformed the way consumers purchase goods and services. With just a click, groceries, clothes, electronics, or even a full meal can be delivered to one's doorstep. This convenience has altered habits so deeply that traditional markets and small family-run businesses are struggling to survive.

Large chains such as D-Mart, Big Basket, and More operate on massive volumes, allowing them to slash prices in ways that no small neighbourhood shop can ever match. The local *kirana* store, once the heartbeat of every community, is now fighting a losing battle. For generations, these shops sustained families, provided credit to neighbours in times of need, and were woven into the very fabric of society. Today, their shutters are closing one by one, silencing not just businesses but entire ways of life. Apart from the fresh unemployed youths, the old people are also joining the "Unemployment Club."

The tragedy extends to the food sector as well. With the dominance of delivery apps, many people prefer to eat at home rather than step into restaurants. The once-bustling fine-dining establishments, where families celebrated milestones and friends gathered for long conversations, are now echoing with emptiness. Some survive only on online orders; others, unable to adapt, have closed their doors forever.

It is not just an economic shift but a cultural one. The marketplace used to be a social space, where relationships were built and trust was exchanged along with goods. Today, those human connections are being replaced by algorithms, discounts, and faceless transactions. While technology offers speed and convenience, it also leaves behind a silent trail of despair—of livelihoods lost, traditions forgotten, and communities fragmented.

The story is not of progress alone, but of displacement. And the true tragedy is that in our pursuit of convenience, we may not realize what we are losing until it is gone.

The rising standards and numbers

If you pause and take a careful look around, you will notice a profound change in the very fabric of our cities and towns. The streets are lined with state-of-the-art wine stores, glowing with neon lights and an endless variety of imported labels. Pharmacies and medical shops now operate 24 hours a day, seven days a week, ensuring that medication is never out of reach. Five-star hospitals stand tall, gleaming with glass and steel, ready to provide the most advanced treatment at a moment's notice. At first glance, all of this might seem like progress, a mark of civilization and modern comfort. But if we pause and reflect deeply, we begin to sense a more troubling undercurrent.

These symbols of modern life — convenience, accessibility, and luxury — are not purely signs of well-being. They are also markers of imbalance, the unintended consequences of technological advancement. Technology, in its brilliance, has given us the gift of time. Tasks that once consumed hours — shopping, banking, ordering food, consulting experts — can now be done with a few taps on a screen. We no longer have to stand in lines, wait for public transportation, or spend hours negotiating prices in a marketplace. In many ways, technology has delivered efficiency, convenience, and comfort.

Yet, with all this saved time, what have we gained? Or more importantly, what have we lost? In our pursuit of speed and efficiency, we have traded our health for convenience. Long hours sitting in front of screens, sedentary lifestyles, stress from constant notifications, late-night meals, and over-reliance on fast solutions have quietly eroded our physical well-being. The same technology that brings food to our doorstep within minutes also encourages a lifestyle of inactivity. The endless availability of medical services — open 24/7 — is both a blessing and a warning: it is a reminder that we are paying the price for the very comforts we sought.

Consider the wine stores and liquor shops. They are a symbol of choice, abundance, and freedom. Yet they also silently reflect the pressures of modern life. People seek pleasure in artificial ways, trying to soothe stress, anxiety, and loneliness. Similarly, five-star hospitals, with their advanced diagnostics, surgeries, and treatments, remind us of the fragility of human health — a fragility that is increasingly manufactured by our lifestyles. We have saved time, yes, but often at the expense of sleep, mental peace, and physical fitness.

Technology has also altered our relationship with money and happiness. We now spend more — not always for enjoyment, but to repair the very health, peace, and joy that our lifestyle erodes. Gym memberships, diet plans, wellness retreats, consultations with nutritionists and therapists — all these are attempts to reclaim what we have lost. We have traded slow, natural living for speed, and in doing so, we find ourselves chasing happiness through money, often without truly finding it.

There is also a social dimension to this transformation. Once, markets were alive with human interactions. The shopkeeper knew your name, the local grocer remembered your preferences, and buying goods was an opportunity to connect, to laugh, to share moments of life. Today, much of this interaction is replaced by apps and automated systems. While technology brings efficiency, it also quietly erodes human connection, leaving behind convenience but emptiness.

The lesson here is subtle but profound. Technology is a double-edged sword. It can save us time and make our lives more comfortable, but without mindfulness, it can also create new forms of suffering. Our health deteriorates, our happiness becomes transactional, and our relationships become more virtual than real. The glowing wine store, the 24-hour pharmacy, the gleaming hospital — these are not just markers of progress; they are reminders of imbalance, of a society rushing ahead without checking what it leaves behind.

Ultimately, the story is not about rejecting technology. Far from it. The story is about awareness, balance, and conscious living. It is a call to remember that while we embrace modern tools, we must not surrender the very things that give life its meaning: good health, genuine happiness, human connection, and the quiet joy of a balanced, mindful existence. Technology should serve life — not dominate it, and certainly not replace the timeless values that sustain well-being.

"If you don't understand MSE,
business is not your playground - **Magada**"

Minimum Scale of Economy (MSE)

After studying various stories of success and failure, one must carefully determine the type of business they can venture into — considering factors such as available resources, technical knowledge, skills, and investment capacity. However, before diving into technology, biology, or any production process, aspiring entrepreneurs must first understand the economics behind it. Grasping the fundamentals of economics is essential, as it forms the foundation upon which every technological or biological innovation can sustainably thrive.

Unless you understand the Minimum Scale of Economy (MSE), one must not venture into any business. MSE is referred as different terminologies in economics. But this MSE can be understood by any common man when it is put it in the simple language without using economic jargons.

Minimum Scale of Economy (MSE) refers to the smallest level of output at which a firm/farm/any business can produce efficiently and achieve the lowest average cost of production.

In business terms:

It's the threshold point where a firm begins to benefit from economies of scale—reductions in cost per unit due to increased production. Producing below this level means the firm faces higher per-unit costs, making it less competitive.

Key Characteristics of MSE:

- **Cost Efficiency**: At MSE, fixed costs (like machinery, rent, admin) are spread over enough units to reduce average costs significantly.
- **Benchmark for Viability**: It acts as a benchmark for deciding whether an enterprise is financially viable or not.
- **Industry-Specific**: The MSE varies by industry. For instance, a software company may reach MSE at a smaller scale than an automobile manufacturer.

Example: If it costs ₹10 lakh per month to run a factory (fixed cost) and it can produce 10,000 units, the **cost per unit is ₹100**. But if it only produces 1,000 units, the **cost per unit becomes ₹1,000**, which may be too high for the market. So, **producing 10,000 units is the Minimum Scale of Economy** for that firm to the keep the CoP at Rs. 100/unit. Always the MSE is decided on the basis of production of a single unit.

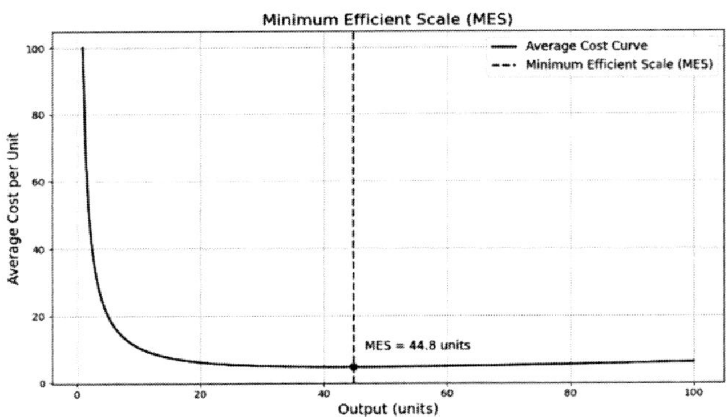

This graph shows how average cost per unit changes with output. The Minimum Efficient Scale (MES) is the output level where average cost is at its lowest – marked by the dashed line. Producing beyond this point does not significantly reduce cost and may even increase it due to diseconomies of scale. Production level anything below the MES point will not be economically viable.

In simpler terms, the Cost-Benefit Ratio (CB Ratio) can be considered to fall at 1.0. This concept is fundamental and must be clearly understood by anyone involved in business operations. However, it is important to recognize that the CB Ratio is not a fixed figure across all situations; it can fluctuate based on various influencing factors such as technological advancements, the quality and availability of human resources (men), and the cost and accessibility of materials. These elements are dynamic and can differ significantly depending on the location, market conditions, and prevailing circumstances. However, drawing from fundamental economic principles, it is essential to conduct a thorough prediction and evaluation of potential outcomes before implementing any project.

Interestingly, among the traditional "4Ms" of business—Men, Material, Machine (Technology), and Money—the element of 'Money' tends to remain relatively constant. Its value and basic function as a medium of exchange do not dramatically shift with geography or season, even though its purchasing power may vary slightly. Therefore, while the other variables introduce complexity and variability into the CB Ratio, Money serves as a relatively stable foundation upon which these fluctuations are assessed.

Understanding these nuances is critical for making informed business decisions and for accurately evaluating the viability and sustainability of any enterprise.

Agriculture Economics

Across India, a significant majority—over 85%—of farmers fall into the category of small and marginal landholders, with an average landholding size of less than 2.5 acres. This structural reality poses substantial challenges to the adoption of advanced scientific agricultural practices and large-scale mechanization. Simply put, such modern techniques often demand a scale and investment that these smallholdings cannot support, rendering them economically unviable under current conditions.

The economic sustainability of agriculture, in general, is under serious strain. Even with government interventions such as the Minimum Support Price (MSP) scheme—designed to provide a financial safety net for farmers—the viability of farming remains questionable. A critical issue lies in the methodology used to calculate MSP: it consciously excludes the managerial or administrative costs borne by the farmer. These include time, effort, decision-making responsibilities, risk management, and other non-labour yet essential contributions, which are integral components in any comprehensive economic evaluation.

In classical economics, the managerial cost is a legitimate and unavoidable factor in the cost of production. By omitting this crucial element, the actual economic burden on farmers is underestimated, leading to policy decisions that do not fully address the realities on the ground. Over time, the cumulative losses incurred by ignoring such hidden costs not only demoralize the farming community but also generate a compounding effect—deepening financial distress, eroding rural livelihoods, and contributing to broader agrarian crises.

Hence, without a structural overhaul in how agricultural economics are assessed and supported, especially for small and marginal farmers, true viability remains elusive. This can be explained very well with the following example.

Economics of Paddy Cultivation

India, the second largest rice growing country and largest exporter in the world, plants rice over an area of about 43 million hectares (mh) and produces around 125 million tonnes (mt) of rice with yield level still remaining low at around 2.85 t/ha. While the global average production is 4.374 t/ha and India stands 57th rank in the paddy yields. Even by considering the commercial paddy growing area, according to data from IndexMundi, India's average milled rice yield is approximately 4.0 metric tons per hectare. India ranks 50th globally in terms of rice yield per hectare.

The average paddy yield in Karnataka state is 2,500 kg per acre (equivalent to 4,000 m^2). The Cost of Cultivation (CoC) for this area is ₹36,000. With the Government's Minimum Support Price (MSP) of Rs. 2300/100 kg, the Gross Revenue (GR) is ₹57,500 (Rs. 2300 X 25), resulting in a Net Profit of ₹21,500 (Rs. 57,500—Rs. 36,000).

To analyze the unit economics, we compute revenue and profit on a per-square-meter basis:

Gross Revenue per m^2 = ₹57,500 ÷ 4,000 m^2 = ₹14.375

Net Profit per m^2 = ₹21,500 ÷ 4,000 m^2 = ₹5.375

To determine the Minimum Scale of Economy (MSE)—i.e., the minimum land area required to recover the CoC—we divide the total cost by the gross revenue per unit area:

MSE = ₹36,000 ÷ ₹14.375 = 2,504.34 m^2

This implies that an area of 2,504.34 m^2 is the break-even point, where the Cost-Benefit (CB) ratio = 1.0. Any production beyond this area (i.e., the remaining 1,495.66 m^2) contributes to economic profit. Thus, cultivating paddy on less than 2,504 m^2 is not economically sustainable under the given cost-revenue structure.

The CB ratio of the above economics is calculated by dividing the gross revenue by net profit and it is:

Rs. 57,500 ÷ Rs. 36,000 =1.597

This implies that for every ₹1 invested in paddy cultivation, a profit of ₹0.597 (59.7 paise) is realized. In economic terms, the minimum viable yield to break even is approximately 1,565 kg per acre (or 3,913 kg per hectare). Yields below this threshold render the enterprise economically unviable.

In many coastal regions of India, the actual paddy yield ranges between 1,200 to 1,400 kg per acre, which falls significantly short of the viability benchmark. As a result, paddy farming in these areas has become economically unsustainable, prompting many farmers to abandon the practice. Additionally, high labour costs in coastal regions further exacerbate the economic unviability of paddy cultivation in these areas.

Here is a graphical representation showing the Minimum Scale of Economy (MSE) and the Profitable Area in paddy cultivation.

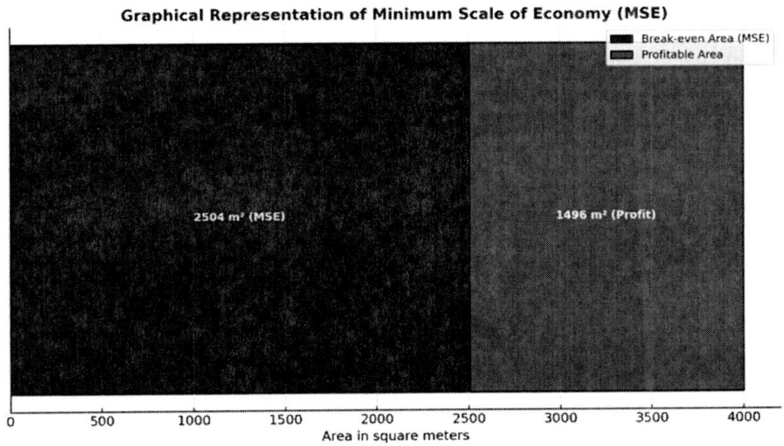

However, the initial analysis does not present the complete economic picture. The earlier calculation overlooks a critical component — managerial or supervisory costs. In practical terms, the manager is expected to visit the paddy field for supervision on approximately 50 out of the 120 days of the cropping cycle. If we attribute a notional managerial cost of ₹500 per day, the total supervisory cost amounts to ₹25,000.

When this cost is factored in, the adjusted net profit becomes:

Net Profit (after managerial cost) = ₹21,500 – ₹25,000 = **–₹3,500**

This implies an effective loss of ₹3,500 from cultivating paddy on one acre. From an opportunity cost perspective, if the same four-month period were allocated to other economically viable activities, the individual might generate a higher return.

Nonetheless, it's important to understand that as the scale of cultivation increases, the cost of cultivation (CoC) per unit area tends to decline, primarily because managerial costs do not increase proportionately with area. For example, if the same cultivation activities are undertaken on one hectare (10,000 m^2) — 2.5 times the original area — the projected profit scales proportionally:

Gross Profit (before managerial cost) = **₹21,500 × 2.5** = **₹53,750**

After accounting for the same fixed managerial cost of ₹25,000:

Adjusted Net Profit (1 hectare) = ₹53,750 – ₹25,000 = **₹28,750**

Spread over four months, this results in a monthly return of ₹7,187.50. Agricultural laborers typically earn between ₹15,000 and ₹18,000 per month. In many cases, their steady income places them in a better financial position than the farmers who employ them.

Thus, these figures underline an essential principle in farm economics: small-scale paddy cultivation may be economically unviable, whereas expanding the area under cultivation can lead to economies of scale, improved profitability, and more rational use of managerial input. These insights are critical for making informed decisions on whether or not to pursue paddy farming as a viable enterprise.

In regions such as Tanjavoor in Tamil Nadu, and Raichur and Sindhanur in Karnataka, India, the paddy yield can reach impressive levels of 3,800 to 4,000 kg per acre. In smaller-scale paddy farms, farmers can typically expect to harvest between 1.5 to 2.0 tons of paddy straw per acre. This straw is a valuable by-product, often sold at a rate of Rs. 4 per kilogram, allowing farmers to generate an additional income of around Rs. 6,000 to Rs. 8,000 per acre from its sale. Throughout the entire process, factors such as natural calamities, pests, diseases, and other related issues have been overlooked.

However, in large-scale paddy farms where mechanical harvesters are employed, the situation is different. These machines tend to cause significant damage to the paddy straw, resulting in little to no straw being available for collection. This mechanical harvesting method, while efficient in terms of time and labour, limits the opportunity for farmers to capitalize on the sale of paddy straw, which can otherwise be a profitable additional-income.

Paradox of Dairy Farming

Dairy farming is one of the oldest and most dependable livelihood activities practiced by rural communities across the world. Traditionally, it was a low-cost enterprise, relying heavily on natural pasturing, green fodder, and farmyard manure. However, with time, the dairy landscape has changed significantly. One of the pressing issues today is the shortage of skilled labour for milking, feeding, and herd management. Unlike in the past, when dairy farming was integrated with cropping and grazing systems, the shrinking landholdings and disappearance of common grazing lands have forced farmers to depend largely on purchased feed inputs, especially commercial concentrates.

The price of concentrate feed has now surged to more than ₹40 per kilogram. A standard feeding practice demands around 1 kg of concentrate for every 2.5 litres of milk produced, significantly raising the input cost for farmers. Despite this, when calculating the Minimum Support Price (MSP) for milk, most government agencies consider only the operational expenditure (OPEX) during the milking period. This is a flawed method, as it completely ignores the expenses incurred during the dry period, as well as management and fixed costs.

In a medium-scale dairy farm, the estimated cost of production (CoP) of milk is around ₹31 per litre, factoring in feed, labour, health care, and basic operational needs. For such farmers to remain viable, the farm gate price of milk should ideally range between ₹40–₹45 per litre. In contrast, small-scale dairy farmers who primarily use family labour and local feed resources manage to produce milk at a lower CoP—around ₹21–₹24 per litre. However, this estimate typically excludes management costs, such as the value of the farmer's time, opportunity cost, and risk management—factors that would never be overlooked in any other business. Unfortunately, this practice of excluding real management costs has become normalized in dairy economics, effectively training farmers to undervalue their own contribution. This not only leads to miscalculated profitability but also enables middlemen and processors to capture disproportionate margins, further weakening the position of the actual milk producers.

Table 3. Scale and profitability of farming

Scale	Profitability Trend	Reason
Small Scale	▲ High per-animal profit	Low overhead, self-labour, minimal waste, low investment risk
Medium Scale	▼ Dip in profit	Higher costs without matching efficiencies (labour, infrastructure, vet)
Large Scale	▲ High total and per-unit profit	Economies of scale, automation, bulk buying, professional management

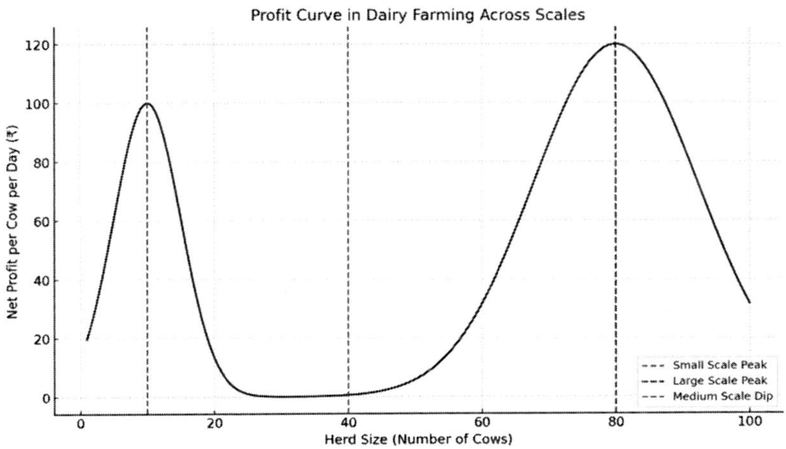

Fig 4. Graphical representation of profit margin against the scale of the dairy farming

- **High profitability at small scale (around 10 cows)** due to self-labour and low overhead.
- **Dip in profitability at medium scale (around 40 cows)** because of increased costs without efficiency.
- **High profitability again at large scale (around 80 cows)** due to economies of scale and professional management.

Though the economics are worked out in the Excel sheet, it is essential for every farmer to understand the basic calculations involved in day-to-day farming activities. This hands-on understanding helps them monitor each input cost more precisely—whether it's labour, seed, water, feed, or fertilizer. When they are aware of what goes into each unit of production, they can better evaluate the overall cost of production. More importantly, this awareness allows them to identify which components are inflating costs unnecessarily, and take corrective action accordingly. In the absence of this understanding, farmers may rely entirely on software or consultants and lose control over their own business decisions. Therefore, knowing simple calculations not only improves financial literacy but also empowers farmers to make timely decisions, improve efficiency, and ultimately increase their profits.

$$\textbf{Cost of Production (₹/kg)} = \frac{\text{Total Cost of Inputs (₹)}}{\text{Total Output (kg)}}$$

$$\textbf{\% Cost Contribution of Component} = \frac{\text{Total Cost of Production}}{\text{Cost of the Component}} \times 100$$

$$\textbf{BC Ratio} = \frac{\text{Total Costs (Costs)}}{\text{Gross Returns (Benefits)}}$$

$$\textbf{RoI (\%)} = \frac{\text{Total Investment}}{\text{Net Profit}} \times 100$$

Fodder Vs Food Crop

Farmers often hesitate to adopt new or diversified farming systems due to a deep-rooted fear of uncertainty and limited capacity to take financial or operational risks. This reluctance is further reinforced by social stigma, where deviating from traditional practices is often frowned upon within their communities. Additionally, a lack of awareness or access to reliable information about alternative farming methods contributes to their continued reliance on monocropping.

Compounding this issue is the fact that many farmers do not maintain detailed economic records of their farming activities. Without proper tracking of input costs, returns, and losses, they are unable to fully assess the profitability or inefficiencies of their current practices. Over time, this lack of financial insight leads to a significant compounding effect—small losses or missed opportunities accumulate, ultimately resulting in long-term economic strain and stagnation in farm productivity and income growth.

Dakshina Kannada, one of the prominent coastal districts of Karnataka, India, is traditionally known for its paddy cultivation. However, the average yield of paddy in this region has been consistently lower than the state average, standing at approximately 1700 to 1800 kilograms per acre, compared to the Karnataka state average of around 2500 kilograms per acre.

When even those farmers who achieve the state average yield are facing economic losses, it raises a critical question—how can coastal farmers, who typically have lower productivity, expect to earn sustainable profits? In such circumstances, it becomes essential for farmers to diversify their agricultural activities based on local demands and regional advantages.

One promising avenue in Dakshina Kannada is dairy farming, which is witnessing steady growth. However, despite this positive trend, there is a significant gap in local fodder availability. Dairy farmers in the region are currently sourcing shredded maize from Belgaum—located nearly 700 kilo meters away—and paddy straw from districts like Hassan and Mandya, which are 200 to 500 kilo meters distant. This heavy reliance on fodder from far-off places not only increases production costs but also reduces the overall profitability and sustainability of the dairy sector.

To address this, local cultivation of green fodder and better integration between crop and livestock systems could be a viable strategy, offering farmers a more self-reliant and cost-effective approach to agricultural diversification.

Fodder maize demonstrate impressive productivity, yielding over 400 tonnes per hectare annually. At a conservative market price of ₹3 per kilogram, this translates to a gross revenue of ₹12,00,000 per hectare. With cultivation costs accounting for approximately 30% of the gross income—estimated at ₹4,00,000 per hectare—the net profit stands at ₹8,00,000 per hectare.

The other varieties like, 'Hybrid Napier-343' yields 150-170 t/ha, while 'Gini grass' yields 120-130 t/ha fetches the gross revenue of Rs. 4,80,000 and Rs. 3,75,000 respectively. Depending on the region, soil type and availability of water, one can chose the right crop.

In contrast, paddy cultivation yields a significantly lower economic return. Assuming two cropping cycles per year with an average gross return of ₹28,750 per crop, the total annual revenue from paddy is ₹57,500 per hectare. When broken down on a monthly basis, paddy cultivation offers an income of approximately ₹4,792, while fodder cultivation yields a more robust monthly return of ₹66,666 from fodder maize, Rs. 28,000 pm while growing Napier and Rs. 21,875 pm from the Gini grass.

This comparison highlights the superior economic viability of fodder cultivation over paddy, especially in regions where market demand for livestock feed is growing and input-output efficiency is critical for profitability.

Continuous Improvement Program

Even in agriculture, agronomic practices cannot remain static. They must evolve and adapt over time in response to changing conditions and new knowledge. This concept is best illustrated through the following example. In the foothill regions of the Western Ghats, paddy cultivation is predominantly based on the popular variety known as 'Bhadra.' However, the average yield of this variety remains relatively low, ranging between 1200 to 1400 kilograms per acre. One of the major agronomic challenges in both the foothills and coastal areas is soil acidity, which hampers nutrient availability and crop performance. Farmers in these regions traditionally rely on the application of cow dung as a natural manure. While this practice supports organic farming principles, it inadvertently contributes to increased soil acidity over time.

Through our field research and soil analysis, it was discovered that a significant deficiency of the essential micronutrient zinc was prevalent in these acidic soils. To address this issue, we recommended the application of zinc sulphate at the rate of 2 kilograms per acre. This simple intervention had a remarkable impact—resulting in a substantial yield increase of nearly 70%. This finding highlights the importance of balanced nutrient management and the need for region-specific soil health interventions to revitalize paddy farming in these ecologically sensitive areas.

It is important to note that even farmers who manage to achieve the state average often find themselves operating at a financial loss due to rising input costs, labour shortages, and market price fluctuations. In this context, one must question: if those attaining higher yields are struggling to make ends meet, how can paddy cultivation in the coastal belt, with significantly lower productivity, remain economically viable?

The consequences of this unprofitable scenario are already visible. Over the past decade, more than 25,000 hectares of paddy fields in Dakshina Kannada have either been converted for non-agricultural purposes such as real estate, infrastructure, and commercial development, or have simply been left uncultivated, turning into fallow lands locally known as *Hadilu*. This shift signals not only a decline in traditional agriculture but also raises serious concerns about food security, rural livelihoods, and the long-term sustainability of land use in the coastal region.

Enhancing paddy production by applying academic and scientific knowledge—such as correcting micronutrient deficiencies with zinc sulphate—is certainly one viable strategy. However, an alternative approach is to market the crop as 'organic produce' by avoiding chemical inputs altogether, which can fetch a premium price in niche markets.

A farmer once approached me with a concern: his small fish pond, measuring just 150 square meters, was overrun with what he considered a weed—lotus plants. I advised him to consider harvesting and selling the lotus instead of removing it. To his surprise, he now earns approximately ₹15,000 annually from selling lotus, with virtually no investment. To achieve the same profit through paddy cultivation, he would have to farm nearly 4,000 square meters of land—demonstrating that sometimes, value lies not in replacing what we see as problems, but in rethinking them.

India's productivity difference in major agricultural and aquaculture crops, comparing with world averages or leading countries

(Based on latest available FAO estimates~)

Crop/Product	India's Average Yield	World Average/Leading Country	Productivity Gap
Rice (Paddy)	2.7–3.0 t/ha	China (6.7 t/ha)	50–60% lower
Wheat	3.5 t/ha	China (5.7 t/ha)	40% lower
Maize	3.0 t/ha	USA (10.9 t/ha)	70% lower
Sugarcane	78–80 t/ha	Brazil (75–80 t/ha)	Comparable
Potato	23–25 t/ha	Netherlands (45–50 t/ha)	45% lower
Onion	5–18 t/ha	South Korea (65 t/ha)	70–75% lower
Garlic	5.5–6 t/ha	China (22 t/ha)	75% lower

Mango	8–10 t/ha	Mexico (13–14 t/ha)	30% lower
Banana	35 t/ha	Global avg. (20–25 t/ha)	Higher than global average
Milk (per animal)	1,700–2,000 l/year	USA (10,000 l/year)	80% lower
Eggs (per hen/year)	80–90 eggs/hen/year	USA (>300 eggs/hen/year)	70% lower
Aquaculture (fish)	3.0–5.5 t/ha/year	China (6–9 t/ha/year)	20–40% lower
Marine Fisheries	2.4 t/vessel/year	Developed Nations (5–6 t/vessel/year)	50–60% lower
Coffee	800 kg/ha	Brazil (2,200 kg/ha)	65% lower
Tea	2,300–2,500 kg/ha	Kenya (3,500 kg/ha)	30% lower
Cotton	500–550 kg lint/ha	China (1,800–2,000 kg/ha)	70% lower

Key Observations

- **Significant Gaps:** India lags significantly behind leading countries in the productivity of several key crops, including rice, wheat, maize, onion, garlic, and cotton. The productivity gap ranges from 40% to 75% lower compared to countries like China, the USA, and South Korea.

- **Comparable Performance:** Sugarcane production in India is comparable to that of Brazil, indicating a relatively strong performance in this sector.
- **Above Average Performance:** Banana production in India exceeds the global average, showcasing a competitive advantage in this area.
- **Dairy and Poultry Deficiencies:** The productivity of milk and egg production is substantially lower in India compared to the USA, with gaps of 80% and 70%, respectively.
- **Fisheries Potential:** Both aquaculture and marine fisheries show productivity gaps, suggesting potential for improvement through better management practices and technology adoption.

Factors Contributing to Productivity Gaps

Several factors contribute to the observed productivity gaps in Indian agriculture:

- **Technology Adoption:** Lower adoption rates of advanced farming technologies, such as precision agriculture, genetically modified seeds, and efficient irrigation systems.
- **Infrastructure:** Inadequate infrastructure, including storage facilities, transportation networks, and cold chain logistics, leads to post-harvest losses and reduced market access.
- **Soil Health:** Declining soil health due to imbalanced fertilizer use, lack of organic matter, and soil erosion.
- **Water Management:** Inefficient water management practices, including over-reliance on groundwater and lack of water conservation techniques.
- **Extension Services:** Weak extension services and limited access to information for farmers regarding best practices and modern techniques.

- **Investment in R&D:** Insufficient investment in agricultural research and development (R&D) to develop high-yielding varieties and climate-resilient crops.
- **Market Access:** Limited access to organized markets and fair pricing mechanisms, which discourages farmers from investing in productivity-enhancing inputs.
- **Climate Change:** Increasing vulnerability to climate change impacts, such as droughts, floods, and extreme weather events, which adversely affect crop yields.

Strategies to Bridge the Productivity Gap

To address the productivity gaps and enhance agricultural output, India needs to focus on the following strategies:

- **Promote Technology Adoption:** Encourage the adoption of modern farming technologies through subsidies, training programs, and demonstration projects.
- **Improve Infrastructure:** Invest in improving rural infrastructure, including storage facilities, transportation networks, and irrigation systems.
- **Enhance Soil Health:** Promote soil health management practices, such as balanced fertilizer use, organic farming, and soil conservation measures.
- **Strengthen Extension Services:** Strengthen agricultural extension services to provide farmers with timely and relevant information on best practices and modern techniques.
- **Increase Investment in R&D:** Increase investment in agricultural R&D to develop high-yielding varieties, climate-resilient crops, and sustainable farming practices.
- **Improve Market Access:** Improve market access for farmers through the development of organized markets, e-commerce platforms, and fair pricing mechanisms.

- **Promote Sustainable Agriculture:** Promote sustainable agricultural practices, such as integrated pest management, conservation agriculture, and water conservation techniques.
- **Address Climate Change:** Develop and implement climate-resilient agricultural strategies to mitigate the impacts of climate change on crop yields.
- **Skill Development:** Focus on skill development and capacity building of farmers to enable them to adopt modern technologies and best practices.
- **Policy Support:** Implement supportive policies and regulations to promote agricultural growth and productivity, including land reforms, credit access, and insurance schemes.

By implementing these strategies, India can significantly enhance its agricultural productivity, improve food security, and boost the rural economy.

"Wrong data will never lead to the right strategy
- **Magada**"

Data Management

"With wrong data, we cannot come out with right strategies" Effective data management is of critical importance in any decision-making or management process. Accurate, timely, and well-organized data forms the foundation upon which sound strategies are built. Without reliable data, even the most well-intentioned plans can go astray. In fact, flawed or incomplete data can lead to misguided strategies, wasted resources, and poor outcomes. As the saying goes, "Garbage in, garbage out"—if the input data is incorrect, the resulting decisions will likely be ineffective or even detrimental. Therefore, investing in proper data collection, validation, and analysis is not just beneficial—it is essential for formulating successful and sustainable strategies.

Data collection does not start after establishing a business. It is a prelude to establish any venture.

In many instances, most of the small business owners do not have the habit of maintaining the data. There are many companies which offer 'Enterprise Resource Planning (ERP)' solutions. ERP is a software system that helps organisations streamline their core business processes—including finance, HR, manufacturing, supply chain, sales, and procurement—with a unified view of activity and provides a single source of truth.

With ERP (Enterprise Resource Planning) software can be configured to manage profit-sharing mechanisms with minimal or no human intervention, depending on the complexity and structure of the scheme. Here's how:

How ERP Can Automate Profit Sharing:

1. **Integrated Financials**: ERP systems track revenues, expenses, and net profits in real-time.
2. **Rule-Based Automation**: You can define rules (e.g., percentage shares, contribution-based models) in the system.
3. **Automatic Calculations**: Based on these rules, the ERP can automatically compute each stakeholder's profit share.
4. **Scheduled Disbursement**: Payments or ledger entries can be scheduled or triggered based on thresholds or timelines.
5. **Audit Trail**: The system maintains records of all transactions, ensuring transparency and traceability.
6. **Alerts & Reports**: Stakeholders can receive automated notifications and reports about their profit shares.

Human Involvement May Still Be Needed for:

- Initial configuration and rule-setting
- Handling exceptions or disputes
- Compliance reviews or audits
- Periodic adjustments based on business changes

So, while ERP software can automate most aspects of profit-sharing, complete removal of human oversight is not advisable—especially in complex or sensitive financial environments.

Not all businesses, especially small or emerging ones, have the financial capacity or technical infrastructure to adopt sophisticated ERP software systems. In such cases, maintaining systematic and organized data manually or through simpler digital tools becomes crucial for informed decision-making.

When data is consistently recorded and analysed, patterns and correlations can often be identified, enabling businesses to make strategic adjustments. Direct correlations—such as increased sales during festive seasons or a rise in costs with inflation—are usually easy to spot. However, it's important to recognize that not all influential factors present clear or immediate connections. Some variables may appear unrelated on the surface but can significantly affect business outcomes over time. These hidden influencers—such as employee morale, weather patterns, or subtle shifts in customer preferences—must be thoughtfully identified and their data diligently recorded.

In essence, even in the absence of ERP systems, a proactive approach to data collection—covering both obvious and subtle factors—can empower businesses to make smarter, evidence-based decisions and improve resilience in an ever-changing market environment.

In many cases, even after diligently collecting relevant data, entrepreneurs may find themselves unable to extract meaningful insights or draw clear conclusions. This can happen due to a lack of analytical expertise, unfamiliarity with data interpretation tools, or the complex nature of the data itself. Raw data, without proper context or analysis, often remains just numbers on a page—failing to inform decision-making.

At such junctures, it becomes essential for business owners to seek guidance from experts—whether they are consultants, domain specialists, or data analysts. These professionals can help interpret the data, identify patterns, uncover hidden relationships, and explain the underlying dynamics that drive business performance. By understanding the broader matrix of business operations—such as market behaviour, financial indicators, customer trends, and operational efficiency—entrepreneurs can make informed, strategic choices.

Adopting this collaborative approach not only enhances the entrepreneur's own understanding but also enables the business to respond more effectively to challenges and opportunities. In essence, when data alone doesn't provide answers, expert insight becomes the bridge between information and impactful action.

In April 2025, I had the opportunity to address a gathering of around 400 coffee growers in Chikkamagalur, a prominent coffee-producing district in Karnataka, India. During my interaction, I posed a simple yet vital question about the economics of coffee cultivation. In response, most planters confidently shared details about the number of bags they produced, the cost associated with each 60-kilogram bag, and their overall returns. This approach seemed to be second nature to them—perhaps shaped by years of industry practice and conventional training.

However, while this method provides a broad overview, it falls short of offering true financial insight. To make informed decisions and achieve sustainable profitability, it is essential to delve deeper—into what is known as "unit economics." This involves understanding the cost and return on a per-unit basis—be it per plant, per kilogram, or per acre—rather than relying solely on aggregate metrics. Without this granular clarity, farmers risk misjudging profitability, overlooking inefficiencies, and missing opportunities for optimization. Transitioning from bulk-based thinking to unit-based financial analysis is critical for modern agricultural entrepreneurship.

Unit economics refers to the direct revenues and costs associated with a single unit of product or service, which helps determine whether the business model is fundamentally profitable at a granular level. It answers the question: "How much do I earn and spend for every unit I produce or sell?"

Key Elements of Unit Economics: For agriculture (like coffee or paddy farming), the "unit" could be:

- 1 plant
- 1 kilogram of produce
- 1 ton

- 1 acre or hectare

For Unit Economics, for each unit, we calculate:

Metric	Explanation
Revenue per unit	Selling price per unit (e.g., ₹500/kg of coffee)
Cost of Production (CoP)	Input costs like fertilizer, labour, water, etc. per unit (May be Rs. 180/kg)
Contribution Margin	Revenue – Variable costs per unit (Revenue-CoP; Rs. 500-Rs. 180 = Rs. 320)
EBITDA **(Earnings before** Interest, Taxes, Depreciation, and Amortization**)**	How much profit is made on each unit (Rs. 320/kg)
Net Profit	EBITDA —ITDA

EBITDA is not the *final or real* profit. It's a proxy for operating performance, useful for comparing companies or evaluating cash flow potential.

It shows how much money a business makes from its core operations before accounting for:

- Loan interest (Interest)
- Government taxes (Taxes)
- Equipment/asset depreciation (Depreciation)
- Long-term asset costs spread over time (Amortization)

Why Unit Economics Matters

- Helps identify if scaling the business is viable.
- Pinpoints inefficiencies in production.
- Informs pricing decisions.
- Supports borrowing or investment with clear financial clarity.

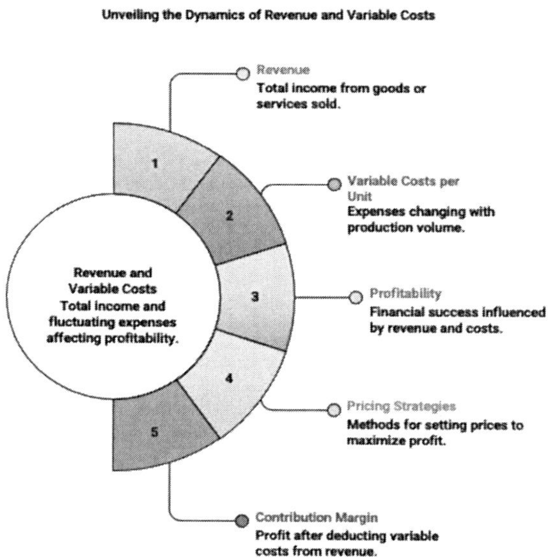

"Numbers don't lie,
but people who ignore numbers do-**Magada**"

Finance Management

Grasping the nuances of finance and effectively managing it is one of the most challenging aspects of running a business. Many entrepreneurs, particularly those from non-financial backgrounds, often lack formal training in financial management. As a result, when they approach banks or financial institutions for loans, they may struggle to fully understand the intricacies of loan agreements—the fine print, the technical terms, and the often complex banking jargon.

In the eagerness to secure funding, entrepreneurs frequently accept all the terms and conditions without fully comprehending their long-term implications. Unfortunately, the true weight of these obligations often becomes apparent only when a problem arises—be it a missed instalment, a sudden interest rate hike, or a penalty clause being triggered.

Adding to this challenge is the fact that modern finance management has become entirely digitized. With online platforms handling most transactions and records, there is little room for negotiation, personal rapport, or selective disclosure. Financial institutions now have real-time access to an entrepreneur's complete financial profile—credit scores, transaction history, liabilities, and cash flow patterns—before extending any assistance. This transparency, while improving efficiency and accountability, also demands that entrepreneurs be more informed, cautious, and strategic in their financial dealings.

Therefore, understanding financial systems, being vigilant about contract terms, and seeking expert advice before making financial commitments are no longer optional—they are essential components of responsible entrepreneurship in today's digital economy.

Understanding Interest Rates

There are different kinds of 'Interest Rates' in Banking systems. Most often, the customer will not read the fine prints in a hurry to avail the loan. There are various types of interest used for different financial products, loans, and investments. Here's a breakdown:

1. Simple Interest

- **Formula**:
  Interest = (Principal × Rate × Time) / 100
- Interest is calculated only on the original principal amount.
- Common in short-term loans and fixed deposits.

2. Compound Interest

- Interest is calculated on principal + accumulated interest from previous periods.
- Compounding frequency can be yearly, half-yearly, quarterly, or monthly.
- Used in long-term loans, savings, and investment schemes.

3. Fixed Interest Rate

- The interest rate remains constant throughout the loan or deposit period.
- Common in fixed-rate loans or fixed deposits.

4. Floating (Variable) Interest Rate

- The interest rate changes based on market benchmarks like repo rate or MCLR (Marginal Cost of Funds-based Lending Rate).
- Common in home loans and education loans.

5. Reducing Balance Interest

- Interest is calculated on the remaining loan balance, not the original amount.
- Used in EMI-based loans like car, personal, or home loans.
- Results in lower total interest compared to flat-rate loans.

6. Flat Interest Rate

- Interest is calculated on the entire principal for the full tenure, regardless of repayments.
- Often used in consumer durable loans and some vehicle loans.

7. Penal Interest

- Charged as a penalty for non-payment or delay in repayment of loans or EMIs.

8. Overdraft Interest

- Charged on the amount overdrawn from a current or savings account.
- Typically daily or monthly compounding.

9. Nominal vs. Effective Interest Rate

- **Nominal**: The stated annual interest rate.
- **Effective**: Includes compounding and gives the true annual return or cost.

If you're not well-versed in the complexities of financial planning or investment strategies, it's wise to seek guidance from qualified financial advisors. Their expertise can help you make informed and strategic decisions, tailored to your income, goals, and risk appetite. Failing to do so may lead to poorly informed choices, and over time, the impact of these decisions can multiply significantly due to the power of compounding. What may seem like a minor oversight initially can accumulate into a substantial financial burden or missed opportunity in the long run.

"The heart of business is not money,
but an idea-**Magada**"

Innovative Business Ideas

In the year 2009, I was approached by Mr. Vinay, a 'Home Stay' owner from Kanakapura, a region in Karnataka, India. He had developed a small farm and was keen to add value to the experience he offered to guests. At the time, his business model was quite straightforward: he charged Rs. 1800 per person per day, which included accommodation, meals, and a few recreational activities. While the concept was appealing to urban visitors seeking a rural escape, the revenue potential was limited due to a lack of innovation and underutilization of available natural resources.

Mr. Vinay requested fish seed to stock a pond located on his farm. Rather than merely providing the seeds, I saw an opportunity to transform his farm into a more dynamic, multi-income generating model through integrated and experience-based farming. I inquired about the layout and existing facilities on his farm and then suggested a comprehensive set of enhancements that could diversify his offerings and substantially increase his income.

One of the first ideas I proposed was the construction of tree huts. These structures not only add aesthetic appeal but also offer a unique accommodation experience that enhances the sense of adventure and connection to nature. Alongside the tree huts, I recommended that he invest in a few trekking tents and place them in scenic, shaded areas around the pond. This would allow him to attract a younger, more adventurous clientele and families interested in spending time in the lap of nature.

Next, I advised Mr. Vinay to rear country fowl and introduce the 'Swarnadhara' breed—a high-performing variety developed by our university. This breed is known for its exceptional egg-laying capabilities, producing over 180 eggs annually, and has a significantly faster growth rate compared to traditional country chickens. By integrating poultry farming into his homestay ecosystem, he could offer guests fresh eggs and chicken meat, both of which would enhance their culinary experience while also creating a new revenue stream.

To make better use of the existing pond, I suggested stocking it with larger fish species suitable for angling. Species selection is crucial, as guests are more likely to enjoy the recreational aspect of fishing if they have the chance to catch larger, more visible fish. I suggest to stock fishes like 'Common Carp', 'Murrel-the snake head', 'Pangasius' etc. To enhance the appeal, garden chairs could be placed around the pond under the shade of trees, allowing guests to sit back and relax. Small packets of fish feed could be sold to guests who wish to feed the fish, adding a new, low-cost income opportunity. The interaction with nature—feeding fish or attempting to catch them—would be both novel and enjoyable for city-dwellers.

Moreover, by offering fishing rods on rent, Mr. Vinay could further engage his guests in angling. In most cases, the guests may not even catch a fish, which means no loss of stock. However, on occasions when a fish is caught, he could charge a premium, labelling the catch as "organic" and offering to cook it as part of a specially prepared meal. This experience would not only command a higher price but also deepen the guest's emotional connection with the farm, making their stay memorable.

By implementing these relatively simple yet high-impact ideas, Mr. Vinay transformed his farm into a vibrant, interactive, and multi-functional space. Within a short span of time, his revenue increased by more than 60%. He achieved this without any major investment in land or infrastructure—only by repurposing existing assets and introducing value-added services.

This case serves as a classic example of how small farm-based enterprises can dramatically enhance their profitability through thoughtful diversification and experience-based offerings. The key lies in understanding the potential of available resources and tailoring the experience to meet and exceed customer expectations. Value addition, in this context, is not merely about increasing the price of a product or service but about enhancing the perceived and real worth of the entire farm experience.

Ultimately, Mr. Vinay's success highlights an important lesson for all rural entrepreneurs: the same piece of land, when approached with creativity and strategic planning, can yield much higher returns. It underscores the importance of integrated farming, customer engagement, and experiential marketing in today's rural tourism and agri-business landscape.

Customised Notebooks

When the demand for commercially produced notebooks declined—largely due to schools beginning to print and distribute their own branded notebooks—several publishing companies faced a significant threat to their traditional business model. In response, a few forward-thinking companies introduced a novel concept: personalized notebooks featuring customers' own photographs on the covers. This customization tapped into the growing appeal of personalization in consumer products, especially among students and parents looking for unique and memorable school supplies.

While this trend may not represent a permanent shift in the market, it has carved out a niche that is likely to remain viable for the next few years. It exemplifies how businesses can adapt creatively within the bounds of their existing operations, using innovation not necessarily to create entirely new products, but to refresh and repackage what already exists in a way that appeals to evolving consumer tastes.

A similar wave of innovation has been observed in the market for other educational supplies such as pens, pencils, erasers, and other stationery items. Recognizing the changing consumer preferences and the growing inclination towards personalization and novelty, several manufacturers have begun offering customized or uniquely packaged versions of these everyday products. These range from pens engraved with names to pencils adorned with attractive characters or motivational quotes, and even eco-friendly variants targeting environmentally conscious users.

While such innovations may not replace the entire conventional market, they introduce a refreshing segment that adds value to the business. By leveraging these creative ideas, companies are able to differentiate themselves in an otherwise saturated market, retain customer interest, and maintain business stability in the face of changing market dynamics. These adaptations reflect a broader trend: the ability to integrate new concepts within existing frameworks can be a vital strategy for sustaining relevance and profitability.

Cold Storages

India's agricultural marketing system includes a well-established framework known as the Agricultural Produce Market Committee (APMC), which was instituted by state governments to regulate the trade of farm commodities. These APMCs operate primarily through designated market yards, commonly referred to as *mandis*, where the sale and purchase of agricultural produce are facilitated under structured rules. The core objectives of APMCs are to promote transparency in transactions, ensure that farmers receive fair and remunerative prices, and enable timely payments through regulated auctions or bidding systems.

However, a major structural limitation within most APMCs is the lack of essential post-harvest infrastructure, especially cold storage facilities. Very few of these markets are equipped with temperature-controlled units, such as chillers maintaining +4 °C for fresh vegetables or deep freezers at –20 °C for perishable commodities like fish, meat, and dairy products. As a result, a significant proportion of perishable produce deteriorates rapidly before reaching the consumer, leading to high levels of post-harvest losses—estimated at 25% to 30%, and in some instances, even higher.

This infrastructural gap not only results in economic loss to farmers, but also contributes to food inflation and nutritional insecurity for consumers. The lack of modern preservation systems hinders value addition, limits the shelf life of goods, and reduces the scope for organized retailing and exports. Addressing this issue through targeted investments in cold chains, packaging, and logistics at the mandi level could significantly improve the efficiency of agricultural markets, boost farm incomes, and reduce the wastage of food—especially in the case of climate-sensitive and highly perishable commodities.

In many instances, meat vendors store perishable products in deep freezers that lack reliable power backup systems. This practice significantly increases the risk of food spoilage, potentially exposing consumers to serious health hazards. The absence of stringent regulatory oversight or routine inspections often allows such practices to continue unchecked, enabling vendors to maximize profits at the expense of public health and food safety.

This situation presents a critical opportunity for responsible entrepreneurship. Individuals or collectives can leverage various government schemes and subsidies offered through departments such as agriculture, fisheries, and food processing to establish properly maintained cold storage facilities. Though the initial investment required for cold chain infrastructure is relatively high, it addresses one of the most significant gaps in India's food supply system—proper storage and preservation. By ensuring hygienic storage and reducing post-harvest losses, such initiatives not only generate sustainable profits but also serve a vital public good by improving food safety and extending shelf life of perishables like meat, fish, fruits, and vegetables.

Modern Sales Outlets

One of the most striking ironies of our current socio-economic reality is that the very system designed to empower individuals—education—has increasingly become a breeding ground for underemployment and frustration. It might be true in many other developing nations. A recent instance in Rajasthan, India underscores this contradiction: over 24.76 lakh applicants competed for just 53,749 peon-level positions in a government department in India. Alarmingly, among the aspirants were individuals holding PhDs, MBAs, and other postgraduate degrees—qualifications that ideally prepare someone for leadership roles, innovation, and entrepreneurship, not for roles requiring minimal formal education or skills.

This example reflects a deeper systemic failure. Education, in its truest purpose, is meant to enable critical thinking, promote innovation, and help individuals either find or create gainful employment. Yet, our current model has become overly focused on degrees rather than skills, resulting in a massive mismatch between what is taught and what the job market demands. Institutions continue to churn out graduates without equipping them with practical knowledge, soft skills, or the entrepreneurial mindset required in today's dynamic economy.

The result? A staggering oversupply of academically qualified individuals competing for limited low-tier jobs, not out of preference but out of sheer desperation. It not only devalues higher education but also reflects the inadequacy of the state and private sectors to create meaningful employment aligned with educational outcomes.

This grim situation calls for immediate structural reforms—curriculum revamps, industry-academia integration, promotion of vocational and skill-based education, and most importantly, creating an ecosystem that nurtures entrepreneurship over mere job-seeking.

From a business standpoint, viewing India merely as a single country significantly underestimates its scale, complexity, and potential. India is, in essence, a conglomerate of 30 or more countries rolled into one—diverse in language, culture, consumer behaviour, income levels, and regional governance. With 17.8% of the world's population residing within its borders, India is not just a large market; it is a microcosm of the global economy, offering business scenarios ranging from rural subsistence to cutting-edge urban innovation.

What makes India especially attractive is its deep connectivity with the global economy—as both a consumer base and a production powerhouse. From IT services and pharmaceuticals to textiles and agri-tech, Indian businesses are increasingly becoming integral to global supply chains. Moreover, India's youthful demographic, with a median age of just over 28 years, represents not only a massive labour force but also a burgeoning consumer segment that is aspirational, digitally active, and open to innovation.

However, the true business potential lies in identifying and addressing the critical gaps—in infrastructure, logistics, retail chains, healthcare delivery, education systems, food preservation, and financial inclusion, among others. These are not just social challenges but untapped market opportunities. Entrepreneurs and businesses that can bridge these gaps by offering cost-effective, scalable, and localized solutions stand to gain significantly—financially and in terms of impact.

India's diversity also demands hyper-localized business models. What works in urban Bengaluru may not work in rural Bihar. This calls for nuanced strategies, regional customization, and grassroots engagement—qualities that agile entrepreneurs and innovative start-ups are uniquely positioned to provide.

India is not a monolithic market—it is a continent-sized opportunity that rewards those with the vision to see gaps not as problems but as possibilities for business creation and sustainable growth. Young individuals must be equipped with the skills to recognize existing market gaps and align them with their core strengths and capabilities.

"Mastery in football begins when the ball is not with you-
Magada"

Non Inventory Businesses

Across the country, millions of individuals are engaged in business activities that follow time-tested and culturally ingrained formats. These small-scale, often informal enterprises play a crucial role in the economy and are widely accepted and trusted by communities. Examples include vegetable vending, grocery shops, stationery outlets, meat and poultry vendors, local canteens, and hotels—each catering to the daily needs of consumers in both rural and urban settings.

These businesses are not confined to mere selling; they are deeply integrated across the entire value chain—beginning from production and processing, extending through trading and distribution, and culminating in retailing. They represent a vast and diverse economic network that functions with remarkable efficiency despite limited formal infrastructure. Their resilience and adaptability underline the strength of grassroots entrepreneurship and the importance of localized business models in ensuring economic stability and employment generation.

Harnessing Micro-Entrepreneurship and Value Addition: A Model for Inclusive Growth

In many developing economies, a significant segment of the youth population remains unemployed—not due to lack of willingness to work, but because of limited access to capital, structured markets, or organized opportunities. However, youth who possess an understanding of basic economic principles and entrepreneurial acumen can play a transformative role in bridging inefficiencies in local markets. One practical model involves aggregating and formalizing unorganized vendors to create a value-added supply chain that benefits all stakeholders: producers, intermediaries, and consumers.

Take, for example, the common sight of fishermen selling dried fish in traditional markets. These vendors often use open gunny sacks or bamboo baskets that expose the product to contamination by dust, flies, and fungi—posing serious health risks to consumers and diminishing product quality. Here lies an economic opportunity: unemployed but educated youth can intervene as value-chain integrators.

The first step involves organizing the vendors into a cooperative or informal collective and educating them about hygiene, food safety standards, and consumer preferences. By introducing simple technologies—such as hygienic stick pouches for packaging—and encouraging product grading and labelling, the perceived value of the same commodity can be significantly enhanced.

From an economic standpoint, this intervention involves *value addition, product differentiation,* and *market segmentation.* If 100 grams of unbranded dry fish sells for Rs. 25 in an open display, the same quantity—when cleaned, graded, packed in a pouch with proper labelling and a price tag—can command Rs. 30 or more. The additional Rs. 5 generated represents *incremental revenue.* After deducting the marginal cost of packaging (approximately Rs. 2 per pouch), the net value-added is Rs. 3 per unit.

This net gain can be shared between the aggregator (entrepreneur) and the vendor, creating a *win-win distribution model.* Vendors receive higher returns for the same product, the aggregator earns income through coordination and innovation, and consumers benefit from safer and better-presented goods. This model not only promotes micro-entrepreneurship but also aligns with broader economic goals such as inclusive growth, formalization of the informal sector, and employment generation with minimal capital investment.

In essence, this approach demonstrates how basic economic restructuring at the grassroots level—through aggregation, quality improvement, and market repositioning—can create sustainable livelihood opportunities while enhancing consumer welfare and food safety.

The same model can be replicated for vegetables, fruits, or any other commodities that are currently sold in an unorganized or unhygienic manner.

Good must be copied

Neither Zomato nor Amazon own the core assets that define their services—Zomato does not run a single restaurant, and Amazon does not manufacture the majority of the products it sells. Yet, both have built massive business empires by strategically leveraging technology and deeply understanding consumer behaviour. They identified inefficiencies in traditional systems and offered seamless, tech-driven solutions that connected consumers to service providers more effectively than ever before. This model demonstrates that ownership of physical infrastructure is not always necessary to build a successful business.

Similarly, within your own means—be it skills, insights, or limited resources—you too can spot existing gaps in the market. If you can offer a value addition that bridges these gaps, whether through better service, organization, hygiene, packaging, convenience, or digital innovation, you can create a business model that is both impactful and profitable. The key lies in innovation, adaptability, and addressing unmet or poorly met needs. Success will follow where there is relevance, efficiency, and value creation.

Project "RAITA": Rental of Agricultural Implements, Tools & Accessories

India has a vast number of tractors—so many that, in theory, they could be used to plough the entire country's arable land. However, the actual utilization rate of these machines is surprisingly low. On average, a tractor is actively and efficiently used for only about 40 to 60 days in a year. For the remaining 300 or more days, these costly machines remain idle, representing underutilized capital.

This pattern is not limited to tractors alone; it extends to other agricultural implements and machinery as well. Without a structured mechanism for sharing or renting, these tools cease to function as productive assets and instead become economic liabilities, tying up capital and space without generating returns.

Encouraging the rental, cooperative ownership, or shared usage models for such equipment could transform this inefficiency into opportunity. By maximizing the utilization rate, farmers can generate secondary income, reduce the cost of ownership, and make agriculture more capital-efficient—especially for small and marginal farmers who cannot afford to purchase machinery outright.

While several state governments have made commendable efforts to promote mechanization and resource-sharing in agriculture through the establishment of 'Custom Hire Centres' (CHCs), the overall success of these initiatives has been limited. Many CHCs failed to achieve sustained impact due to issues such as bureaucratic inefficiencies, poor maintenance of machinery, lack of trained operators, limited outreach to small and marginal farmers, and absence of a strong entrepreneurial model.

This brings us to a crucial principle of governance: the role of the government should not be to directly engage in selling goods or managing day-to-day commercial operations. Rather, the government should focus on selling transformative ideas, enabling frameworks, and facilitating innovation. Its primary responsibility lies in designing effective policy ecosystems, ensuring transparency, building capacity, and monitoring implementation.

By encouraging private sector participation, cooperative ownership, youth-led enterprises, and digital platforms for booking and renting machinery, governments can ensure better efficiency and sustainability. In this context, the government should act as a catalyst and regulator—mobilizing communities, de-risking innovation, and fostering an environment where ideas take root and scale. Ultimately, the state must lead by empowering, not by micromanaging.

Young individuals with a sound understanding of software technology—particularly those familiar with digital platforms like Ola and Uber—hold tremendous potential to revolutionize the agricultural sector. By creating digital applications or web-based systems to aggregate and map the availability of agricultural implements and machinery across villages, districts, or states, these youth can establish efficient rental networks for farm tools. This model mirrors the ride-hailing industry, where idle resources are monetized through a demand-driven, technology-enabled service model.

Such an approach would ensure better utilization of underused farm equipment—tractors, harvesters, threshers, tillers, and more—that often lie idle for most of the year. The rental income generated through this shared economy model would offer an additional revenue stream for farmers, known as *'Ancillary Agricultural Income.'* It is particularly critical in the current scenario, where primary farm incomes are stagnating due to shrinking landholdings, climate uncertainties, and volatile market prices.

These auxiliary sources of income—ranging from equipment rentals and processing services to logistics and storage—can help cushion farmers from economic vulnerability and enhance rural employment. Thus, leveraging digital technologies for asset optimization not only supports individual farmers but also contributes to the larger goal of agricultural sustainability and rural development.

Human Resources as Capital

- One of the most pressing issues facing the agricultural sector today is the so-called 'labour problem.' At first glance, this seems paradoxical, especially in a country like India, which boasts a population of approximately 1.43+ billion people. How can there be a labour shortage in such a populous nation? In my view, the problem does not lie in the actual supply of labour, but rather in a mismatch between the availability of workers and the specific demands of the agricultural sector.

In most Indian cities, one can find designated corners, circles, or public squares where groups of daily-wage laborers gather every morning. These workers—men, women, and in some unfortunate cases even children—stand in hope that landowners, estate managers, contractors, or householders will arrive to hire them for a day's work. The wages usually range between ₹600 and ₹1,200 per day, depending on the state and type of labor.

However, the conditions at these informal labor hubs are far from humane. There is rarely any shelter from the sun or rain, no access to clean drinking water, and no public toilets. Despite waiting for hours, 20–40% of these workers often return home without securing employment for the day, carrying back disappointment and uncertainty.

Paradoxically, while laborers struggle to find work, many farm owners and households complain about not getting reliable manpower when they need it. This paradox highlights a deeper systemic issue—a disconnect between labor demand and supply, aggravated by the absence of proper platforms to bridge the two.

The situation is not merely an economic challenge but also a human dignity issue. When workers are left exposed to harsh conditions and unpredictability, the cycle of poverty perpetuates. For management professionals and policymakers, this reflects the urgent need for structured interventions: digital platforms to match demand and supply, basic infrastructure at labor points, and skilling programs that can open more opportunities for these workers.

Ultimately, these daily gatherings at city squares are not just about wages; they are a reminder of the fragile balance between human effort and opportunity, and how society must evolve to provide dignity, security, and consistency in livelihoods.

This mismatch arises from several factors. Firstly, there's a growing reluctance among the younger generation to engage in farming or agricultural labour due to its physically demanding nature, low social prestige, and often unsteady income. Secondly, rapid urbanization and migration trends have drawn a large portion of the rural workforce toward cities in search of better-paying, less strenuous jobs. As a result, even though the labour pool exists, it is either unavailable or unwilling to meet the sector's needs.

Moreover, this problem is exacerbated by the seasonal and regional nature of agricultural work, which makes it difficult to maintain a steady and reliable workforce. What we are witnessing, therefore, is not a genuine shortage of people, but a failure to align the labour force with the right opportunities through better incentives, mechanization, skill training, and efficient labour management systems.

By leveraging modern technology, a dedicated team of professionals can effectively organize agricultural labour and address some of the critical challenges facing the sector. A successful example of this approach can be found in Kerala, where an initiative called "Friends of Paddy"—locally known as "Nel Nalkar"—demonstrated the potential of collective action and community involvement in revitalizing rice farming.

"Friends of Paddy" represents a network of individuals and groups committed to supporting paddy cultivation. This includes traditional and organic farmers, as well as grassroots organizations such as the 'Padasekhara Samithies,' which promote group farming practices. Together, they cultivate a variety of rice strains, encourage sustainable agricultural methods, and work to secure fair prices and stronger institutional support for farmers. Their coordinated efforts have shown that with the right organizational structure and technological support, it is entirely possible to overcome labour shortages and rejuvenate agricultural productivity.

Urban Company, formerly known as UrbanClap, is an online platform that connects individuals with professionals for a wide range of home services. The platform facilitates booking services like beauty, cleaning, repairs, and more. It acts as a marketplace, matching customers with vetted service providers based on their needs and location.

Green Army

The concept can be envisioned as an organized workforce platform for agricultural laborers, much like what *UrbanClap* (now Urban Company) did for urban services. This initiative, tentatively called **"Green Army"**, could establish units in different regions, bringing together the available labor force within each agro-ecological zone.

The first step would be to map and document the skill sets of every member—whether in planting, harvesting, irrigation management, machinery handling, livestock care, or allied activities—and categorize them accordingly. Such classification ensures that the right person is deployed for the right job, enhancing efficiency and satisfaction on both sides.

The organization would then serve as an intermediary, receiving requests from farmers, estate owners, agribusinesses, or even households, and assigning laborers with predetermined wages under transparent "Terms of Reference." Pricing could be flexible:

- If the service seeker provides travel, food, and other essentials, the charges would be lower.
- For distant work locations, the Green Army could arrange transportation and logistics, charging accordingly.

By creating this structured system, the probability of workers securing consistent employment increases significantly, ensuring better livelihood security.

Beyond mere placement, the Green Army could also take responsibility for capacity building and welfare:

- Providing regular upskilling and technical training.
- Educating members on workplace safety, first aid, sex education, family planning and healthy living practices.
- Facilitating access to health and life insurance.
- Assisting in savings, pensions, and other financial inclusion measures aligned with government schemes—and potentially exceeding them through corporate social responsibility initiatives.

In essence, the Green Army would not just be a manpower supply chain but a social enterprise model that brings dignity, structure, and long-term growth opportunities to agricultural laborers, while simultaneously addressing the chronic labor shortages faced by farm owners and agribusinesses.

"Entrepreneurs add. Enterprisers multiply -
Magada"

Entrepreneur to Enterpriser

I was visiting Davanagere- one of the districts in the central Karnataka, India to address women entrepreneurs. After that session, I thought of addressing ICAR-Krishi Vigyan Kendra's Scientists in the same town. I called Dr Devaraj-Head of that KVK and expressed that I would like to speak on "Becoming Entrepreneur to Enterpriser". He laughed at me and said there is no word called "Enterpriser." He is a well-read fellow, so, I did not argue with him. After my talk he agreed with my concept in a very humble way.

However, the entire business ecosystem often becomes overly dependent on the entrepreneur. If, for any reason, the entrepreneur is removed or steps aside, the organization may face significant setbacks. The business might experience a sharp decline in efficiency, profitability, or even face collapse. This often happens because the knowledge, strategies, and methods that led to success are seldom institutionalized or shared with others in the organization. Instead, much of the operational and strategic acumen remains locked within the founder.

This phenomenon is evident in the history of some leading Kannada tabloids such as 'Lankesh Patrike' and 'Hi Bangalore'. Both publications had a commanding presence in Karnataka's media landscape for decades. They were driven by the formidable journalistic and entrepreneurial spirits of P. Lankesh and Ravi Belagere, respectively. These founders infused their ventures with vision, creativity, and operational discipline. However, following their demise, the publications were handed over to their children — and both began to struggle. The successors inherited the businesses, but not the writings, leadership ethos or enterprise-building capacity that had sustained them.

On the other hand, JRD Tata, Infosys Narayana Murthy, Steve Jobs and Jeff Bezos are the best example for the enterprisers. They built the system based on the core competence, system ethics, governance, and institutional values that grow beyond the leadership.

An enterpriser is someone who goes beyond merely running a business — they focus on understanding and applying the principles that drive long-term success, rather than getting bogged down in the day-to-day operational processes. Unlike an entrepreneur who may rely heavily on personal involvement and instinct, an enterpriser builds a system-driven organization where performance is consistent, scalable, and sustainable.

Central to their approach is the creation and implementation of Standard Operating Procedures (SoPs) that clearly define how each task should be performed, ensuring uniformity, accountability, and efficiency across the organization. They don't just manage people and materials — they strategically organize them, ensuring that roles are defined, responsibilities are delegated, and outcomes are measurable.

An enterpriser also invests in supply chain management, ensuring that the flow of goods, services, and information is streamlined from procurement to delivery. Additionally, they give due importance to branding and marketing, recognizing that the value of a product or service lies not only in its quality but also in how it is perceived by the market.

One of the hallmark qualities of an enterpriser is their ability to create an interconnected system where every department, function, and individual is part of a larger, cohesive mechanism. This system is designed in such a way that efficiency is rewarded and inefficiency is easily detectable. A weak link in this chain becomes immediately visible, prompting timely corrections, while strong links continue to propel the business forward.

In essence, an enterpriser builds a resilient, self-sustaining enterprise that thrives not because of the constant presence of the founder, but because of the systems, values, and structures put in place.

An entrepreneur often seeks to expand their business within the same or a closely related domain. This approach allows them to build upon their existing expertise, networks, and resources. They typically rely on hands-on involvement and replicate their initial success by repeating familiar processes. Their expansion is often driven by personal effort, intuition, and direct control over operations.

An enterpriser, on the other hand, possesses a broader and more strategic vision. While they may also scale within the same field, their true strength lies in their ability to apply the underlying principles of success across different sectors. They can translate the knowledge, systems, and organizational frameworks from one industry into another — even if the products or services are entirely unrelated. This ability to replicate success by leveraging system-based thinking, not just domain expertise, is what sets them apart.

The fundamental distinction between the two lies in their approach to leadership and growth.

- An entrepreneur typically builds and runs a business by steering all aspects personally. Their model of success often depends on their presence, decisions, and energy.
- In contrast, an enterpriser creates a self-sustaining system that functions effectively even in their absence. They focus on building institutional structures, sharing leadership, delegating knowledge, and embedding resilience and adaptability into the organization's DNA.

Thus, while both roles are vital in the business ecosystem, the enterpriser's ability to scale ideas into institutions — not just businesses — is what makes their model more enduring and transformational. A successful enterpriser does not get caught up in day-to-day operations; instead, they focus on creating efficient systems that run smoothly, allowing them to concentrate on scaling and expanding the business.

Kodak that stopped making sound

As per the 'Historical Facts' the Kodak Invented Digital Photography in 1975 and Still Went Bankrupt by 2012. In 1975, inside a quiet Kodak lab, a 24-year-old engineer named 'Steve Sasson' built a strange, toaster-sized contraption. It looked nothing like a camera. It recorded grainy black-and-white images onto a cassette tape. Its resolution? Just 0.01 megapixels.

But it was revolutionary.

What Sasson had built wasn't just a camera—it was the world's first digital camera. A device that could capture moments without film, without processing, without chemicals. The future had just clicked into existence.

But Kodak didn't celebrate. They shelved it.

Why? Because Kodak didn't fear innovation—they feared disruption. They were making billions from selling film. Sasson's invention threatened that. The thought of embracing a future that would destroy their present profits was too much to bear. So instead of leading the digital revolution, Kodak decided to wait.

And while they waited, others moved forward. By the 1990s, companies like Sony and Canon were racing into the digital age. Kodak tried to catch up, but by the time they embraced digital fully, it was too late. In 2012, they filed for bankruptcy, the once-mighty giant crushed under the weight of their own fear.

It wasn't the technology that failed—it was the mindset.

Kodak saw the future. They built it. But they didn't have the courage to believe in it.

And that's the real warning. Innovation doesn't always fail because of bad ideas—it fails when good ideas are ignored in favour of comfort. When the present feels safer than the future.

Steve Sasson still works in imaging technology today. His invention changed the world—but not for the company that first held it. The original digital camera stored its images on a cassette tape, and it took 23 seconds to capture a single image.

This story serves as a powerful reminder that those who resist change risk becoming obsolete. In a world increasingly driven by technology and artificial intelligence, disruption is inevitable across industries and professions. Traditional ways of working are rapidly evolving, and clinging to outdated methods or mindsets can lead to stagnation or even extinction.

However, this era of transformation is not without hope. With every disruption comes opportunity—new roles, industries, and avenues of innovation emerge for those who are willing to learn, adapt, and grow. By continuously upskilling and staying attuned to the shifting landscape, individuals can not only survive but thrive. Embracing change is no longer optional; it is the key to relevance and resilience in the modern age.

"Failure is not the opposite of success;
it is a part of it-**Magada**"

Learning from the Mistakes

There is no such thing as a fool-proof technology. Whether it is a creation of nature or a product of human innovation, everything must follow a natural cycle of emergence, utility, and eventual decline. Every process, practice, or product—no matter how advanced or well-received—comes with an inherent shelf life. What may be considered appropriate, efficient, or ethical today may be deemed outdated, inefficient, or even harmful in the future.

With the continuous evolution of knowledge and the rise of public awareness, all established systems and practices are subject to scrutiny. As people become more informed and conscious, even long-standing methods will be questioned, reassessed, and, where necessary, challenged. The widespread acceptance of a flawed or unethical practice does not justify its continuation. Majority consensus does not equate to moral or practical correctness. Sustainable progress demands that we remain open to change, accept constructive criticism, and adapt our systems in response to new evidence and evolving societal values.

Cadbury Re-'Covered'

Cadbury, one of the world's most iconic chocolate brands, enjoyed widespread popularity in India until a major setback in 2003. Just before the festive season of Diwali, the brand was hit by a controversy widely known as the "Worm Infestation Scandal."

In October 2003, consumers in Mumbai reported finding worms in Cadbury Dairy Milk chocolate bars, prompting an investigation by the Maharashtra Food and Drug Administration (FDA). The FDA traced the contamination to the company's Pune manufacturing facility, citing inadequate packaging and poor hygiene practices as the root causes. Authorities subsequently seized large quantities of chocolate from the plant.

Initially, Cadbury attributed the issue to improper storage conditions at retail outlets. However, as consumer outrage grew and sales dropped by nearly 30%, the company realized the need for immediate and effective damage control.

In response, Cadbury launched *Project Vishwas,* a retailer education campaign aimed at training over 190,000 vendors on appropriate storage techniques. Simultaneously, the company invested ₹15 crore in state-of-the-art packaging technology, introducing metallic poly-flow wrappers to improve product safety and shelf life.

To win back public trust, Cadbury brought in Bollywood legend Amitabh Bachchan as the face of a new national advertising campaign. These strategic steps helped the company regain its footing, and by early 2004, both sales and consumer confidence had significantly recovered.

Lessons Learned

The Cadbury incident is now regarded as a textbook example of successful crisis management. It underscores the vital importance of swift, transparent responses, proactive solutions, and strategic communication in protecting brand reputation and consumer loyalty during challenging times.

Maggi-the Lead(er): A Tale of Taste, Turmoil, and Trust

Maggi instant noodles have long been a go-to comfort food for many — from busy bachelors to school kids — often offering a quick fix to hunger pangs. Its popularity soared, becoming a household staple across India. However, this success story hit a major bump in 2015 when Maggi was embroiled in a significant food safety controversy.

In May 2015, food safety authorities in Uttar Pradesh reported that samples of Nestlé India's Maggi 2-Minute Noodles contained lead — a toxic heavy metal — in quantities far exceeding permissible limits. Some batches were found to have up to 17 times the allowed level. Additionally, there were concerns about the presence of monosodium glutamate (MSG), despite the product's packaging claiming "No added MSG."

These alarming findings prompted several Indian states, including Delhi and Gujarat, to impose temporary bans on Maggi. On June 5, 2015, the Food Safety and Standards Authority of India (FSSAI) ordered a nationwide recall of all nine approved variants of Maggi noodles, declaring them "Unsafe and Hazardous" for human consumption. Nestlé India responded by undertaking one of the largest food recalls in the country's history, withdrawing approximately 38,000 tonnes of noodles and destroying them at 11 cement plants nationwide.

Challenging the FSSAI's decision, Nestlé India appealed to the Bombay High Court, arguing that the testing procedures were flawed and that Maggi was safe to consume. The court ordered retesting at three independent laboratories accredited by the National Accreditation Board for Testing and Calibration Laboratories (NABL). The new results confirmed that Maggi noodles met safety standards and contained lead within permissible limits.

Consequently, on August 13, 2015, the Bombay High Court lifted the nationwide ban. Production and sales resumed by November 2015. In a bid to restore consumer trust, Nestlé India launched widespread marketing efforts, including the release of a "Maggi anthem" by comedian Vir Das and the band Alien Chutney, reinforcing its commitment to quality and safety.

Lessons Learned

The Maggi episode serves as a powerful reminder of the critical importance of stringent quality control, transparent public communication, and prompt crisis response in the food industry. It also underlines the necessity for accurate labelling and unwavering adherence to food safety regulations to uphold consumer trust and confidence.

Asset Building

The Irony of Middle-Class Investments: A Personal Reflection

Asset building is often considered the ultimate hallmark of financial wisdom. Yet, for a long time, it remained an abstract art I could never quite grasp—until my son, with his sharp, modern financial sense, sat me down and patiently decoded it for me. His insights revealed a truth that I had lived but never questioned.

Like most middle-class Indians, we were conditioned to believe that owning a house and a car were not just aspirations—they were symbols of stability, respectability, and success. And so, we too chased that dream, pouring our hard-earned money into buying a house and a car, feeling proud that we were finally "settled." What we didn't fully grasp was the cost hidden in plain sight—not just in rupees, but in lost opportunities.

By the time the loans were paid off, we had spent nearly double the actual worth of what we owned. The EMIs, the interest rates, the maintenance, the insurance—it all added up, slowly bleeding us over the years. In hindsight, had we opted for a well-maintained rented house and invested the difference wisely, we could have afforded a larger home later, without the burden of interest or the emotional shackles of loan repayments.

We assumed real estate would appreciate at the mythical rate of 30–40%, justifying every rupee spent. The reality? In over 98% of the localities, real estate barely grows at 8–10% annually, sometimes even less—barely beating inflation. The story of quick returns turned out to be a comforting illusion we fed ourselves to avoid financial discomfort.

Therein lies the irony. The middle class, in its quest for security, often walks straight into the traps of financial rigidity. We mistake ownership for empowerment, and in doing so, we lock our freedom behind EMI schedules and long-term debt. We celebrate assets that depreciate the moment they're bought, and ignore investments that grow quietly, invisibly, over time. Perhaps it's not just an error in judgment, but a legacy of generational thinking—a belief that physical possessions equal wealth. It took the voice of the next generation—my son—to help me unlearn, to see that true asset building lies not in what we own, but in how wisely we invest our choices.

Take a closer look at the wealthiest individuals across the globe—you'll notice a recurring pattern. They are not salaried employees. They are investors, entrepreneurs, visionaries, and creators. They are the players of the financial and business world, not the spectators. They take risks, build systems, create opportunities, and often fail—only to rise again.

Of course, there may be a rare exception or two—a highly paid executive or a uniquely skilled professional—but even they often become wealthy by eventually investing, founding companies, or owning stakes in something bigger than themselves.

The underlying truth is this: long-term wealth rarely comes from trading time for money. It comes from creating value, building assets, and leveraging ideas. Employees may earn a living, but entrepreneurs and investors create legacies.

So, if your goal is not just to survive but to thrive—to rise beyond the ordinary—consider stepping out of the safe zone. Dare to build, to invest, to play the bigger game. Because the world remembers, and rewards, the ones who choose to lead the game, not just play by its rules.

*"Persistence is the most powerful force on Earth, it can move mountains -**Albert Einstein**"*

The Dung Beetle

I have always been fascinated by the dung beetle — a seemingly insignificant creature, yet carrying within it a profound lesson from nature. At first glance, it may appear as a lowly insect rolling waste across the ground. But pause and reflect, and you begin to see the wisdom embedded in its existence. The dung beetle does not complain, does not chase glory, nor seek validation. It simply does what it must — with purpose, consistency, and resilience. It transforms waste into life by laying its eggs inside what the world considers filth. In that, it reminds us that even what appears worthless can become a cradle of hope and new beginnings.

Nature, in its quiet brilliance, offers us countless teachers — if only we learn to observe. The dung beetle teaches us humility, focus, and perseverance. It reminds us that every being has its role, that dignity lies not in status but in purpose. In a world obsessed with image, the dung beetle calls us back to substance.

If we open our eyes and hearts, nature becomes a mirror — showing us what we need to unlearn, to evolve, and to live with deeper harmony. True wisdom is not in domination, but in alignment — in tuning ourselves to the rhythm of life around us. Only then we can live meaningfully, with reverence for all that lives and moves — even a beetle rolling its sacred burden beneath the stars.

In my journey through life, I have often come across people who seem to have failed — not because they made an attempt and didn't succeed, but because they never dared to try in the first place. It is a quiet kind of failure, one that is often masked by excuses, fear, or the comfort of the known. But in truth, I hesitate to even place them in the category of 'failure,' for to fail, one must have made an effort. One must have stepped into the arena, faced uncertainty, and risked loss.

There is dignity in failure that comes from genuine effort. The person who has failed after trying carries the weight of experience, the scars of courage, and a heart that was willing to strive. Such people are far more accomplished than those who never moved beyond contemplation. They are the ones who carry lessons, not regrets. Their 'failures' often become seeds of strength, resilience, and future success.

On the other hand, those who avoid trying—paralyzed by fear of judgement or defeat—remain untouched by both failure and growth. They are like seeds that refused to break open and missed the chance to become trees. Life doesn't honour mere intentions; it rewards action. It recognizes the courage of those who stood up and said, 'Let me try,' even if the outcome was uncertain.

In the book of life, those who have failed with effort are written in ink; those who never tried are only faint shadows pencilled in the margins. True failure is not falling short—it is staying in the game till you win. It is choosing to compete, boldness over hesitation, and faith over doubt. And so, I say with certainty: those who failed after trying are far greater than those who never dared at all. The world remembers the players—the ones who stepped onto the field, who dared, who played—regardless of whether they won or lost. Ask yourself, do you recall the person who handed the World Cup trophy to Messi? Or the dignitary who presented the IPL trophy to the winning team in India? Likely not. Because history doesn't remember the presenters—it remembers the performers.

So stop waiting for perfect conditions or applause. Don't aim to be remembered for standing beside greatness—strive to be part of it. Step into your arena, embrace your calling, and play your game with all your heart. That's the only way to be remembered. Just that. Go, and play in your field

The Dung Beetle Within – A Story for Unemployed Youth

In the silent corners of the earth, far from admiration or spotlight, lives a tiny creature—the dung beetle. Just 10 milli meters in size, often dismissed as insignificant, this little insect performs one of nature's most astonishing feats. It can pull 1,411 times its own body weight—the human equivalent of lifting two fully loaded 18-wheel trucks.

Most would laugh at the idea of learning from a dung beetle. After all, it lives in waste, survives in struggle, and thrives in filth. But that is exactly where the lesson lies—for those who are walking through the muddy fields of unemployment, rejection, and hopelessness.

The Return of Reshi: A Journey from Drift to Determination

Reshi was once celebrated as a brilliant student—a boy who outshone many of his peers with his sharp mind and sky-high ambitions. Scoring an impressive 96.8 percentile in the Joint Entrance Examination, he secured admission to the Indian Institute of Information Technology (IIIT), Jabalpur, India, National Institute of Technology, Suratkal, Karnataka and finally leaving those two institutes, joined prestigious RV College of Engineering, Bangalore, a dream for many aspiring engineers across the country.

But life, as it often does, took a detour.

Somewhere along the way, Reshi was drawn into the fast-paced, glittering world of digital media. He became a successful influencer, earning not just popularity but a decent income. The thrill of instant validation and financial independence slowly eroded his interest in structured education. One decision followed another, and with the reluctant consent of his parents, he made a bold move—he discontinued his studies.

The world around him whispered in disappointment:

"*Such a wasted potential…*"
"*A bright spark dimmed by distraction…*"

But behind those whispers stood two silently hopeful figures—his parents. His father, an academician, and his mother, a postgraduate in Philosophy, were pained but patient. They understood that brilliance sometimes goes astray before it finds its true course.

And then came a moment. Not a grand epiphany or dramatic turning point—just a quiet, deep realization: Reshi began to believe again. Not because someone forced him to, but because something within him stirred—a voice that whispered louder than the world:

"*You were meant for more.*"

With renewed purpose, he returned to college. Not as the same boy who left in confusion, but as a young man burning with resolve. He faced the impossible—14-18 subjects pending—and cleared them all in one determined stretch. The very subjects that once seemed like mountains were now stepping stones.

He had once convinced himself that he couldn't study, that academics were not for him. But one day of clarity, one decision of discipline, shattered that illusion. Today, Reshi is preparing for the Indian Administrative Service (IAS)—one of the toughest and most respected competitive exams in the world.

Whether he cracks it or not is beside the point. He is in the process with great positive energy…

What matters is that he reclaimed his journey. That he proved to himself—and to others—that failure is not the end, but a bend in the road, and that potential is never wasted as long as you're willing to pick it up again.

Sometimes, youth stumble not because they lack intelligence, but because they lose direction in a noisy world that rewards distraction. But those who turn inward, even briefly, often find a strength that can rebuild what was lost.

Reshi's story is not just about exams or engineering or IAS. It's about the courage to begin again.
And that, more than marks or ranks, is the true test of greatness.

One evening, sitting on a dusty park bench, I watched an insect rolling a ball of dung across the path. Curious, I leaned closer. The beetle struggled, slipped, pushed again, and again—relentlessly. It didn't care about who watched or what filth it was rolling. It had a goal. It had a purpose.

This night, go and search: *"Strongest insect in the world"*. It will stun you:

"The dung beetle (*Anthophagus taurus*), 10 mm long, can pull 1,411 times its body weight—the human equivalent of lifting two fully loaded 18-wheelers."

You stare at the screen, then go and stand in front of the mirror. Say it yourself that "*If a beetle can drag mountains through dirt... why can't I pull myself through this phase?*"

That very night, you make decision to yourself: you wouldn't stop, no matter how dirty the path looked. you take up a pending work you wanted to finish. You learn new skills, you struggle, make mistakes, but never give up. Let the days turned to months. Opportunities come—not glamorous ones, but stepping stones. You grab every one of them.

Years later, you become leader by yourself and you will be addressing unemployed youths. In every motivational talk you start and end with the same line:

“If you feel worthless, jobless, or stuck, remember: the dung beetle doesn’t complain about the dirt—it moves it. Find your strength. Pull your weight. You are stronger than you think.”

Unemployment is not the end. It is the dirt you must walk through. Society may mock your struggle, just as it mocks the dung beetle. But strength is not in size or status—it is in how much you carry without giving up.

Be the dung beetle. Get inspired. Lift… Roll… Move… Repeat.

"One day, your story will inspire someone who is sitting where you once sat—in silence, in doubt, in darkness. So start preparing now, for the time will come when you’ll share that story with the world."

Wisdom of Simplicity

"This is the only body and the only life you have—live it -**Magada**"

We have entered an era where technological disruptions can no longer be paused or reversed. Innovation has gained a momentum of its own — transforming the way we live, work, and relate to one another. These waves of change will inevitably displace millions of jobs while simultaneously creating new opportunities for those equipped to adapt. Yet, the unsettling truth remains: our governments, educational institutions, and social systems are far less prepared for this transformation than the industries driving it.

In today's world, industries race ahead with purpose, urgency, and survival instincts, while many academic institutions still conduct research merely as a means of livelihood rather than as a pursuit of life itself. The gap between knowledge creation and its real-world application widens every day. The role of government is not to control this unstoppable tide of technology, but to facilitate a smooth and equitable transition — ensuring that human dignity and employment are not sacrificed in the name of progress.

However, even as technology continues to shape our outer world, it is vital that we shape our inner world. The antidote to disruption is not resistance, but simplicity. As machines grow more intelligent, humans must become more conscious. We must learn to live with less — not as a sign of deprivation, but as a symbol of freedom.

Adopting a minimalist mindset does not mean renouncing ambition; it means redefining success on our own terms. After you have proved your worth to society, whether you travel by car or by bicycle makes little difference. The irony is that we spend most of our lives trying to impress a society that has an exceptionally short memory. It celebrates success briefly and forgets swiftly.

So, live not to prove, but to experience. Live not for applause, but for inner peace. Define your comforts, your happiness, and your success based on your own intuition — not society's fleeting standards. The true art of living in this age of disruption lies in finding balance: embracing progress with awareness and simplicity with pride.

The Simplicity of Mr Sridhar Vembu: Success Rooted in Stillness

In a world where success is often measured by visibility, luxury, and valuation, Sridhar Vembu, the Founder and CEO of *Zoho Corporation*, stands as a quiet contradiction. While many global entrepreneurs chase spotlight and scale, Vembu has redefined success through simplicity, purpose, and deep connection with the grassroots of India.

A billionaire by any economic measure, he chooses to live in a small village near Tenkasi in Tamil Nadu, far from the glittering skylines of Bengaluru, Mumbai, or Silicon Valley. His office is a modest structure surrounded by fields and hills, and his commute is often on a bicycle. Yet from this unassuming setting, *Zoho*—a homegrown technology company—serves over 100 million users worldwide, competing with some of the biggest names in the global software industry.

Vembu's philosophy is profound: technology must empower, not alienate. He believes that true progress lies not in urban migration or material accumulation but in enabling people to thrive where they are. His decision to build Zoho's R&D centres in rural India is not a symbolic gesture—it is a statement that innovation does not belong only to cities or elite institutions. It can arise from any place where curiosity, commitment, and purpose converge.

Despite his achievements, Sridhar Vembu lives with a monk-like simplicity. His daily life mirrors the values he preaches—minimal possessions, maximum purpose. For him, simplicity is not a retreat from ambition but a refinement of it. It strips away distraction and helps preserve clarity, empathy, and integrity in decision-making.

His life offers a timeless lesson: wealth and simplicity are not opposites. One can build billion-dollar enterprises without surrendering to the illusion of extravagance. The truest measure of success, as Vembu demonstrates, is not how much we accumulate but how little we need to remain content and purposeful.

In an age of noise, Sridhar Vembu reminds us that leadership is not about being seen—it is about *being grounded.* His simplicity is not a strategy; it is his way of being—a living example of how technology and humility can coexist, and how greatness can emerge quietly from the heart of simplicity.

"It is better to be hated for what you are, than to be loved for what you are not-**Andre Gide**"

From Intelligence to Intuition

In many instances, intelligence will not play a significant role. Most of the position are replaceable. World is advancing at a greater pace. As greatest philosopher Sri Thiruvallavar said "Wisdom is to live in tune the mode of the changing world." Intuitions are always genetical, historical, infallible and they don't go wrong. Osho says "Meditation is simply knocking on the doors of intuition. Intuition is completely ready. It doesn't grow; you have inherited that too from existence. Intuition is your consciousness, your being. Whereas, intellect is your mind. Instinct is your body and just as instinct functions perfectly on behalf of body, intuition functions perfectly as for as your consciousness concerned."

According to Microsoft CEO Mr Satya Nadella 'Humans can't rely on brains alone to succeed at workplace.' One of the finest examples of intuition and calm leadership rising above pure intelligence comes from aviation history. It shows how, in moments when logic fails and data is missing, human intuition and presence of mind can achieve the impossible. The story below illustrates how intuition, composure, and adaptive wisdom saved hundreds of lives — proving that the human mind's deepest strength is not intelligence alone.

All four engines died at 37,000 feet—and the captain's announcement became the calmest statement in aviation history.

June 24, 1982. Seven miles above the Indian Ocean.

British Airways Flight 9—a Boeing 747 carrying 263 souls—was cruising peacefully through the night when something impossible began.

First, the crew noticed St. Elmo's fire. An eerie blue glow crackling across the cockpit windows like electricity dancing on glass.

Then shimmering sparks appeared along the wings, as if the aircraft were trailing fire through darkness.

Captain Eric Moody and his crew had thousands of flying hours between them. They'd seen unusual weather. They'd handled emergencies.

But they'd never seen anything like this.
Then came the alarm they dreaded most.
Engine four had failed.
Before they could process it, engine two quit.

Then engine one.
Then engine three.
In less than 90 seconds, all four engines had stopped.
Complete silence.

At seven miles above the ocean.
A commercial jet losing one engine is manageable. Losing two is a serious emergency. Losing three is catastrophic.
Losing all four?
That's not supposed to happen. Ever.
Yet here was Captain Moody, flying a 300-ton glider with 263 people aboard, no engines, no power, and no idea why.
The 747 was descending—losing altitude at an alarming rate. Below them: the dark Indian Ocean and the mountainous Indonesian coastline.
They had minutes to figure out what happened and somehow restart the engines.
In the cabin, passengers saw strange sparks outside their windows. Oxygen masks dropped. Thick, acrid smoke filled the air, smelling

like sulphur.

People began writing farewell notes.

Then Captain Moody's voice came over the intercom with what would become one of the most famous announcements in aviation history:

"Ladies and gentlemen, this is your captain speaking. We have a small problem. All four engines have stopped. We are doing our damnedest to get them going again. I trust you are not in too much distress."

A small problem.

All four engines stopped.

Seven miles in the sky.

That's not just British understatement. That's leadership—keeping 263 people calm while facing catastrophe.

In the cockpit: controlled chaos.

Senior First Officer Roger Greaves' oxygen mask had broken, leaving him gasping in the thin air. Moody immediately descended—trading precious altitude for breathable air.

Flight Engineer Barry Townley-Freeman worked frantically through engine restart procedures while First Officer Barry Fremantle handled communications with Jakarta.

They tried restarting the engines.

Nothing.

Again. Nothing.

Ten attempts. Twelve. Fifteen.

Each failure meant less altitude. Less time. Less sky.

The aircraft descended through 15,000 feet. Then 14,000. Then 13,000.

Below them, somewhere in darkness, were Java's mountains.

They were running out of options.

At 13,500 feet—with terrain looming—engine four suddenly coughed, sputtered, and roared back to life.

Then engine three.

Then engine one.

Finally, engine two.

All four engines—dead for 13 minutes and 13,000 feet of descent—had somehow restarted.

They had power. They had control.

But they still weren't safe.

Whatever had killed the engines had also destroyed the windscreen. The windows were opaque, sandblasted to translucence by millions of tiny particles traveling at 500 mph.

Captain Moody could barely see through them.

They had to land this crippled aircraft essentially flying blind.

They used side windows for glimpses. Relied on instruments. Followed radio guidance from Jakarta, trusting voices from the ground.

And somehow, impossibly, Captain Moody brought the battered 747 down safely at Jakarta's Halim Perdanakusuma Airport.

Not a single person died.

All 263 passengers and crew walked away.

Only after landing did investigators discover the truth.

Mount Galunggung in Java had been erupting. On June 24, it sent a massive ash cloud eight miles high—spreading across flight paths.

Flight 9 had flown directly through it in darkness.

Volcanic ash is pulverized rock—microscopic glass shards suspended in air. Invisible to weather radar. Nearly impossible to see at night.

When jet engines running at over 1,000 degrees ingest it, the ash melts instantly, coating components like molten glass and choking the engines completely.

The engines restarted only because Moody's descent brought them below the ash cloud, where cooler air allowed the melted glass to solidify and break off.

It was luck as much as skill.

But the skill kept them alive long enough for the luck to matter.

British Airways Flight 9 changed aviation forever.

Before June 24, 1982, volcanic ash was considered a minor nuisance.

After Flight 9:

Global volcanic ash detection systems were established
Airlines receive real-time eruption alerts
Flight paths are immediately rerouted around ash clouds
The International Airways Volcano Watch was created

Captain Moody's experience—and his crew's quick thinking—saved not just 263 people that night.
It potentially saved thousands in the decades since.
Captain Moody continued flying until retirement. He's remembered not just for his skill, but for that famous announcement—the calm understatement quoted in aviation training worldwide.
"We have a small problem. All four engines have stopped."
That's leadership. Keeping people calm when the world is falling apart. Refusing to give up when giving up would be understandable.
The lesson:
The impossible sometimes happens. Prepare anyway.
Calm leadership saves lives. Panic kills.
Never give up. Moody's crew tried over 15 times to restart those engines. The 15th attempt worked. If they'd stopped at 14, everyone dies.
June 24, 1982.
All four engines died at 37,000 feet.
The crew had 13 minutes to solve an impossible problem.
They couldn't see why the engines failed.
They couldn't see the ash cloud killing them.
They couldn't see the runway when they landed.
But they could think. They could try. They could refuse to quit.
And 263 people survived because four men in a cockpit refused to accept the impossible.
That's not just an aviation story.
That's a reminder that even when all four engines fail—literally and

metaphorically—you keep trying. You stay calm. You don't give up.
Because sometimes, the 15th attempt is the one that works.

Go with Intuition

In moments of profound uncertainty—when one stands at a crossroads and rational analysis fails to reveal a clear direction—intuition often emerges as an essential decision-making mechanism. In management science, intuition is understood not as guesswork, but as a rapid, subconscious form of cognition derived from accumulated experiences, pattern recognition, and deeply embedded instinctual responses.

Instinct theory suggests that human beings retain evolutionarily inherited behavioural tendencies that enable swift judgments, especially in ambiguous or high-pressure situations. These instinctive impulses are shaped by ancestral survival mechanisms and refined through one's personal learning history. Modern neuroscience also supports this view: the brain encodes long-term experiential memory in neural circuits that activate automatically when confronted with complex choices.

Thus, what we commonly call "intuition" is actually an integration of instinctual intelligence, subconscious pattern processing, and tacit knowledge. It draws upon what behavioural theorists refer to as *heuristic pathways*—internal shortcuts developed through repeated exposure to similar contexts.

When we listen to our intuitive signals, we are effectively accessing a deep reservoir of cognitive and genetic memory. This internal guidance system evaluates risks, opportunities, and personal alignment far more rapidly than deliberate reasoning alone. As a result, intuition often leads individuals toward decisions that are not only contextually appropriate but also aligned with one's values, competencies, and long-term goals.

In leadership and strategic management, acknowledging intuition as a complementary decision-making tool—especially when data is incomplete—allows for more holistic and adaptive choices. In this sense, the "right path" is often the one illuminated by this silent yet powerful internal intelligence.

Throughout human history, tribes and ancient societies relied profoundly on intuition as a guiding force in their collective decision-making. Long before scientific instruments, forecasting models, or structured analytical frameworks existed, intuition served as their primary strategic tool. Whether predicting rainfall, sensing the onset of disease, anticipating enemy attacks, or interpreting natural warnings of earthquakes and volcanic eruptions, these communities trusted an inner intelligence that was deeply intertwined with the rhythms of nature.

Remarkably, their intuitions rarely failed. This was not magic or superstition—it was the result of sustained observation, pattern recognition, and an embodied understanding of their environment. Over generations, they developed a heightened sensitivity to subtle cues: changes in wind patterns, animal behaviour, plant responses, or atmospheric shifts. Their intuition was, in essence, an early form of data analytics—processed not through machines, but through the human nervous system and collective memory.

When we, too, observe nature—or any complex system—closely and patiently, we begin to see how scattered signals connect. Patterns emerge. Insights sharpen. What appears as sudden intuition is often the subconscious synthesis of countless observations accumulated over time.

In modern leadership and management, this ancient wisdom remains profoundly relevant. Intuition complements rational analysis by allowing leaders to see beyond numbers, detect emerging trends, and sense risks before they materialize. When we learn to "connect the dots," we arrive at conclusions that are not speculative but rooted in an intimate engagement with our environment—just as our ancestors did.

Thus, intuition is not opposed to logic; it is the highest form of logic, refined through experience, awareness, and silent observation. In a world flooded with information yet scarce in wisdom, reconnecting with this intuitive intelligence can provide leaders with a decisive strategic edge.

Intuition and Business

The moment an individual begins contemplating a new business venture, the brain activates a complex interplay of neural systems that generate a flood of ideas, possibilities, risks, and imagined outcomes. This sudden surge of thoughts is not random—it is the brain's cognitive network scanning through stored memories, past experiences, emotional associations, and learned patterns to produce intuitive signals.

However, decisions made in moments of heightened emotion—whether excitement, happiness, fear, or frustration—are neurologically compromised. When a person is overly happy, dopamine levels spike; when upset, cortisol floods the system. Both neurotransmitters temporarily impair the brain's prefrontal cortex, the region responsible for rational judgment, impulse control, and long-term planning. In such states, intuition becomes unreliable because emotional noise interferes with the brain's natural pattern-recognition abilities.

Neuroscience shows that intuition functions optimally only under neutral or balanced emotional conditions. In that state, the brain draws on what scientists call *implicit memory*: the deeply stored knowledge acquired from years of experience, observation, and learning. This memory operates below conscious awareness and enables rapid, accurate judgments—what we commonly call "gut feeling."

When we are unbiased and emotionally regulated, intuition becomes a powerful internal compass that can reveal which business aligns with our skills, temperament, and long-term ambitions. Yet, humans often suppress or dismiss these intuitive signals, choosing instead to follow external pressures, social expectations, or momentary impulses. Behavioural science suggests that ignoring authentic intuition in favour of external cues often leads to poor decisions and, in many cases, business failure.

In entrepreneurial decision-making, intuition can provide critical guidance in areas such as investment size, business location, scalability, partnerships, and opportunity selection. Importantly, intuition is not separate from logic—it is the subconscious integration of every logical experience we have ever accumulated. What feels like a sudden insight is actually the brain synthesizing thousands of data points too quickly for conscious reasoning to process.

Thus, intuition is not a mysterious force but a sophisticated neural mechanism shaped by experience, emotion regulation, and environmental awareness. When harnessed correctly—free from emotional distortion and cognitive bias—intuition becomes an invaluable strategic tool for entrepreneurs navigating uncertainty and complexity.

"What more can one ask of God when life itself is a miracle?"

The Economics of Human Values

I often travel to different institutions, organisations, and communities across the country—sometimes to speak about science, other times about philosophy, agriculture, art, or the environment. On the surface, I go there to teach. But the truth is, I return with far more than I give. Each interaction feels like a classroom of its own, where every person becomes a teacher and every experience a lesson.

In villages, cities, classrooms, farms, and conference halls, I meet people whose wisdom cannot be measured by degrees or titles. Some individuals in our society possess insights equivalent to three PhDs—not because they studied in prestigious universities, but because life itself has been their greatest teacher. Their analytical ability, their understanding of human nature, and their sense of balance with the world often leave me mesmerised. They remind me that intelligence is not confined to laboratories and libraries; it also resides in the fields, fish farms, markets, homes, and hearts of ordinary people.

I am often reminded of an anonymous philosopher's words:
"If you want to live for a year, grow paddy;
If you want to live for a hundred years, grow coconut;
But if you want to live eternally, grow people."

This statement holds a profound truth—investing in people is the most sustainable and eternal form of growth. Paddy feeds the year, coconut sustains the century, but nurturing people creates a legacy that outlives time itself. Knowledge shared, values instilled, and confidence ignited in one person can ripple across generations.

However, this timeless investment requires one essential skill—identifying the right people. Machines come with manuals. Tools come with specifications. Modern industries follow 'Sigma Six' management strategies to evaluate precision, performance, and efficiency. But when it comes to human beings, no such perfect measurement exists. There are guidelines, rules, laws, and psychological frameworks, but there is no universally accepted metric to measure a person's potential, sincerity, or character.

Human beings are beautifully complex. Their worth cannot be captured in checklists or ratings. Therefore, identifying the right people becomes an art—an art sharpened by intuition, experience, empathy, and observation. When we invest our time, skill, and energy in the right minds and hearts, it never goes to waste. They grow, they transform, and they carry forward the wisdom we shared with them.

Lesson from Dr Ayyappan

Dr. S. Ayyappan was one of India's finest agricultural scientists—a man who headed the mighty Indian Council of Agricultural Research, a research empire so huge that even Google Maps would get confused trying to mark all its institutes. Yet, despite holding such a massive position, he was the kind of person who could walk into a room without anyone realizing a VIP had arrived. No airs, no aura—just pure simplicity.

One fine evening, I decided to visit him at Shastri Bhavan in New Delhi—right opposite the office of the Minister of Agriculture. Now, if there is a place in India where even a mosquito needs security clearance to enter, it is Shastri Bhavan. And I, being the brave-hearted Mangalorean that I am, went there without an appointment. After all, we both studied in the same college… what could possibly go wrong?

Well, everything.

The guards looked at me as if I was trying to enter the Prime Minister's bedroom. I proudly flashed my identity card, expecting them to salute. Instead, they stared at it the way students stare at calculus—completely confused and absolutely uninterested.

"No entry," they said, firmly.

But I was not ready to give up. Without losing a second, I called Dr. Ayyappan on his cell phone.

"Sir, I am downstairs," I said, hoping he remembered me.

"Oh nice… just a minute," he replied casually, as if I had called him from the next room.

Within moments, he appeared. Yes—the Director General of one of the world's largest agricultural research networks came down *himself* to receive me. The armed policemen were shocked. They looked at me as if I had suddenly turned into the President of India. Their expressions clearly said, "Ayyo… we almost stopped a very big man!"

With chest out and confidence rising like India's inflation, I walked beside Dr. Ayyappan towards his office. Even my footsteps had a VIP sound.

When we entered his chamber, two senior Members of Parliament were already seated. They stood up slightly, as if wondering who this important-looking fellow was. Dr. Ayyappan immediately told them, "Please wait for a few minutes. A great scientist has come all the way from Mangalore. Let me talk to him first."

The MPs nodded respectfully.
I nodded respectfully.
Even my ego nodded respectfully.

We walked into his inner chamber, and I started talking to him in my usual casual college-friend language. The MPs outside must have been thinking, "Who is this guy? A Nobel Prize winner? A secret advisor? Or the person who actually runs the country from behind the scenes?"

Meanwhile, I was still basking in those twenty glorious minutes—minutes in which hierarchy had melted, protocol had dissolved, and simple human warmth had taken centre stage. When our conversation finally ended and I prepared to leave, Dr. Ayyappan did something that senior officials rarely do.

He walked with me.

Not just up to the door of his chamber, but all the way to the downstairs exit.

His footsteps were unhurried, his presence unassuming, and his gesture so natural that it felt as if humility itself had borrowed his body for a brief walk. At that moment, the imposing corridors of Shastri Bhavan felt like they were bowing slightly—not to a title, not to an office, but to the grace of a man who understood what true leadership meant.

I couldn't resist asking him,
"Sir, do you do this for everyone who visits your office?"

He smiled gently, the kind of smile that comes from years of wisdom and a heart untouched by arrogance.

"Yes," he said. Just that.
A simple "Yes"—but filled with a philosophy deeper than any textbook on management.

He turned to go back upstairs. But my mind was overflowing with thoughts—questions about behaviour, about humility, about the quiet power of kindness. I stopped him just as he was about to climb the first step. It all happened in a few seconds, like a scene from a play where the curtain suddenly pauses mid-air.

"Sir," I said, "I will copy this and practice it for my lifetime."

He didn't give a lecture. He didn't preach. He simply smiled again—a smile that said, ***learning is complete, if we don't grow people***—and shook my hand with a firmness that sealed the lesson permanently in my memory. Then he slowly walked back upstairs, climbing step by step, like a sage returning to his quiet mountain cave. In fact, I did not understand the second set of words in his sentence.

I remained standing there.

Just standing.
Absorbing.
Thinking.

A few seconds later, he appeared again at the top and waved at me. As if to remind me that humility is not a gesture—it is a way of being. His presence at that moment was like a second, unplanned blessing.

By this time, the armed policemen were watching me with great confusion. Their eyes spoke louder than words:
"Sir, please move. This is not a museum. Important people need to pass."

But I couldn't move. Because in that still moment, I realised something profound:

The greatness of a man is not in the height of the chair he sits on, but in the depth of the gesture he offers.

In that vast administrative fortress called Shastri Bhavan—surrounded by protocols, ranks, titles, and armed security—I, a simple visitor from Mangalore, felt like the most important man in the building. Not because of who I was, but because of who he was.

And sometimes, that is all it takes:
One humble soul to make another soul feel seen.

In every institution I visit, I realise this truth repeatedly:
We do not just teach; we shape.
We do not just share knowledge; we sow seeds.
And when we grow people, we grow eternity.

Net Practice at KVK

Two years later, in 2016, destiny placed me in a role where leadership was not just a responsibility, but an opportunity to redefine the culture of service. I became the Head of the Krishi Vigyan Kendra (KVK)—a Farm Science Centre that serves as the extension arm of the agricultural universities and the agriculture department. With more than 700 such KVKs across the country, each one stands as a bridge between scientific knowledge and the daily life of farmers.

The moment I assumed office, I felt a deep sense of mission. Farmers—the backbone of our nation, the silent granaries of our civilization—deserve not only technical support but respect, dignity, and human warmth. So in one of my very first meetings, I called all my scientists: agronomists, soil scientists, horticulturists, veterinarians, fisheries experts, and every other staff member who played a role in the KVK.

I told them something very simple, yet profoundly transformative:

"Whenever a farmer visits your chamber, rise from your seat.
Give them undivided attention.
Listen to them with empathy.
Solve their problems with sincerity."

There was silence in the room.
Not the silence of agreement—but the silence of confusion.

A few thought I was doing all of this for publicity.

Some suspected I was using theatrical techniques—after all, they knew I was a playwright, actor, and director. They might have even imagined spotlights and background music hidden somewhere behind my chair.

But leadership is not about convincing everyone—it is about moving the first stone so the rest begin to roll.

I insisted.
I explained.
I persuaded.
And finally, I made them agree—some willingly, some reluctantly, and a few purely because they had no alternative.

Then began my inspection journey.

Whenever farmers walked into the campus, I quietly followed them—like a detective of compassion—to see whether my scientists were actually rising from their chairs. And yes, they were! At least when they sensed my presence nearby. But even that was a start.

Slowly, the practice became a habit.
And the habit became a culture.
And the culture became our identity.

Within a few months, something magical happened.

The KVK became alive.
Not just a centre of technology, but a centre of humanity.

Farmers felt valued.
Scientists felt more connected.
Conversations became warmer.
Solutions became quicker.
And trust blossomed like a well-irrigated crop.

Our activities multiplied—literally multiplied.

Field visits increased.
Demonstrations became more frequent.
Innovations took birth.
The smile of the farmers became our daily reward.

And then came the recognition.

Almost every day, we were in the news—
Not for controversies or conflicts,

But for good work, meaningful work, work that touched people's lives.

Our popularity soared, not because we were shouting for attention, but because sincerity is a music people naturally hear.

In less than a year, we transformed from "just another KVK" into a model of farmer-centric service.
And all of it began with a simple act—Rising from a chair. May that is what Dr Ayyappan said "Grow people"

Sometimes leadership is not about big reforms.

It is about small gestures repeated consistently until they become the soul of an institution.

In most institutions—whether they are research centres, universities, corporations, or government departments—there is rarely a shortage of knowledge. Ideas flow abundantly. Funds, though sometimes limited, can still be mobilized with the right proposals. Technology keeps improving. Infrastructure continues to expand. On paper, everything looks perfect.

Yet, despite all this, something subtle but essential is often missing: **human values**.

You may fill an office with brilliant minds, but brilliance without empathy becomes arrogance. You may equip a lab with the latest technology, but technology without integrity becomes dangerous. You may pour money into projects, but money without compassion never creates trust.

Institutions do not collapse because of lack of intelligence. They weaken because of lack of humanity.

If even one person in an organization begins to nurture human values—respect, sincerity, kindness, honesty, humility, and responsibility—something remarkable begins to happen. Values grow silently, just like roots grow quietly beneath the soil. They spread from one mind to another, from one room to the entire building.

People begin to listen better.
Conflicts reduce.
Collaboration increases.
Work becomes meaningful instead of mechanical.

And gradually, the institution begins to flourish—not merely in terms of numbers or reports, but in terms of culture, identity, and purpose.

An organization grows from the inside, not outside.
And it grows only when its people grow.

Human values are not expenses;
They are investments that yield the highest returns—
returns in trust, in harmony, in innovation, and in lasting success.

Behavioural experts often remind us of a profound truth: **we are the average of the five people we spend the most time with.** In other words, our mind is like a river—shaped not only by its own flow but also by the landscapes it passes through. The company we keep quietly sculpts our thoughts, choices, and ultimately our destiny.

This makes it essential to choose our inner circle wisely. But wisdom should never become arrogance. Selecting the right people does not mean disrespecting the ones you do not resonate with. After all, every person is fighting a battle we may not understand, and no soul deserves to be insulted simply because we walk in different directions.

You may spend time with everyone—colleagues, acquaintances, strangers, even critics—but you must not open the doors of your inner world to all of them. Presence is allowed for many; influence must be reserved for a few. Influence is sacred—it is the currency of the soul. If we let everyone shape us, we lose our shape.

Therefore, choose to open up only with those who elevate your thinking, protect your energy, and bring a sense of clarity to your life. These are the sensible and positive people, the ones who make you feel lighter after every interaction.

Yet, amid all this selectiveness, maintain a universal principle: **Believe everyone.**

Not blindly—but respectfully. Believe that every person carries a story, an intention, or a struggle. Believe in their intrinsic goodness, even if you do not adopt their behaviour. Belief builds bridges; suspicion builds walls.

But at the same time—**do not keep your gunpowder dry.** This ancient metaphor simply means: trust, but do not be unprepared. Have hope, but also have wisdom. Open your heart, but not so wide that your judgment escapes. Keep your inner strength ready, your values protected, and your boundaries firm.

In life, balance is the ultimate mastery:

- Trust without being naïve.
- Be kind without being exploited.
- Stay open without becoming vulnerable to manipulation.
- Embrace people without losing yourself.

Because in the end, your circle doesn't just reflect you—**it creates you.**

"Your answers reveal your knowledge while your questions reflect your thinking. Ask questions...preferably,

right questions"

Embracing Technology

Technology is growing fast in the recent fast. I am lucky enough to witness the tint of past and fast pace of new technology. Technology is making lecture based universities irrelevant. Majority are taking the advantage of technology and making few people rich and do not know how to use such technology to enhance their finance and livelihood. This country do not need many IAS or IPS officers. Hardly there are 3000 jobs a year. But, just young boys and girls are earning 10 times more than these people. Technology allows low skill person to do higher work. So, one must embrace the technology and make best out of it. Now, the girls from Uttarakhand, Sikkim make reels and promoting their homestays, food, culture.

In one of recent classes, I asked the students to introduce themselves and they were blank after two statements. They were looking smart and rich. I told them to follow and attend some "Communication" classes online and get updated. When you are skilled, without a flashy dress and money, you look smart. Your skill makes you look smart. In fact, in many instances, the tertiary education becomes meaningless. Some of the youtubers and influences earn better income than the chairman of the Indian Space Research Organisation (ISRO). It does not mean that the science has no relevance for progress, but technological revolution will offer new kind of jobs for the ones who upgrade with the time.

In the present context, competencies such as data literacy, effective use of digital tools, application of the Internet of Things (IoT), ethical utilisation of AI tools, understanding of blockchain technology, awareness of plagiarism, cybersecurity preparedness, and the strategic use of digital applications for learning and business are essential. **"Use your cellphones to learn and earn, not to waste time, but to make time work for you."**

"Once a cowboy watching a train. Now the author of this book. Persistence can rewrite anyone's story—even yours."

Beyond the CGPA

From the Buffalo Fields to the Boardrooms of Learning

In the early 1970s, a barefoot cowboy stood beside his family's buffaloes in a small rural village, his feet soaked in mud and his mind filled with wonder- the author himself. His world was simple and unhurried. The sound of a train whistling in the distance would send shivers of excitement through his tiny frame. To him, the train was not just a machine — it was a symbol of power, direction, and freedom. His greatest dream was modest yet vast: to board a train one day, or perhaps, to become a lorry driver. He was fascinated by how a single human could command such a mighty creation of iron and steam. Each time a train passed, he waved eagerly at the strangers leaning from its windows, imagining their destinations, their stories, and their unknown possibilities.

On his way back home, he would stop by the pastures, gathering cow dung to make fuel cakes for cooking — a task that most considered menial. Yet, for him, that muddy corner became a silent classroom. It was there he first observed the **dung beetle**, a creature of astonishing patience and purpose. He watched as it rolled its sphere of life, never deterred by its size or the weight of its task. The beetle became his first teacher — a symbol of transformation, direction, and quiet persistence. It taught him that greatness does not come from where you stand, but from how you move — with purpose, no matter how small the step.

As life unfolded, he stumbled many times on the uneven path of learning. He failed his 12th standard examination — an event that could have ended the dreams of many from a humble background. Later, he faltered again in several subjects during his college days. His low CGPA barred him from moving forward with his batchmates, forcing him to walk alongside juniors. To many, it appeared as a mark of failure. But to him, it was a test of endurance. Perhaps he was not in a hurry to earn a degree — he was in a hurry to understand life. He knew that education was not just about passing exams; it was about building the courage to continue when the world gives up on you.

He once said, *"I didn't fail; I was being prepared."* Those delays were divine pauses — moments where he was being moulded, polished, and strengthened. He had silently told himself, "One day, I will win," and he did — not with noise or pride, but with grace, patience, and conviction.

Like the dung beetle that once rolled its tiny world through the dust, he began shaping his own destiny. From the muddy fields of rural Karnataka, he rose through perseverance and purpose to become one of the youngest professors in the country, and years later, the Dean of the very institute from which he once struggled to graduate. Life had indeed come full circle. Happiness doesn't last for long. The new set of enemies were born. He was troubled by his own peers. He never bothered. He became a "Zen" and moved with great happiness to win life. As Shakespeare said *"When a person doesn't know what he has lost, he has not lost anything."*

Yet, his journey was not just about personal triumphs. From the very start of his professional life, he chose to be more than an academic. He became a teacher who listened, a motivator who inspired, and an artist who expressed. His lectures were not confined to classrooms; they were dialogues on life. His writings were not merely research; they were reflections of human experience. He evolved into a motivational speaker, author, playwright, and philosopher, touching countless lives with his words and warmth.

In his own words, *"Life is not a competition; it is a composition."* He believed that each of us has our own rhythm — some move faster, some slower, but all reach the destination meant for them if they walk with faith and focus. His life became a testament to that truth.

Today, when he looks back, he sees not the failures, but the footprints — each one a lesson, each stumble a silent teacher. From waving at strangers on passing trains to waving at audiences filled with students, colleagues, and dreamers, he has travelled far — not just in distance, but in depth.

He smiles and says, "What more can one ask of God?" For he has learned that true success is not about what we become, but about how meaningfully we travel the distance.

To every student struggling in classrooms or caught in the maze of expectations, his life whispers a message:

"Don't let grades measure your greatness. Don't let failure silence your fire. Life will test you, delay you, and even detour you — but if you keep rolling like the dung beetle, with purpose and faith, the world will roll in your direction one day."

The insect dung beetle (Anthophagus taurus)-a 10 mm long can pull up to 1411 times of its own body weight-which is an equivalent of an average man lifting two fully loaded 18-wheel truck: Let's get inspired by "Dung Beetle"

References

Bargh, John A.; Chartrand, Tanya L. (1999). *"The Unbearable Automaticity of Being"*. American Psychologist.

Basu, Kaushik (25 July 2007). India's demographic dividend. BBC News. Retrieved 24 September 2011.

Dane, Erik; Pratt, Michael G. (20 October 2007). *"Exploring Intuition and its Role in Managerial Decision Making"*. Academy of Management Review.

Darwin, Charles (1872). *"The Expression of the Emotions in Man and Animals"*. John Murray.

Ericsson, K. Anders; Charness, Neil (12 November 1994). *"Expert Performance: Its Structure and Acquisition"*. American Psychologist.

Ferrante, Malcolm Scerri (6 May 2018). "Life with the NAS Daily crew". Times of Malta. Retrieved 10 August 2018.

Gigerenzer, Gerd (2007). *"Gut Feelings: The Intelligence of the Unconscious"*. Penguin Books.

Horowitz, Jason; Lorenz, Taylor (2 June 2021). Khaby Lame, the Everyman of the Internet. The New York Times. Retrieved 7 November 2023

India overtakes China to become world's most populous nation with 1.428 billion people: UN. The Economic Times. 20 April 2023. Retrieved 1 August 2023.

India's population growth will come to an end: the number of children has already peaked. Our World in Data. Retrieved 28 May 2021.

Intuition: Knowing Beyond Logic by Osho (2001). St Martin's Griffin, New YorkJaffe-Hoffman, Maayan (26 June 2019). "NAS Daily's evaluation of the Start-up Nation". The Jerusalem Post. Retrieved 10 June 2021.

Jung, Carl G. (11 February 1964). *"Man and His Symbols"*. Aldus Books.

Kahneman, Daniel (2011). *"Thinking, Fast and Slow"*. Farrar, Straus and Giroux.

Keegan, Rebecca (21 May 2022). Cannes Diary: The Content Creators Have Conquered the Croisette. The Hollywood Reporter. Retrieved 18 September 2023.

Khaby Lame, world's most-followed TikTok creator, joins 'Italia's Got Talent' as juror. NBC News. 2 March 2023. Retrieved 4 March 2023.

Klein, Gary (1998). *"Sources of Power: How People Make Decisions"*. MIT Press.

Lieberman, Matthew D. (2000). *"Intuition: A Social Cognitive Neuroscience Approach"*. Psychological Bulletin.

Logan, Nick (5 August 2018). "Nuseir Yassin quit his job, started NAS Daily and brought the world to your Facebook newsfeed". Globalnews.ca. Retrieved 10 August 2018.

Lorenz, Konrad (1950). *"The Comparative Method in Studying Innate Behaviour Patterns"*. Symposia of the Society for Experimental Biology.

Median age – The World Factbook. Central Intelligence Agency. Retrieved 16 May 2022.

Mercado, Darla (12 April 2017). "Facebook video star refuses to cash in via YouTube". CNBC. Retrieved 10 August 2018.

Mintzberg, Henry (1 July 1976). *"Planning on the Left Side and Managing on the Right"*. Harvard Business Review.

Polanyi, Michael (1966). *"The Tacit Dimension"*. Doubleday. Archived from the original on 15 April 1966. Retrieved 23 January 2025.

Population growth (annual %). World Bank. Retrieved 20 January 2015.

Rick Gladstone (29 July 2015). India Will Be Most Populous Country Sooner Than Thought, U.N. Says. The New York Times. Archived from the original on 3 January 2022. Retrieved 7 November 2016.

Sadler-Smith, Eugene (2008). *"Inside Intuition"*. Routledge.

Samuel, Barimah (2 July 2023). "NAS Daily Biography". Youtube Creators Festival. Archived from the original on 2 July 2023. Retrieved 23 October 2023.

Sternlicht, Alexandra (14 September 2022). The world's most followed TikToker gets paid as much as $750K per post, but to reach his greatest business goal Khaby Lame is binge-watching American cartoons. Fortune. Retrieved 7 November 2023.

Tooby, John; Cosmides, Leda (1992). *"The Psychological Foundations of Culture"*. In The Adapted Mind.

United States Census Bureau – International Data Base (IDB). Census.gov. Archived from the original on 25 June 2011. Retrieved 24 September 2011.

Vivarelli, Nick (1 March 2023). Khaby Lame, World's Most-Followed TikTok Creator, Joins 'Italia's Got Talent' as Juror. Variety. Retrieved 18 September 2023.

Acknowledgment

I wish to express my heartfelt gratitude to all the individuals and organizations mentioned in this book. The names and examples I have referred to while narrating various stories are included solely to inspire aspiring entrepreneurs and readers. Some anecdotes are supported with proper references, while others could not be fully acknowledged due to the unavailability of accurate information about the original contributors. I offer my sincere respect to all such thinkers whose ideas have shaped this work, even if their names are not explicitly cited.

I am deeply thankful to **Dr. Stephen David**, International Aquaculture Consultant, USA and alumnus of my college, for generously sponsoring my previous book. His support enabled me to bring this book to completion much earlier than expected, a task that might otherwise have remained pending for several more months.

I also owe a special thanks to the legendary trio—Mr. Dinesh (Director, Innosolv), Mr. Pradeep Haniya aka Subbi (Founder, Innosolv, Bengaluru), and my son, Reshi Magada. These three formed a highly efficient "Book Supply Chain," delivering English novels to me on a strict **no-return policy**.

The first two at least had the courtesy to read the books before passing them on. My son, however, took a different strategic approach: he handed them to me *without* reading, then closely monitored me like a personal productivity officer—just to ensure I finished them instead of wasting time on my mobile! Thanks to their combined efforts, I finally became a disciplined reader—whether I liked it or not!

I would also like to thank M/s. Blue Rose Publications and their wonderful team for bravely taking on the job of publishing my books—especially Mr. Karthik who deserve a special award for patiently handling my "critical replies" and surviving them with a smile!